AF564426

Corporate Governance and Accountability

Corporate Governance and Accountability

Dr. Sandeep Sharma

Corporate Governance and Accountability

ISBN 978-93-5111-230-3

Published in 2014 in India by

Reprint 2019

RANDOM PUBLICATIONS

4376-A/4B, Gali Murari Lal, Ansari Road
New Delhi-110 002
Phone : +91-11-43580356, +91-11-23289044
e-mail: randomexports@gmail.com, sales@randompublications.com,
info@randompublications.com

Type Setting by : Keystoneprintads, Delhi-110051
Printed at : Mehra Printers, Delhi-110 092

Preface

To account is to give a description or depiction of something that happens or happened. Accountability would therefore be taken to literally mean the process of giving an account of an event. The tricky part; about it, is that for the people to whom the account is being given, the accuracy and probity of the story is very important. To achieve this, accountability usually moves hand in hand with seven other principles. These include, "delegation, responsibility, disclosure, autonomy, authority, power and legitimacy."

The separation of ownership from management can cause conflict if there is a breach of trust by managers either by intentional acts, omission of key facts from reports, neglect, or incompetence. One way in which this can be avoided is for entities (in their entirety) to act with transparency and be accountable to the shareholders and other stakeholders. Therefore apart from just being a component of corporate governance, there are many advantages of accountability.

Firstly, it is a key to economic prosperity. If there is poor accountability by players in the economy, stakeholders may lose the confidence they have in it and hence become reluctant to put in their best. For instance; for some developing countries, lack of accountability may lead to a fall in the participation rate in their development programmes by their co operating partners- a situation that leads to further deterioration in the development process. Accountability is also a key to performance measurement. The more accountable corporate governors are, the more likely it is that results of performance measurement processes are going to be a true and fair representative of the performance being measured.

Accountability is a very important pillar of corporate governance. Without it, the agency problem would be hard to defeat. With it, the confidence of stakeholders is increased. It is achieved through faithfulness in various aspects of corporate governance especially reporting. The strength and accuracy of the reporting is also strengthened by various standards and regulations.

The book gives a thorough insight into how this is to be done, and what are the current trends and practices which circumscribe this field.

I thank all members of my team who have helped in the preparation of the book. My special thanks go to "Random Publications" who have published the book.

– Dr. Sandeep Sharma

Contents

1

Corporate Governance

Executive compensation as a governance device is an increasingly important part of the strategic management process. If the board makes the wrong decision in compensating the firm's strategic leader, the shareholders and the firm suffer. Compensation is used to motivate CEOs to act in the best interests of the firm—in particular, the shareholders. When they do, the firm's value should increase. What is a CEO's actions worth? The Opening Case suggests that they are increasingly worth a significant amount in the United States. While some critics argue that U.S. CEOs are paid too much, the hefty increases in their incentive compensation in recent years ostensibly have come from linking their pay to their firms' performance, and U.S. firms have performed better than many companies in other countries. However, research suggests that firms with a smaller pay gap between the CEO and other top executives perform better, especially when collaboration among top management team members is more important.

The performance improvement is attributed to better cooperation among the top management team members. Other research suggests that CEOs receive excessive compensation when corporate governance is the weakest. Also, as noted in the Opening Case, there has been a shift in compensation practices used for top executives over the last several years, given new policies regarding governance and increasingly critical media attention. Corporate governance is the set of mechanisms used to manage the relationship among stakeholders that is used to determine and control the strategic direction and performance of organizations.

At its core, corporate governance is concerned with identifying ways to ensure that strategic decisions are made effectively. Governance can also be thought of as a means corporations use to establish order between parties whose interests may conflict. Thus, corporate governance reflects and enforces the company's values. In modern corporations— especially those in the United States and the United Kingdom—a primary objective of corporate governance is to ensure that the interests of top-level managers are aligned with the interests of the shareholders. Corporate governance involves oversight in areas where owners, managers, and members of boards of directors may have conflicts of interest. These areas include the election of directors, the general supervision of CEO pay and more focused supervision of director pay, and the corporation's overall structure and strategic direction. Corporate governance has been emphasized in recent years because, as the Opening Case illustrates, corporate governance mechanisms occasionally fail to adequately monitor and control top-level managers' decisions. This situation has resulted in changes in governance mechanisms in corporations throughout the world, especially with respect to efforts intended to improve the performance of boards of directors. These changes often cause confusion about the proper role of the board.

According to one observer, "Depending on the company, you get very different perspectives: Some boards are settling for checking the boxes on compliance regulations, while others are thinking about changing the fundamental way they govern, and some worry that they've gotten themselves into micromanaging the CEO and company. There's a fair amount of turmoil and collective searching going on." A second and more positive reason for this interest is that evidence suggests that a well-functioning corporate governance and control system can create a competitive advantage for an individual firm. For example, one governance mechanism—the board of directors—has been suggested to be rapidly evolving into a major strategic force in U.S. business firms.

Thus, in this chapter, we describe actions designed to implement strategies that focus on monitoring and controlling mechanisms, which can help to ensure that top-level managerial actions contribute to the firm's strategic competitiveness and its ability to earn above-average returns. Effective corporate governance is also of interest to nations. As stated by one scholar, "Every country wants the firms that operate within its borders to flourish and grow in such ways as to provide employment, wealth, and satisfaction, not only to improve standards of living materially but also to enhance social cohesion. These aspirations cannot be met unless those firms are competitive internationally in a sustained way, and it is this medium- and long-term perspective that makes good corporate governance so vital."

Corporate governance, then, reflects company standards, which in turn collectively reflect societal standards. In many corporations, shareholders hold top-level managers accountable for their decisions and the results they generate. As with these firms and their boards, nations that effectively govern their corporations may gain a competitive advantage over rival countries. In a range of countries, but especially in the United States and the United Kingdom, the fundamental goal of business organizations is to maximize shareholder value. Traditionally, shareholders are treated as the firm's key stakeholders, because they are the company's legal owners. The firm's owners expect top-level managers and others influencing the corporation's actions to make decisions that will result in the maximization of the company's value and, hence, of the owners' wealth. In the first section of this chapter, we describe the relationship that is the foundation on which the modern corporation is built: the relationship between owners and managers. The majority of this chapter is used to explain various mechanisms owners use to govern managers and to ensure that they comply with their responsibility to maximize shareholder value. Three internal governance mechanisms and a single external one are used in the modern corporation. The three internal governance mechanisms we describe in this chapter are:

- Ownership concentration, as represented by types of shareholders and their different incentives to monitor managers;
- The board of directors; and
- Executive compensation.

We then consider the market for corporate control, an external corporate governance mechanism. Essentially, this market is a set of potential owners seeking to acquire undervalued firms and earn above-average returns on their investments by replacing ineffective top-level management teams. The chapter's focus then shifts to the issue of international corporate governance. We briefly describe governance approaches used in German and Japanese firms whose traditional governance structures are being affected by the realities of global competition. In part, this discussion suggests that the structures used to govern global companies in many different countries, including Germany, Japan, the United Kingdom, and the United States, are becoming more, rather than less, similar. Closing our analysis of corporate governance is a consideration of the need for these control mechanisms to encourage and support ethical behavior in organizations.

Importantly, the mechanisms discussed in this chapter can positively influence the governance of the modern corporation, which has placed significant responsibility and authority in the hands of top-level managers. The most effective managers understand their accountability for the firm's performance and respond positively to corporate governance mechanisms. In addition, the firm's owners should not expect any single mechanism to remain effective over time. Rather, the use of several mechanisms allows owners to govern the corporation in ways that maximize strategic competitiveness and increase the financial value of their firm. With multiple governance mechanisms operating simultaneously, however, it is also possible for some of the governance mechanisms to be in conflict. Later, we review how these conflicts can occur.

SEPARATION OF OWNERSHIP AND MANAGERIAL CONTROL

Historically, U.S. firms were managed by the founder-owners and their descendants. In these cases, corporate ownership and control resided in the same persons. As firms grew larger, "the managerial revolution led to a separation of ownership and control in most large corporations, where control of the firm shifted from entrepreneurs to professional managers while ownership became dispersed among thousands of unorganized stockholders who were removed from the day-to-day management of the firm." These changes created the modern public corporation, which is based on the efficient separation of ownership and managerial control. Supporting the separation is a basic legal premise suggesting that the primary objective of a firm's activities is to increase the corporation's profit and, thereby, the financial gains of the owners.

The separation of ownership and managerial control allows shareholders to purchase stock, which entitles them to income from the firm's operations after paying expenses. This right, however, requires that they also take a risk that the firm's expenses may exceed its revenues. To manage this investment risk, shareholders maintain a diversified portfolio by investing in several companies to reduce their overall risk. As shareholders diversify their investments over a number of corporations, their risk declines. The poor performance or failure of any one firm in which they invest has less overall effect. Thus, shareholders specialize in managing their investment risk. In small firms, managers often are high percentage owners, so there is less separation between ownership and managerial control. In fact, there are a large number of family-owned firms in which ownership and managerial control are not separated.

In the United States, at least one-third of the S&P top 500 firms have substantial family ownership, holding on average about 18 percent of the outstanding equity. And family-owned firms perform better when a member of the family is the CEO than when the CEO is an outsider. In many countries outside the United States, such as in Latin America, Asia, and some European countries, family-owned firms represent the dominant form. The primary purpose of most of these firms is to increase the family's wealth, which explains why a family CEO often is better than an outside CEO. There are at least two critical issues for family-controlled firms. First, as they grow, they may not have access to all of the skills needed to effectively manage the firm and maximize its returns for the family. Thus, they may need outsiders. Also, as they grow, they may need to seek outside capital and thus give up some of the ownership.

In these cases, protection of the minority owners' rights becomes important. To avoid these potential problems, when these firms grow and become more complex, their owner-managers may contract with managerial specialists. These managers make major decisions in the owner's firm and are compensated on the basis of their decision-making skills. As decision-making specialists, managers are agents of the firm's owners and are expected to use their decision-making skills to operate the owners' firm in ways that will maximize the return on their investment. Without owner specialization in risk bearing and management specialization in decision making, a firm may be limited by the abilities of its owners to manage and make effective strategic decisions. Thus, the separation and specialization of ownership and managerial control should produce the highest returns for the firm's owners. Shareholder value is reflected by the price of the firm's stock. As stated earlier, corporate governance mechanisms, such as the board of directors or compensation based on the performance of a firm, is the reason that CEOs show general concern about the firm's stock price. As the Opening Case describes, CEO incentive compensation generally reflected the gain in the S&P 500 firms in 2004.

AGENCY RELATIONSHIPS

The separation between owners and managers creates an agency relationship. An agency relationship exists when one or more persons hire another person or persons as decision-making specialists to perform a service. Thus, an agency relationship exists when one party delegates decision-making responsibility to a second party for compensation.

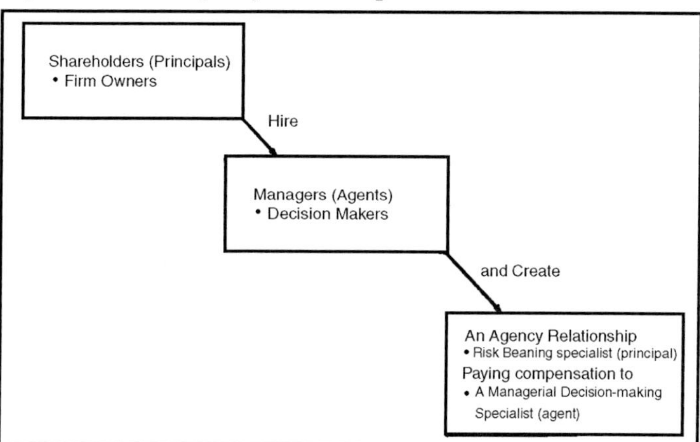

Fig. An Agency Relationship

In addition to shareholders and top executives, other examples of agency relationships are consultants and clients and insured and insurer. Moreover, within organizations, an agency relationship exists between managers and their employees, as well as between top executives and the firm's owners. In the modern corporation, managers must understand the links between these relationships and the firm's effectiveness. Although the agency relationship between managers and their employees is important, in this chapter we focus on the agency relationship between the firm's owners and toplevel managers because this relationship is related directly to how the firm's strategies are implemented. The separation between ownership and managerial control can be problematic.

Research evidence documents a variety of agency problems in the modern corporation. Problems can surface because the principal and the agent have different interests and goals, or because shareholders lack direct control of large publicly traded corporations. Problems also arise when an agent makes decisions that result in the pursuit of goals that conflict with those of the principals. Thus, the separation of ownership and control potentially allows divergent interests to surface, which can lead to managerial opportunism. Managerial opportunism is the seeking of self-interest with guile. Opportunism is both an attitude and a set of behaviors. It is not possible for principals to know beforehand which agents will or will not act opportunistically. The reputations of top executives are an imperfect predictor, and opportunistic behavior cannot be observed until it has occurred. Thus, principals establish governance and control mechanisms to prevent agents from acting opportunistically, even though only a few are likely to do so. Any time that principals delegate decision-making responsibilities to agents, the opportunity for conflicts of interest exists. Top executives, for example, may make strategic decisions that maximize their personal welfare and minimize their personal risk. Decisions such as these prevent the maximization of shareholder wealth. Decisions regarding product diversification demonstrate these possibilities.

PRODUCT DIVERSIFICATION AS AN EXAMPLE OF AN AGENCY PROBLEM

As explained in Chapter 6, a corporate-level strategy to diversify the firm's product lines can enhance a firm's strategic competitiveness and increase its returns, both of which serve the interests of shareholders and the top executives. However, product diversification can result in two benefits to managers that shareholders do not enjoy, so top executives may prefer product diversification more than shareholders do. First, diversification usually increases the size of a firm, and size is positively related to executive compensation. Also, diversification increases the complexity of managing a firm and its network of businesses and may thus require more pay because of this complexity.

Thus, increased product diversification provides an opportunity for top executives to increase their compensation. Second, product diversification and the resulting diversification of the firm's portfolio of businesses can reduce top executives' employment risk. Managerial employment risk is the risk of job loss, loss of compensation, and loss of managerial reputation. These risks are reduced with increased diversification, because a firm and its upperlevel managers are less vulnerable to the reduction in demand associated with a single or limited number of product lines or businesses. For example, Kellogg Co. was almost entirely focused on breakfast cereal in 2001 when it suffered its first ever market share leadership loss to perennial number two, General Mills, Inc. Upon appointing Carlos Gutierrez, a longtime manager at Kellogg, to the CEO position, the company embarked on a new strategy to overcome its poor performance. The competitive environment was difficult because of the emergence of premium-product private labels and frequent price wars. Furthermore, retail consolidation squeezed overall industry sales and caused an extensive focus on cost reduction. In order to reduce the risk of a takeover attempt because of low stock price, Kellogg purchased Keebler Foods Co. in 2001.

As a result, its overall revenue increased from $6 billion to $8.3 billion in 2002. While its diversified scope increased, it also focused on a change from "volume to value" and implemented a second strategy called "managing for cash," in which it significantly increased its incentive compensation for division managers, encouraging them to focus on improved innovation at more decentralized divisions. Through this approach, Kellogg's earnings were substantial enough so that it could raise its dividend by 10 percent in 2005, which was the first dividend increase in five years. Kellogg's stock price doubled during Gutierrez's tenure as CEO, and through this diversification move, his risk of job loss was substantially reduced. Another concern that may represent an agency problem is a firm's free cash flows over which top executives have control.

Free cash flows are resources remaining after the firm has invested in all projects that have positive net present values within its current businesses. In anticipation of positive returns, managers may decide to invest these funds in products that are not associated with the firm's current lines of business to increase the firm's level of diversification. The managerial decision to use free cash flows to overdiversify the firm is an example of self-serving and opportunistic managerial behavior. In contrast to managers, shareholders may prefer that free cash flows be distributed to them as dividends, so they can control how the cash is invested.

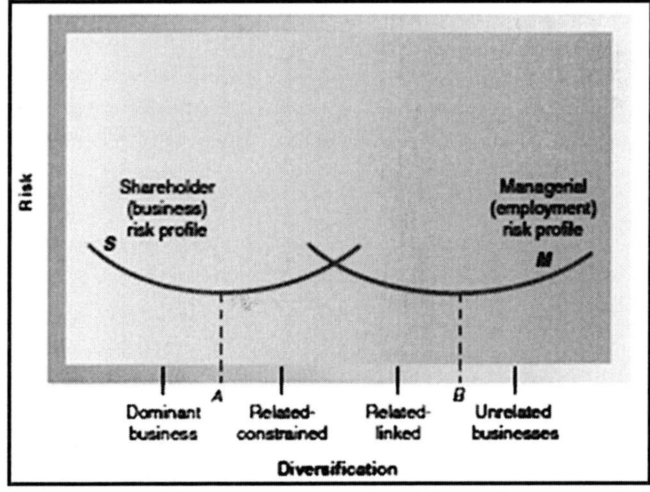

Fig. Manager and Shareholder Risk and Diversification

Curve *S* in Figure depicts the shareholders' optimal level of diversification. Owners seek the level of diversification that reduces the risk of the firm's total failure while simultaneously increasing the company's value through the development of economies of scale and scope. Of the four corporate-level diversification strategies shown in Figure, shareholders likely prefer the diversified position noted by point *A* on curve *S*—a position that is located between the dominant business and related-constrained diversification strategies. Of course, the optimum level of diversification owners seek varies from firm to firm.

Factors that affect shareholders' preferences include the firm's primary industry, the intensity of rivalry among competitors in that industry, and the top management team's experience with implementing diversification strategies. As do principals, upper-level executives—as agents—also seek an optimal level of diversification. Declining performance resulting from too much product diversification increases the probability that corporate control of the firm will be acquired in the market. After a firm is acquired, the employment risk for the firm's top executives increases substantially. Furthermore, a manager's employment opportunities in the external managerial labor market are affected negatively by a firm's poor performance. Therefore, top executives prefer diversification, but not to a point that it increases their employment risk and reduces their employment opportunities. Curve *M* in Figure shows that executives prefer higher levels of product diversification than do shareholders.

Top executives might prefer the level of diversification shown by point *B* on curve *M*. In general, shareholders prefer riskier strategies and more focused diversification. They reduce their risk through holding a diversified portfolio of equity investments. Alternatively, managers obviously cannot balance their employment risk by working for a diverse portfolio of firms. Therefore, top executives may prefer a level of diversification that maximizes firm size and their compensation and that reduces their employment risk. Product diversification, therefore, is a potential agency problem that could result in principals incurring costs to control their agents' behaviors.

AGENCY COSTS AND GOVERNANCE MECHANISMS

The potential conflict illustrated by Figure, coupled with the fact that principals do not know which managers might act opportunistically, demonstrates why principals establish governance mechanisms. However, the firm incurs costs when it uses one or more governance mechanisms. Agency costs are the sum of incentive costs, monitoring costs, enforcement costs, and individual financial losses incurred by principals because governance mechanisms cannot guarantee total compliance by the agent. If a firm is diversified, governance costs increase because it is more difficult to monitor what is going on inside the firm.

In general, managerial interests may prevail when governance mechanisms are weak, as is exemplified by allowing managers a significant amount of autonomy to make strategic decisions. If, however, the board of directors controls managerial autonomy, or if other strong governance mechanisms are used, the firm's strategies should better reflect the interests of the shareholders. More recently, governance observers have been concerned about more egregious behavior beyond inefficient corporate strategy. Due to fraudulent behavior such as that found in Enron and WorldCom, concerns regarding corporate governance has been increasing. In 2002, the U.S. Congress enacted the Sarbanes-Oxley Act, which increased the intensity of corporate governance mechanisms as it was implemented in 2003 and 2004. These governance changes and associated reactions are described in the Strategic Focus detailing the changes enacted by the SOX Act.

Research suggests that more intensive application of governance mechanisms may produce significant changes in strategies. William Donaldson, then chairman of the SEC, argued that the collapse of investor confidence after the Enron and other scandals suggests that corporate America needs more intense governance in order for continued investment in the stock market to facilitate growth. Donaldson has said, "The shortterm costs of compliance, particularly efforts to improve internal control and corporate governance over financial reporting, should be viewed as an investment. In the long term, the reforms realized from SOX will result in more sound corporate practices and more reliable financial reporting." However, others argue that the indirect costs of SOX—the impact on strategy formulation and implementation—are even more influential.

That is, because of more intense governance, firms may make a lot fewer risky decisions and thus decrease potential shareholder wealth significantly. Stephen Odland, the new CEO of Office Depot, is a supporter of the law but has said, "If we frighten managers to the point that they're not willing to risk anything we could damage our economy and our ability to compete in the world." Jack Lambeth, vice president of information technology and leading the SOX-compliant effort at Blackboard, an education-technology company, will spend about $1.5 million implementing SOX by the end of 2005. Blackboard went public in 2004 and earned $5.6 million in its initial year.

Accordingly, the money spent on implementing SOX is costing the company a significant portion of its earnings power. Lambeth said, "A dollar spent making sure we are SOX-compliant could have been spent increasing our sales territory or investing in our Web-hosting infrastructure." As a result, he suggests, SOX will force many start-up companies to consider selling out to a large company rather than going public, as for example Ask Jeeves was acquired by IAC. This could reduce the number of venture capital investments and ultimately reduce the number of IPOs. One observer noted: "Many boards have been vigilant in their oversight role in regard to corporate value. However, CEOs and directors have been distracted from more important strategic issues in order to meet detailed compliance deadlines provided by the Sarbanes-Oxley Act. Boards need to refocus on three critical strategic processes: strategic planning, risk assessment and renewal which includes succession planning." Next, we explain the effects of different governance mechanisms on the decisions managers make about the choice and the use of the firm's strategies.

OWNERSHIP CONCENTRATION

Both the number of large-block shareholders and the total percentage of shares they own define ownership concentration. Large-block shareholders typically own at least 5 percent of a corporation's issued shares. Ownership concentration as a governance mechanism has received considerable interest because large-block shareholders are increasingly active in their demands that corporations adopt effective governance mechanisms to control managerial decisions. In general, diffuse ownership produces weak monitoring of managers' decisions.

Among other problems, diffuse ownership makes it difficult for owners to effectively coordinate their actions. Diversification of the firm's product lines beyond the shareholders' optimum level can result from ineffective monitoring of managers' decisions. Higher levels of monitoring could encourage managers to avoid strategic decisions that harm shareholder value. In fact, research evidence shows that ownership concentration is associated with lower levels of firm product diversification. Thus, with high degrees of ownership concentration, the probability is greater that managers' strategic decisions will be intended to maximize shareholder value.

As noted, such concentration of ownership has an influence on strategies and firm value. Interestingly, research in Spain showed a curvilinear relationship between shareholder concentration and firm value. At moderate levels of shareholder concentration, firm value increased; at high levels of concentration, firm value decreased for shareholders, especially minority shareholders.

When large shareholders have a high degree of wealth, they have power relative to minority shareholders in extracting wealth from the firm, especially when they are in managerial positions. The importance of boards of directors in mitigating expropriation of minority shareholder value has been found in the United States relative to strong family ownership who have incentives to appropriate shareholder wealth. Such expropriation is often found in countries such as Korea where minority shareholder rights are not as protected as they are in the United States. However, in the United States much of this concentration has come from increasing equity ownership by institutional investors.

THE GROWING INFLUENCE OF INSTITUTIONAL OWNERS

A classic work published in the 1930s argued that the "modern" corporation had become characterized by a separation of ownership and control. This change occurred primarily because growth prevented founders-owners from maintaining their dual positions in their increasingly complex companies. More recently, another shift has occurred: Ownership of many modern corporations is now concentrated in the hands of institutional investors rather than individual shareholders. Institutional owners are financial institutions such as stock mutual funds and pension funds that control largeblock shareholder positions. Because of their prominent ownership positions, institutional owners, as large-block shareholders, are a powerful governance mechanism. Institutions of these types now own more than 50 percent of the stock in large U.S. corporations, and of the top 1,000 corporations, they own, on average, 56 percent of the stock. Pension funds alone control at least one-half of corporate equity.

These ownership percentages suggest that as investors, institutional owners have both the size and the incentive to discipline ineffective top-level managers and can significantly influence a firm's choice of strategies and overall strategic decisions. Research evidence indicates that institutional and other large-block shareholders are becoming more active in their efforts to influence a corporation's strategic decisions. Initially, these shareholder activists and institutional investors concentrated on the performance and accountability of CEOs and contributed to the ouster of a number of them. They are now targeting what they believe are ineffective boards of directors. For example, CalPERS provides retirement and health coverage to over 1.3 million current and retired public employees. As the largest public employee pension fund in the United States, CalPERS is generally thought to act aggressively to promote governance decisions and actions that it believes will enhance shareholder value in companies in which it invests. The largest institutional investor, TIAA-CREF, has taken actions similar to those of CalPERS, but with a less publicly aggressive stance. To date, research suggests that these institutions' activism may not have a direct effect on firm performance, but that its influence may be indirect through its effects on important strategic decisions, such as those concerned with international diversification and innovation. With the increased intensity of governance associated with the passage of the SOX Act, institutional investors as well as other groups have been emboldened in their activism.

BOARD OF DIRECTORS

Typically, shareholders monitor the managerial decisions and actions of a firm through the board of directors. Shareholders elect members to their firm's board. Those who are elected are expected to oversee managers and to ensure that the corporation is operated in ways that will maximize its shareholders' wealth. Even with large institutional investors having major equity ownership in U.S. firms, diffuse ownership continues to exist in most firms, which means that in large corporations, monitoring and control of managers by individual shareholders is limited. Furthermore, large financial institutions, such as banks, are prevented from directly owning stock in firms and from having representatives on companies' boards of directors, although this is not the case in Europe and elsewhere. These conditions highlight the importance of the board of directors for corporate governance.

Unfortunately, over time, boards of directors have not been highly effective in monitoring and controlling top management's actions. As noted in the Strategic Focus, boards are experiencing increasing pressure from shareholders, lawmakers, and regulators to become more forceful in their oversight role and thereby forestall inappropriate actions by top executives. If changes are instituted as explained in the Strategic Focus, boards will have even more power to influence the actions of managers and the directions of their companies. Furthermore, boards not only serve a monitoring role, but they also provide resources to firms.

These resources include their personal knowledge and expertise as well as their access to resources of other firms through their external contacts and relationships. The board of directors is a group of elected individuals whose primary responsibility is to act in the owners' interests by formally monitoring and controlling the corporation's top-level executives. Boards have the power to direct the affairs of the organization, punish and reward managers, and protect shareholders' rights and interests. Thus, an appropriately structured and effective board of directors protects owners from managerial opportunism such as that found in Enron and WorldCom. Board members are seen as stewards of their company's resources, and the way they carry out these responsibilities affects the society in which their firm operates. Generally, board members are classified into one of three groups.

Insiders are active top-level managers in the corporation who are elected to the board because they are a source of information about the firm's dayto-day operations. *Related outsiders* have some relationship with the firm, contractual or otherwise, that may create questions about their independence, but these individuals are not involved with the corporation's day-to-day activities. *Outsiders* provide independent counsel to the firm and may hold top-level managerial positions in other companies or may have been elected to the board prior to the beginning of the current CEO's tenure. Historically boards of directors were primarily dominated by inside managers. A widely accepted view is that a board with a significant percentage of its membership drawn from the firm's top executives tends to provide relatively weak monitoring and control of managerial decisions. Managers have been suspected of using their power to select and compensate directors and exploiting their personal ties with them.

In response to the Securities and Exchange Commission's proposal to require audit committees to be made up of outside directors, in 1984 the New York Stock Exchange, possibly to preempt formal legislation, implemented an audit committee rule requiring outside directors to head the audit committee. Subsequently, other rules required important committees such as the compensation committee and the nomination committees to be headed by independent outside directors. These requirements were instituted after the Sarbanes-Oxley Act was passed, and policies of the New York Stock Exchange as well as the American Exchange now require companies to maintain boards of directors that are composed of a majority of outside independent directors and to maintain full independent audit committees. Thus one can clearly see that corporate governance is becoming more intense through the board of directors mechanism.

Critics advocate reforms to ensure that independent outside directors represent a significant majority of the total membership of a board. Alternatively, others argue that having outside directors is not enough to resolve the problems; it depends on the power of the CEO. In some cases, the CEO is powerful enough to reduce the effectiveness of outside board members. The Strategic Focus proposes that boards need to reduce the power of the CEO by separating the chairperson of the board's role and the CEO's role on the board so that the same person does not hold both positions. From the Strategic Focus, it is clear that the increased emphasis on separating the roles of the CEO and the chairperson provides more power and independence to the independent outside directors relative to the CEOs. This should lead to more CEO dismissals when things go wrong such as when Carly Fiorina was fired from Hewlett- Packard. Because of recent problems associated with egregious use of CEO power, CEOs who have recently been appointed by boards must meet tougher standards. As a result, often the selection process takes longer. At Computer Associates, John Swainson, replacing a CEO who was accused of unethical behavior, was scrutinized for three months before being appointed to the position: "[E]very aspect of my personal life was investigated before I took the job." Most companies no longer prohibit consensual romances between employees, but because of high ethical standards at Boeing, especially due to ethical concerns associated with government contracting, Harry Stonecipher lost his CEO position at Boeing because of an affair with a female employee. Although the Sarbanes-Oxley implementation has created stronger scrutiny in regard to finances, the legislation and concern in the media has heightened scrutiny on a range of candidate traits beyond the leader's actual ability to run the company's businesses.

Alternatively, having a large number of outside board members can also create some problems. Outsiders do not have contact with the firm's day-to-day operations and typically do not have easy access to the level of information about managers and their skills that is required to effectively evaluate managerial decisions and initiatives. Outsiders can, however, obtain valuable information through frequent interactions with inside board members, during board meetings and otherwise. Insiders possess such information by virtue of their organizational positions. Thus, boards with a critical mass of insiders typically are better informed about intended strategic initiatives, the reasons for the initiatives, and the outcomes expected from them. Without this type of information, outsider-dominated boards may emphasize the use of financial, as opposed to strategic, controls to gather performance information to evaluate managers' and business units' performances. A virtually exclusive reliance on financial evaluations shifts risk to top-level managers, who, in turn, may make decisions to maximize their interests and reduce their employment risk. Reductions in R&D investments, additional diversification of the firm, and the pursuit of greater levels of compensation are some of the results of managers' actions to achieve financial goals set by outsider-dominated boards.

ENHANCING THE EFFECTIVENESS OF THE BOARD OF DIRECTORS

Because of the importance of boards of directors in corporate governance and as a result of increased scrutiny from shareholders—in particular, large institutional investors—the performances of individual board members and of entire boards are being evaluated more formally and with greater intensity. Given the demand for greater accountability and improved performance, many boards have initiated voluntary changes. Among these changes are:

- Increases in the diversity of the backgrounds of board members,
- The strengthening of internal management and accounting control systems, and
- The establishment and consistent use of formal processes to evaluate the board's performance. Additional changes include
- The creation of a "lead director" role that has strong powers with regard to the board agenda and oversight of non-management board member activities, as suggested in the Strategic Focus, and
- Modification of the compensation of directors, especially reducing or eliminating stock options as a part of the package.

Boards have become more involved in the strategic decision-making process, so they must work collaboratively. Some argue that improving the processes used by boards to make decisions and monitor managers and firm outcomes is the key to increasing board effectiveness. Moreover, because of the increased pressure from owners and the potential conflict among board members, procedures are necessary to help boards function effectively in facilitating the strategic decision-making process. Increasingly, outside directors are being required to own significant equity stakes as a prerequisite to holding a board seat. In fact, some research suggests that firms perform better if outside directors have such a stake. Other research suggests that diverse boards help firms make more effective strategic decisions and perform better over time. One activist concludes that boards need three foundational characteristics to be effective: director stock ownership, executive meetings to discuss important strategic issues, and a serious nominating committee that truly controls the nomination process to strongly influence the selection of new board members. Once on the job, the outside director needs to seek effectiveness through three linked sets of behaviors that suggest the non-executive director should be "engaged but non-executive", "challenging but supportive" and "independent but involved".

EXECUTIVE COMPENSATION

As the Opening Case illustrates, the compensation of top-level managers, and especially of CEOs, generates a great deal of interest and strongly held opinions. One reason for this widespread interest can be traced to a natural curiosity about extremes and excesses. Another stems from a more substantive view, that CEO pay is tied in an indirect but tangible way to the fundamental governance processes in large corporations: Who has power? What are the bases of power? How and when do owners and managers exert their relative preferences? How vigilant are boards? Who is taking advantage of whom? Executive compensation is a governance mechanism that seeks to align the interests of managers and owners through salaries, bonuses, and long-term incentive compensation, such as stock awards and options.

As noted in the Opening Case, long-term incentive plans have become a critical part of compensation packages in U.S. firms. The use of longer-term pay helps firms cope with or avoid potential agency problems by linking managerial wealth to the wealth of common shareholders. Because of this, the stock market generally reacts positively to the introduction of a long-range incentive plan for top executives. Sometimes the use of a long-term incentive plan prevents major stockholders from pressing for changes in the composition of the board of directors, because they assume that the long-term incentives will ensure that top executives will act in shareholders' best interests. Alternatively, stockholders largely assume that top-executive pay and the performance of a firm are more closely aligned when firms have boards that are dominated by outside members. However, sometimes the persistence of institutional investors pays off in regard to questioning actions by boards regarding pay packages.

This is certainly the case at Hollinger International, Inc. where the persistent questions of Christopher H. Browne, a managing director of Tweedy, Browne Company, who is Hollinger's largest shareholder, lead to the CEO's dismissal. Conrad Black, Hollinger's then CEO, and other managers were overpaid for a number of years. Brown simply asked the important question as to the background of the pay being provided to Black and others. A report sponsored by the board found that over $400 million between 1997 and 2003 had been transferred to Hollinger's key managers, including Black. This amounted to approximately 95 percent of the company's entire net income during this period.

Ultimately, key managers lost their positions and the firm was broken up into pieces; the collective share price went from $7.70 in March 2003 to around $17.00 in late 2004. Effectively using executive compensation as a governance mechanism is particularly challenging to firms implementing international strategies. For example, the interests of owners of multinational corporations may be best served when there is less uniformity among the firm's foreign subsidiaries' compensation plans. Developing an array of unique compensation plans requires additional monitoring and increases the firm's potential agency costs. Importantly, levels of pay vary by regions of the world. For example, managerial pay is highest in the United States and much lower in Asia. Compensation is lower in India partly because many of the largest firms have strong family ownership and control. As corporations acquire firms in other countries, the managerial compensation puzzle becomes more complex and may cause additional executive turnover.

A COMPLICATED GOVERNANCE MECHANISM

Executive compensation—especially long-term incentive compensation—is complicated for several reasons. First, the strategic decisions made by top-level managers are typically complex and nonroutine, so direct supervision of executives is inappropriate for judging the quality of their decisions. The result is a tendency to link the compensation of toplevel managers to measurable outcomes, such as the firm's financial performance. Second, an executive's decision often affects a firm's financial outcomes over an extended period, making it difficult to assess the effect of current decisions on the corporation's performance. In fact, strategic decisions are more likely to have long-term, rather than short-term, effects on a company's strategic outcomes. Third, a number of other factors affect a firm's performance besides top-level managerial decisions and behavior. Unpredictable economic, social, or legal changes make it difficult to discern the effects of strategic decisions.

Thus, although performance-based compensation may provide incentives to top management teams to make decisions that best serve shareholders' interests, such compensation plans alone are imperfect in their ability to monitor and control managers. Still, incentive compensation represent a significant portion of many executives' total pay. Although incentive compensation plans may increase the value of a firm in line with shareholder expectations, such plans are subject to managerial manipulation. For instance, as firms are being forced to expense stock options, *Forbes* magazine has reported that many firms are using "creative accounting" to reduce the expense associated with these options by changing the "expectations of volatility." The idea is that the value of options increases as the stock price varies. If the stock price does not vary as much, then stock options are valued lower. This creates a lower expense for firms using options simply by changing the accounting formula.

Additionally, annual bonuses may provide incentives to pursue short-run objectives at the expense of the firm's long-term interests. Supporting this conclusion, some research has found that bonuses based on annual performance were negatively related to investments in R&D when the firm was highly diversified, which may affect the firm's long-term strategic competitiveness. However, research has found a positive relationship between investments in R&D and long-term compensation in non-family firms. Although long-term, performance-based incentives may reduce the temptation to underinvest in the short run, they increase executive exposure to risks associated with uncontrollable events, such as market fluctuations and industry decline. The longer term the focus of incentive compensation, the greater are the long-term risks borne by top-level managers. Also, because long-term incentives tie a manager's overall wealth to the firm in a way that is inflexible, such incentives and ownership may not be valued as highly by a manager as by outside investors who have the opportunity to diversify their wealth in a number of other financial investments. Thus, firms may have to overcompensate managers using long-term incentives, as the next section suggests.

THE EFFECTIVENESS OF EXECUTIVE COMPENSATION

The primary reason for compensating executives in stock is that the practice affords them an incentive to keep the stock price high and hence aligns managers' interests with shareholders' interests. However, there may be some unintended consequences. Managers who own more than 1 percent of their firm's stock may be less likely to be forced out of their jobs, even when the firm is performing poorly. Furthermore, a review of the research suggests that over time, firm size has accounted for more than 50 percent of the variance in total CEO pay, while firm performance has accounted for less than 5 percent of the variance. Thus, the effectiveness of pay plans as a governance mechanism is suspect. While some stock option–based compensation plans are well designed with option strike prices substantially higher than current stock prices, too many have been designed simply to give executives more wealth that will not immediately show up on the balance sheet. Research of stock option repricing where the strike price value of the option has been lowered from its original position suggests that action is taken more frequently in high-risk situations.

However, repricing also happens when firm performance was poor, to restore the incentive effect for the option. Evidence also suggests that politics are often involved. Additionally, research has found that repricing stock options does not appear to be a function of management entrenchment or ineffective governance. These firms often have had sudden and negative changes to their growth and profitability. They also frequently lose their top managers. Interestingly, institutional investors prefer compensation schemes that link pay with performance, including the use of stock options. Again, this evidence shows that no internal governance mechanism is perfect. While stock options became highly popular as a means of compensating top executives and linking pay with performance, they also have become controversial of late. It seems that option awards became a means of providing large compensation packages, and the options awarded did not relate to the firm's performance, particularly when boards showed a propensity to reprice options at a lower strike price when stock prices fell precipitously. Because of the large number of options granted in recent years and the increasingly common practice of repricing them, this was one of the reasons for the pressure to expense options. As noted in the Opening Case, this action is quite costly to many firms' stated profits and appears to have dampened the excessive use of options.

MARKET FOR CORPORATE CONTROL

The market for corporate control is an external governance mechanism that becomes active when a firm's internal controls fail. The market for corporate control is composed of individuals and firms that buy ownership positions in or take over potentially undervalued corporations so they can form new divisions in established diversified companies or merge two previously separate firms. Because the undervalued firm's executives are assumed to be responsible for formulating and implementing the strategy that led to poor performance, they are usually replaced. Thus, when the market for corporate control operates effectively, it ensures that managers who are ineffective or act opportunistically are disciplined. The market for corporate control is often viewed as a "court of last resort." This suggests that the takeover market as a source of external discipline is used only when internal governance mechanisms are relatively weak and have proven to be ineffective.

Alternatively, other research suggests that the rationale for takeovers as a corporate governance strategy is not as strong as the rationale for takeovers as an ownership investment in target candidates where the firm is performing well and does not need discipline. Additionally, a study of active corporate raiders in the 1980s showed that takeover attempts often were focused on above-average performance firms in an industry. Taken together, this research suggests that takeover targets are not always low performers with weak governance. As such, this research suggests that the market for corporate control may not be as efficient as a governance device as theory suggests. At the very least, internal governance controls would be much more precise relative to this external control mechanism. Although the market for corporate control may be a blunt instrument as far as corporate governance is concerned, the takeover market has continued to be very active. In fact, research suggests that more intense governance environment may have fostered an increasingly active takeover market. Because institutional investors have more concentrated ownership, they may be interested in firms that are targeted for acquisition. Target firms earn a substantial premium over the acquiring firm.

At the same time, managers who have ownership positions or stock options are likely to gain in making a transaction with an acquiring firm. There is even more evidence that this may be the case given the increasing number of firms that have golden parachutes which allow up to three years of additional compensation plus other incentives if a firm is taken over. These compensation contracts reduce the risk for managers if a firm is taken over. In fact, research suggests that there was a friendlier environment in the 1990s for takeovers due to these ownership and governance arrangements. Although the 1980s had more defenses put up against hostile takeovers, the current environment has been much more friendly, most likely due to the increased intensity of the governance devices on both the buyer side as well as the corporate management side.

The idea that CEOs who have substantial ownership or stock options in the target firm do well in the friendly transactions in the 1990s and into the 21st century is also supported by research. The market for corporate control governance mechanism should be triggered by a firm's poor performance relative to industry competitors. A firm's poor performance, often demonstrated by the firm's earning below-average returns, is an indicator that internal governance mechanisms have failed; that is, their use did not result in managerial decisions that maximized shareholder value. This market has been active for some time. As noted in Chapter 7, the decade of the 1990s produced the largest number and value of mergers and acquisitions. The major reduction in the stock market resulted in a significant drop in acquisition activity in the first part of the 21st century. However, the number of mergers and acquisitions began to increase and the market for corporate control has become increasingly international, with over 40 percent of the merger and acquisition activity involving two firms from different countries.

While some acquisition attempts are intended to obtain resources important to the acquiring firm, most of the *hostile* takeover attempts are due to the target firm's poor performance. Therefore, target firm managers and members of the boards of directors are highly sensitive about hostile takeover bids. It frequently means that they have not done an effective job in managing the company. If they accept the offer, they are likely to lose their jobs; the acquiring firm will insert its own management. If they reject the offer and fend off the takeover attempt, they must improve the performance of the firm or risk losing their jobs as well. For example, Oracle made a hostile bid for PeopleSoft; PeopleSoft rejected the offer, but Oracle remained in the takeover battle. The takeover attempt invited considerable attention from regulatory authorities in both the United States and Europe. Ultimately, the takeover was consummated and the CEO of PeopleSoft was dismissed before the two firms were integrated.

MANAGERIAL DEFENSE TACTICS

Hostile takeovers are the major activity in the market for corporate control governance mechanism. Not all hostile takeovers are prompted by poorly performing targets, and firms targeted for hostile takeovers may use multiple defense tactics to fend off the takeover attempt. Historically, the increased use of the market for corporate control has enhanced the sophistication and variety of managerial defense tactics that are used to reduce the influence of this governance mechanism. The market for corporate control tends to increase risk for managers. As a result, managerial pay is often augmented indirectly through golden parachutes. Golden parachutes, similar to most other defense tactics, are controversial.

Among other outcomes, takeover defenses increase the costs of mounting a takeover, causing the incumbent management to become entrenched, while reducing the chances of introducing a new management team. For example, though People- Soft's management ultimately succumbed to a takeover by Oracle, the company's takeover defense strategy allowed it to hold Oracle at bay for roughly a year and a half. As one observer noted, "PeopleSoft had a number of defense mechanisms, including a board with staggered terms. In addition, its board was authorized to increase or decrease its own size without shareholder approval, and its directors could only be removed for cause and only by a vote of 66.67 percent of entitled voters." In addition, PeopleSoft had a poison pill in place "entitling holders of its common stock to buy any acquirer's shares at a very cheap price in the event of a hostile takeover. That provision forced Oracle to take it to court in an effort to avoid the hefty dilution that might be triggered by the poison pill."

Some defense tactics necessitate only changes in the financial structure of the firm, such as repurchasing shares of the firm's outstanding stock. Some tactics require shareholder approval, but the greenmail tactic, wherein money is used to repurchase stock from a corporate raider to avoid the takeover of the firm, does not. These defense tactics are controversial, and the research on their effects is inconclusive. Alternatively, most institutional investors oppose the use of defense tactics. TIAA-CREF and CalPERS have taken actions to have several firms' poison pills eliminated. Many institutional investors have also been opposed to severance packages and the opposition is growing significantly in Europe as well. But there can be advantages to severance packages because they may encourage executives to accept takeover bids that are attractive to shareholders.

Also, as in the case of Carly Fiorina at HP, a severance package may encourage a CEO doing a poor job to depart. A potential problem with the market for corporate control is that it may not be totally efficient. A study of several of the most active corporate raiders in the 1980s showed that approximately 50 percent of their takeover attempts targeted firms with above-average performance in their industry—corporations that were neither undervalued nor poorly managed. The targeting of high-performance businesses may lead to acquisitions at premium prices and to decisions by managers of the targeted firm to establish what may prove to be costly takeover defense tactics to protect their corporate positions. Although the market for corporate control lacks the precision of internal governance mechanisms, the fear of acquisition and influence by corporate raiders is an effective constraint on the managerial-growth motive. The market for corporate control has been responsible for significant changes in many firms' strategies and, when used appropriately, has served shareholders' interests. But this market and other means of corporate governance vary by region of the world and by country. Accordingly, we next address the topic of international corporate governance.

INTERNATIONAL CORPORATE GOVERNANCE

Understanding the corporate governance structure of the United Kingdom and the United States is inadequate for a multinational firm in today's global economy. While the stability associated with German and Japanese governance structures has historically been viewed as an asset, the governance systems in these is changing, just as it is in other parts of the world. These changes are partly the result of multinational firms operating in many different countries and attempting to develop a more global governance system.

While the similarity is increasing, differences remain evident, and firms employing an international strategy must understand these differences in order to operate effectively in different international markets.

CORPORATE GOVERNANCE IN GERMANY

In many private German firms, the owner and manager may still be the same individual. In these instances, there is no agency problem. Even in publicly traded German corporations, there is often a dominant shareholder. Thus, the concentration of ownership is an important means of corporate governance in Germany, as it is in the United States. Historically, banks have been at the center of the German corporate governance structure, as is also the case in many other European countries, such as Italy and France. As lenders, banks become major shareholders when companies they financed earlier seek funding on the stock market or default on loans. Although the stakes are usually under 10 percent, the only legal limit on how much of a firm's stock banks can hold is that a single ownership position cannot exceed 15 percent of the bank's capital.

Through their shareholdings, and by casting proxy votes for individual shareholders who retain their shares with the banks, three banks in particular—Deutsche, Dresdner, and Commerzbank— exercise significant power. Although shareholders can tell the banks how to vote their ownership position, they generally do not do so. A combination of their own holdings and their proxies results in majority positions for these three banks in many German companies. Those banks, along with others, monitor and control managers, both as lenders and as shareholders, by electing representatives to supervisory boards. German firms with more than 2,000 employees are required to have a two-tiered board structure that places the responsibility for monitoring and controlling managerial decisions and actions in the hands of a separate group.

While all the functions of direction and management are the responsibility of the management board, appointment to the Vorstand is the responsibility of the supervisory tier. Employees, union members, and shareholders appoint members to the Aufsichtsrat. Proponents of the German structure suggest that it helps prevent corporate wrongdoing and rash decisions by "dictatorial CEOs." However, critics maintain that it slows decision-making and often ties a CEO's hands. In Germany the power sharing may have gone too far because it includes representation from the local community as well as unions. Accordingly, the corporate governance framework in Germany has made it difficult to restructure companies as quickly as can be done in the United States when performance suffers. Because of the role of local government and the power of banks in Germany's corporate governance structure, private shareholders rarely have major ownership positions in German firms. Large institutional investors, such as pension funds and insurance companies, are also relatively insignificant owners of corporate stock. Thus, at least historically, German executives generally have not been dedicated to the maximization of shareholder value that occurs in many countries. However, corporate governance in Germany is changing, at least partially, because of the increasing globalization of business. Many German firms are beginning to gravitate toward the U.S. system. Recent research suggests that the traditional system produced some agency costs because of a lack of external ownership power. Alternatively, firms with stronger external ownership power were less likely to undertake governance reforms. Firms that adopted governance reforms often divested poorly performing units and achieved higher levels of market performance.

CORPORATE GOVERNANCE IN JAPAN

Attitudes toward corporate governance in Japan are affected by the concepts of obligation, family, and consensus. In Japan, an obligation "may be to return a service for one rendered or it may derive from a more general relationship, for example, to one's family or old alumni, or one's company, or the country. This sense of particular obligation is common elsewhere but it feels stronger in Japan." As part of a company family, individuals are members of a unit that envelops their lives; families command the attention and allegiance of parties throughout corporations. Moreover, a *keiretsu* is more than an economic concept; it, too, is a family. Consensus, an important influence in Japanese corporate governance, calls for the expenditure of significant amounts of energy to win the hearts and minds of people whenever possible, as opposed to top executives issuing edicts. Consensus is highly valued, even when it results in a slow and cumbersome decision-making process.

As in Germany, banks in Japan play an important role in financing and monitoring large public firms. The bank owning the largest share of stocks and the largest amount of debt—the main bank—has the closest relationship with the company's top executives. The main bank provides financial advice to the firm and also closely monitors managers. Thus, Japan has a bank-based financial and corporate governance structure, whereas the United States has a market-based financial and governance structure. Aside from lending money, a Japanese bank can hold up to 5 percent of a firm's total stock; a group of related financial institutions can hold up to 40 percent. In many cases, main-bank relationships are part of a horizontal keiretsu. A keiretsu firm usually owns less than 2 percent of any other member firm; however, each company typically has a stake of that size in every firm in the keiretsu. As a result, somewhere between 30 and 90 percent of a firm is owned by other members of the keiretsu. Thus, a keiretsu is a system of relationship investments. As is the case in Germany, Japan's structure of corporate governance is changing. For example, because of Japanese banks' continuing development as economic organizations, their role in the monitoring and control of managerial behavior and firm outcomes is less significant than in the past. The Asian economic crisis in the latter part of the 1990s made the governance problems in Japanese corporations apparent. The problems were readily evidenced in the large and once-powerful Mitsubishi keiretsu. Many of its core members lost substantial amounts of money in the late 1990s. Still another change in Japan's governance system has occurred in the market for corporate control, which was nonexistent in past years. Japan experienced three recessions in the 1990s and is dealing with another early in the 21st century. As a whole, managers are unwilling to make the changes necessary to turn their companies around.

As a result, many firms in Japan are performing poorly, but could, under the right guidance, improve their performance. For example, Sony Corporation was shaken by the appointment of Howard Stringer, originally from Wales in the United Kingdom, as the new CEO. It is likely that the appointment of a non-Japanese CEO would not have been possible without a set of strong independent outsiders on the board such as Carlos Ghosn, a Brazilian CEO who facilitated Nissan's return to profitability. Outside directors are increasing their influence. Cross-shareholding, which has largely prevented the market for corporate control from developing, has been reduced from 50 to 20 percent over the last decade. As Japan's commercial legal code softens in regard to foreign ownership, foreign investment banks have been looking to buy Japanese domestic firms in order to enter the market, filling the vacuum left by lower cross-shareholding. Interestingly, research suggests that the Japanese stewardship-management approach, historically dominated by inside managers, produces greater investments in longterm R&D projects than does the more financially oriented system in the United States. As the potential for a stronger takeover market increases, some Japanese firms are considering delisting and taking their firms private in order to maintain long-term "strategic flexibility."

GLOBAL CORPORATE GOVERNANCE

The 21st-century competitive landscape is fostering the creation of a relatively uniform governance structure that will be used by firms throughout the world. For example, as markets become more global and customer demands more similar, shareholders are becoming the focus of managers' efforts in an increasing number of companies in Korea and Taiwan. Investors are becoming more and more active throughout the world, as evidenced by the growing shareholder outrage at severance packages given to executives in Europe. Changes in governance are evident in many countries and are moving the governance models closer to that of the United States. Firms in Europe, especially in France and the United Kingdom, are developing boards of directors with more independent members. Similar actions are occurring in Japan, where the boards are being reduced in size and foreign members added. Even in transitional economies, such as those of China and Russia, changes in corporate governance are occurring. However, changes are implemented more slowly in these economies.

Chinese firms have found it helpful to use stock-based compensation plans, thereby providing an incentive for foreign companies to invest in China. Because Russia has reduced controls on the economy and on business activity much faster than China has, the country needs more effective governance systems to control its managerial activities. In fact, research suggests that ownership concentration leads to lower performance in Russia, primarily because minority shareholder rights are not well protected through adequate governance controls.

GOVERNANCE MECHANISMS AND ETHICAL BEHAVIOR

The governance mechanisms described in this chapter are designed to ensure that the agents of the firm's owners—the corporation's top executives—make strategic decisions that best serve the interests of the entire group of stakeholders, as described in Chapter 1. In the United States, shareholders are recognized as a company's most significant stakeholder. Thus, governance mechanisms focus on the control of managerial decisions to ensure that shareholders' interests will be served, but product market stakeholders and organizational stakeholders are important as well. Therefore, at least the minimal interests or needs of all stakeholders must be satisfied through the firm's actions.

Otherwise, dissatisfied stakeholders will withdraw their support from one firm and provide it to another. The firm's strategic competitiveness is enhanced when its governance mechanisms take into consideration the interests of all stakeholders. Although the idea is subject to debate, some believe that ethically responsible companies design and use governance mechanisms that serve all stakeholders' interests. There is, however, a more critical relationship between ethical behavior and corporate governance mechanisms.

The Enron disaster illustrates the devastating effect of poor ethical behavior not only on a firm's stakeholders, but also on other firms. This issue is being taken seriously in other countries such as Japan as well. In addition to Enron, scandals at WorldCom, HealthSouth, and Tyco show that all corporate owners are vulnerable to unethical behaviors by their employees, including top-level managers—the agents who have been hired to make decisions that are in shareholders' best interests. The decisions and actions of a corporation's board of directors can be an effective deterrent to these behaviors.

In fact, some believe that the most effective boards participate actively to set boundaries for their firms' business ethics and values. Once formulated, the board's expectations related to ethical decisions and actions of all of the firm's stakeholders must be clearly communicated to its top-level managers. Moreover, as shareholders' agents, these managers must understand that the board will hold them fully accountable for the development and support of an organizational culture that increases unethical decisions and behaviors. As explained in Chapter 12, CEOs can be positive role models for improved ethical behavior. Only when the proper corporate governance is exercised can strategies be formulated and implemented that will help the firm achieve strategic competitiveness and earn above-average returns. As the discussion in this chapter suggests, corporate governance mechanisms are a vital, yet imperfect, part of firms' efforts to select and successfully use strategies.

2

Corporate Public Relations

Corporate public relations are often underestimated by companies. A corporate PR team must work together to provide a variety of resources to a company. For venture capital, it is extremely important to have a corporate PR team to handle the public attention. A corporate PR team must provide experts in their particular field, necessary tools, resources, information, and media relationships. They must be able to provide as much information about the company to as many people as possible.

Corporate public relations are in charge of finding investors and others that can invest money in your company. A good corporate PR team will be able to identify those investors you may not have been able to find on your own. Most angel investors are looking for different companies to invest in and they will contact some companies that look promising, but it doesn't hurt to contact them first. Every company wants to increase public awareness about their company, service, or product. Without a good corporate PR team, potential investors could be overlooked and missed. The awareness a corporate PR team raises needs to show the company in a good light and build its reputation. It is important to promote the corporate name and build an identity in the marketplace. The more public awareness a person can generate, the better chance you have at increased sales and revenue for the company.

The larger the corporation, the larger the corporate PR team. A corporate PR team must create effective PR campaigns and implement them within the organization. An effective PR campaign takes time, something that most corporations don't have. Several companies don't create PR campaigns because they don't want to deal the hassle of creating one or the hassle of paying for one. A public relations firm will take care of all your PR needs, but they cost a lot of money. Utilizing a PR firm will decrease your companies' chances at building an effective PR team within the organization, especially if the PR firm is in charge of handling all the media relations.

It is important to create a PR campaign to generate public interest about your company. A PR campaign is similar to a marketing campaign. The PR campaign focuses on generating interest for the company, service, or product and building upon the reputation of a company. A PR campaign needs to identify its target audience and create a campaign that focuses on them. Every individual on the corporate PR team needs to be trained with excellent written and verbal communication skills since they alone are in charge of the reputation of the company.

Creating a good corporate PR campaign is pretty simple. Like the marketing campaign, you need to begin with a basic outline. The outline will consist of various ideas from creative staff members. Corporate public relations needs to be thought of as a team effort that needs everyone's input and advice. This is why it is so important to call a brainstorming meeting to discuss everyone's opinion. Individuals hired to be on the corporate public relations team need to be able to strategize and be creative. The goal of corporate PR is to publicize the company and gain awareness. Several corporate PR campaigns work with marketing campaigns to gain awareness about a specific product or service.

The first part of creating an outline for your corporate PR campaign will include deciding who your target audience is and what the best forms of media are to reach them. Decide how big you would like to focus your target on such as local, national or international. Several corporate PR campaigns follow a regional approach and divide the country up into northwest, west, east, south, etc. Once you have decided where you want to target and how you want to target, you need to begin looking at your media contacts. Management often has larger contacts that can be used by the corporate PR team, so be sure you ask for them. The contacts need to include various members of the media including journalists in newspapers, magazines, television, radio, and internet media.

One of the best corporate PR strategies to use is to piggyback on an existing topic. If there is a large media topic at the time, find a way to exploit it by offering expert advice on the topic. Large corporations often have several staff members with expertise in different fields of study. When a media topic has hit the public attention, look for ways to send out press releases to news media members informing them how you can help their story. Contact your close media friends and talk about possibly giving a quote on a story. Developing a good relationship with the media will only help your company grow and increase its public exposure.

There are several ways to promote your business in the corporate PR strategy. Since PR individuals are in charge of building and maintaining the reputation of a company, it is important for them to attend social gatherings where they can network the company with others. Your goal is to establish your credibility in the particular field and establish the image of the company. Several corporations have begun writing weekly or daily blogs that allows them to discuss their expertise in their particular field.

A web site is a very important piece of good corporate public relations. Interested investors and other parties can go to the web site and expect to find detailed content about the products and services of the company. A web site needs to include information about the corporate structure of a company including its officers, directors, and strategic planners. Other information about the company that should be included are the following: a history of the company, how it began and how it grew into the company it is today, information that sets your company apart from your competitors, and additional information that establishes your companies expertise in their field.

In order for interested parties to find your web site, they must be looking for it or for something you promote. Search Engine Optimization is one of the best ways to increase web site exposure and gain new clients or customers. Search Engine Optimization involves not only listing your web site on the major search engines but using marketing strategies to gain more web site visitors. Generally included with search engine optimization is pay-per-click marketing. Pay-per-click marketing involves placing a 2 line ad on the search engines and gaining exposure for the company. When an interested party clicks on your advertisement, you will be charged per click. The web site must also include a link to the blog page. Since blogging has become one of the most popular ways to expand knowledge on particular subjects, thousands of people are posting blogs daily. Using the blog page, you can write articles about particular areas of interest and establish the reputation of the company.

Another excellent way to build the reputation of the company is to write editorials to the newspaper and magazines. You can write articles for both print media materials and see if they will either run your article in full or publish a portion of it. Some journalists will even write a story on a topic of interest that was generated by your PR department and will contact them for expert quotes on the subject matter.

Press releases are one of the easiest ways to gain exposure for your company and build the reputation of a company. Press releases need to be written in the third person and they need to be interesting. One of the most important question to ask yourself with a press release is: "why is this topic interesting to me and why would a media member run a story on it?" A well-written press release will almost certainly be read by a journalist and it will inspire them to write a story based off your press release.

While it may be difficult to get your articles published in the newspaper or magazines, you still have a chance at getting it published on an internet site. Internet articles are easier to get published. Simply write an article that is of interest and submit it to the article submission web sites. Once the article is published, you need to provide a direct link to it through your web site. The more published work you have, the greater chance you have at being considered an expert in your particular field.

Corporate PR teams are also responsible for planning and executing corporate events. Most corporate events are called at "meet and greet" because the guests were invited so the PR people could network with them. A meet and greet is an effective way to build your network of contacts and increase the exposure of the company.

A corporate PR team is responsible for various tasks, the most important is to keep the reputation of the company positive. If media attention is drawn to a negative aspect of the company, it is the corporate PR team's job to fix it and show the company in a positive manner.

DEFINITIONS AND TERMINOLOGY

A fundamental problem in the field of corporate social responsibility (CSR) is that there is no universally accepted definition of the concept. Bowen offered one of the earliest definitions seeing CSR as the "obligations of businessmen to pursue those policies, to make those decisions, or to follow those lines of action which are desirable in terms of the objectives and values of our society". Since then, the field has evolved assuming different names such as corporate social responsiveness and corporate social performance. This evolution also reflects an increase in awareness in important areas of action and performance that the early definitions had overlooked.

For the purposes of this study, we adopted Bowd, Harris, and Cornelissen's definition of CSR, which was derived from the views of scholars such as Carroll, Wood, Freeman, and Friedman. Bowd also incorporated recent industry reports such as Commission of the European Communities and the Financial Times Top 100 Index to define the term:

- CSR is corporations' being held accountable by explicit or inferred social contract with internal and external stakeholders, obeying the laws and regulations of government and operating in an ethical manner which exceeds statutory requirements....

Addressing the vagueness of the term "ethical manner," Bowd, et. al. offered examples of ethical behavior such as proactive community involvement, philanthropy, corporate governance, and commitment to the environment. This definition also entails a commitment to accountability, where the organization is obliged to measure and audit its CSR strategy, aims, principles, and manifestations, while simultaneously continuing its focus on generating profits for investors.

We adopted Bowd definition because we believe it is comprehensive, embracing the dominant academic and industry views on CSR. We next conducted a review of literature – a body which we see more as a collection of approaches rather than a coherent theoretical body of knowledge. The lack of a unified body of knowledge is also indicative of the relative novelty of this field. We have divided the dominant literature in this domain to three categories: the business and society approach, economic approach and stakeholder approach. Using these approaches, we first describe how CSR is practiced around the world, in Asia, and finally in Singapore – the primary focus of this paper and identify the research questions for this study.

BUSINESS AND SOCIETY APPROACH

The view that corporations have an obligation to society developed at a time when corporations were enjoying unprecedented levels of power – especially over citizens – while exercising little social responsibility. Carroll's model of CSR, which came into prominence during the 1970s, framed business responsibilities into four components: economic, legal, ethical, and discretionary. When the author reformulated the model in 1991, he depicted it in the form of a pyramid, with economic performance being the most basic function and moving up to legal, ethical and philanthropic components.

Carroll's CSR pyramid stated that a socially responsible corporation should simultaneously "strive to make a profit, obey the law, be ethical, and be a good corporate citizen". He specifically distinguished between philanthropic and ethical responsibilities noting that many corporations assume that they are being socially responsible by being good corporate citizens in the community. Interestingly, several scholars and economists have in fact rejected philanthropy as a legitimate corporate action. Carroll himself stated that philanthropy, while highly desirable, is actually less important than the first three components of CSR. It should be noted that even though the four components have been discussed as separate constructs, they are not mutually exclusive.

Building on Carroll's work, Lantos classified CSR into three forms: ethical, altruistic, and strategic. Ethical CSR is the minimal, mandatory fulfillment of a corporation's economic, legal, and ethical responsibilities to its publics. Lantos argued that strategic CSR, where corporations participate only in those philanthropic actions that will financially benefit them by attracting positive publicity and goodwill, should be practiced over altruistic CSR, which constitutes making philanthropic contributions at the possible expense of stockholders. He stated that altruistic CSR is not legitimate. Despite their different orientations, these scholars have put forth a common notion that corporations do not operate in isolation from the society where they exist. This symbiotic relationship was summarized by Wood: "Business and society are interwoven rather than distinct entities".

ECONOMIC APPROACH

Contrary to the proponents of the business and society approach, classical economists separated social functions from economic functions, asserting that businesses have the basic responsibility of maximizing profits for their owners or shareholders. Adam Smith, perhaps the first to espouse the market value maximization perspective, argued that by pursuing profits, corporations produce the greatest social good because the invisible hand of the capitalist market ultimately helped solve society's problems. Lantos used the term Economic CSR to refer to profit-oriented CSR activities, which absolves corporations from social contribution because they pay taxes and wages to employees rather than enslaving them. Some economists have gone as far as to argue that the only social responsibility corporations have is to obey the law.

Like Carr, Nobel laureate economist Milton Friedman offered the dominant and well known view representing the economic approach separating social functions from business functions, asserting that the "business of business is business.". However, Friedman did recognize a spectrum of moral and ethical responsibilities, positing that the social responsibility of corporations is to "make as much money as possible while conforming to the basic rules of the society, both those embodied in law and those embodied in ethical custom."

STAKEHOLDER APPROACH

The economic approach overlooked the fact that in the effort to maximize profits, corporations do affect multiple stakeholders. The stakeholder approach to CSR viewed the corporation as "a set of interrelated, explicit or implicit connections between individuals and or groups of individuals" that include anybody who "can affect or is affected by the achievement of the organization's objectives". This approach distinguishes between primary and secondary (e.g. the media and NGOs) stakeholders according to their relative impact on the corporation. It advocates that corporations are responsible for addressing the interests of the various stakeholders – not just those of the owners and/or shareholders – because they make other, non-monetary investments, albeit at varying levels depending on the corporation's objectives.

OPERATIONALIZING AND MEASURING CSR

A prevailing criticism against the functional conceptualization of CSR is that the term is too inclusive and "too vague to be useful". Rowe and Schlacter argued that the vagueness of the term has played a key role in corporations being hesitant to embrace CSR. The difficulty in measuring the manifestations and effects of CSR has proved to be another factor that has deterred managers from embracing the concept. Evidence that can prove the assumed links between CSR and the achievement of corporate goals would perhaps be the "best and most effective argument to encourage uptake of CSR".

Since the 1980s, there has been a growing interest in the field to reconcile theory with practice. Increasing attention is given to the development of measurement initiatives. Cochran and Wood's empirical study represented one of the early attempts to operationalize CSR and linking it to profitability. They used the Moskowitx index - a reputation index that categorized corporations as "outstanding," "honorable mention," or "worst" to measure CSR. They however, conceded in the same study that this measure has its limitations and called for new evaluation tools. Aupperle, Carroll and Hatfield operationalized Carroll's theoretical four-part definition of CSR and used it as a measurement tool. Their study confirmed executives' priorities of Carroll's CSR components in the order: economic, legal, ethical and philanthropic.

CSR AND PROFITABILITY

In recent years, there has been growing evidence in academia suggesting that the relationship between CSR practices and financial performance is at minimum neutral but quite likely positive. To date, there are no generally accepted models for auditing CSR practices, although the Global Reporting Initiative (GRI) and the International Organization for Standardization (ISO) did make significant attempts at providing guidelines for social responsibility. However, these do not constitute an overarching approach to auditing CSP as a result of which many corporations either contract auditing corporations to conduct traditional verification, draw on area expert consultancies, or use customized processes to measure their CSR activities.

CSR AROUND THE WORLD

Although it originated in Western liberal democracies, the CSR movement has evolved into a global movement that includes multiple sectors such as businesses, governments, NGOs, and the general public. Increasing attention is given to CSR in the corporate and public spheres, alongside the proliferation of academic and management literature on the subject. A study by Echo Research found that media coverage on CSR issues in the UK, US, France, and Germany increased by a dramatic 407 % from 2001 to 2002. Today, CSR is receiving increasing attention around the world and has become a legitimate issue on the international diplomatic agenda. Several inter-governmental agreements, such as the International Labor Organization convention, have been in place for years. At the meeting of the World Economic Summit in Davos in 2000, UN Secretary-General Kofi Annan launched Global Compact in an attempt to get corporations around the world to voluntarily incorporate CSR into their operations. Ten principles covering four key areas – human rights, labor standards, environmental protection, and anticorruption – have been established and corporations are asked to voluntarily adopt these principles and self-regulate. Further, at the ISO's international conference on social responsibility, which was attended by stakeholders from 66 countries, there was a consensus among the participants in favor of ISO's work on CSR, affirming that social responsibility is globally relevant and there exists a clear demand for it around the world.

The US is one of the first countries where many corporations had acknowledged CSR as a legitimate business concern as far back as 1971. Competition is the primary driver for corporations to be more socially responsible. A survey by the Centre for Corporate Citizenship at Boston College found that more than 80% of American CEOs polled believed that good CSR practices are beneficial to the bottom-line. The survey also found that a majority of the CEOs wanted CSR to be voluntary and not regulated or governed by law. Significantly, this contrasted with the European approach to CSR, where the preference was towards legislation and government intervention.

PRESSURE ON CORPORATIONS TO BE SOCIALLY RESPONSIBLE

Globalization has played a significant role in being the catalyst for corporate social responsibility. It is not surprising that multinational corporations (MNCs) are the main proponents of CSR since much is at stake for them. Most leading MNCs are headquartered in Western liberal democracies where organizations are pressured by government regulation, the mass media, and citizen groups (NGOs) to be socially responsible. MNCs have a presence around the world, with supply chains and manufacturing factories situated in numerous countries. In addition, business operations have become more transparent with the advancement of modern information and communication technologies. This heightened visibility ensures that unethical or irresponsible corporate actions are increasingly susceptible to public scrutiny and criticism. For example, Nike struggled to regain its reputation years after a sweatshop labor scandal despite its efforts to implement better working conditions. A 2001 Social and Environmental study ranked Nike at the top of the list of corporations that had failed to fulfill their corporate responsibilities.

CSR IN ASIA AND SINGAPORE

The awareness about, and adoption of, CSR practices is generally low in Asia compared to the developed countries of the West. Globalization appears to be the single largest factor that has propelled the CSR movement in Asia. Corporations based in Asia that venture into international markets have to improve their CSR standards to measure up to the expectations of their global stakeholders in order to remain competitive. The way CSR is perceived and practiced is shaped by culture, religion, political, and socio-economic conditions. Thus, there is likely to be significant differences in the way CSR is conducted across different countries and regions.

Especially after the non-profit Centre for CSR was set up in this city-state in 2003, Singapore has seen an increase in attention on CSR among the mass media, academia, government agencies, and corporations although overall awareness level is still considered low. Many early studies used the disclosure method, which analyzed corporations' self-reported CSR performances via corporate annual reports or websites, when studying CSR in Singapore. As CSR can be difficult to quantify, reports provide a means of determining the quality of corporations' commitment to CSR. A study of Singapore's banking, food, and beverage industries during the period 1986-93 showed that 16 of 33 corporations had no references to social responsibility or community involvement. In the remaining 17, CSR reporting was focused largely on employee matters. Although Tsang's paper aimed to stimulate similar studies with the hope of making longitudinal comparisons, we could not find a more recent study to determine whether the situation has changed in the last seven years.

The disclosure method, despite its popularity, has several drawbacks as a measure of CSR practices. For example, corporate social reporting may lag behind actual involvement and might not be an accurate reflection of corporate behavior. This method also may ignore the behavior of smaller corporations who tend to have lower disclosure rates. There is also a concern that the information provided by corporations in their annual reports and websites could be driven by publicity motives.

Recent studies appear to move away from the disclosure method, preferring the stakeholder perspective. A study of nine Asia-pacific countries including Singapore interviewed different stakeholders such as consumers and corporate executives and found that stakeholders in Asia-Pacific are increasingly (a rise from 29% in 2003 to 36% in 2004) concerned with the needs of the community beyond their own needs. About 65% of the stakeholders interviewed for the study felt that corporations need to be socially responsible, compared with 35% in 2003 – almost doubling in just one year.

Interviewees ranked Community welfare as having the lowest priority and saw offering top quality products and services as the most important factor. While the study by Edelman provided good insights on stakeholders' perspectives, the findings were not specific to Singapore and did not account for significant differences in economic development and culture across the countries studied. Hung and Ramasamy also conducted a comparative study of CSR awareness but limited their analysis to only one stakeholder – employees. However, this is consistent with Clarkson's finding that "stakeholder satisfaction" should be used as a measure when evaluating CSR.

Besides the growing attention from scholars and the media, Singapore has hosted an increasing number of CSR conferences. In 2004, three significant conferences on CSR were held in the city-state involving organizations such as the British High Commission, Centre for CSR and UN Global Compact. The conferences were attended by executives of multinational and domestic corporations, small-and-medium-enterprises, and private and public sector organizations. This is indicative of the increasing interest in CSR across a wide spectrum of corporations in Singapore.

At the conference organized by the British High Commission, Nottingham University surveyed the delegates. More than half of the respondents said that there was a person in their organization dedicated to CSR and more than 80% said that they were required to consider CSR implications when doing their job. We feel these results appear to be highly optimistic and note that the sample was skewed as those choosing to attend the conference can be assumed to have heightened interest and a favorable disposition toward CSR from the very outset.

The Nottingham University survey also found that in Singapore, customers, shareholders, and employees were recognized as the most important stakeholders while suppliers, competitors, and NGOs were the least important. This finding corresponds with the stakeholder approach where corporations are more concerned with primary stakeholders. An inconsistency here would be the perceived lack of primacy of suppliers and business partners among the respondents although these stakeholders have direct transactions with the corporation. The researchers noted that the respondents may not pay enough attention to the ability of these groups to do harm to the corporation's reputation – a trap Nike fell into when it believed it could keep the sweatshop practices of suppliers and partners out of its doorstep.

Research Questions Our review of the relevant literature on CSR led us to conclude that the existing research pertaining to CSR in Singapore consists either of studies that measure social reporting or comparative studies between CSR in Singapore and other nations. The current body of knowledge fails to provide information on the current status of CSR in Singapore. We therefore designed this study to assess the current status of CSR among a sample of corporations in Singapore.

3

Corporate-Level Strategy

Our discussions of business-level strategies and the competitive rivalry and competitive dynamics associated with them concentrate on firms competing in a single industry or product market. In this chapter, we introduce you to corporatelevel strategies, which are strategies firms use to *diversify* their operations from a single business competing in a single market into several product markets and most commonly, into several businesses. Thus, a corporate-level strategy specifies actions a firm takes to gain a competitive advantage by selecting and managing a group of different businesses competing in different product markets. Corporate-level strategies help companies select new strategic positions—positions that are expected to increase the firm's value.

As explained in the Opening Case, Brinker International competes in five different markets of the casual dining segment of the restaurant industry. Each of Brinker's dining concepts represents a different business holding a different strategic position in the casual dining segment. As is the case with Brinker International, firms use corporate-level strategies as a means to grow revenues and profits. But the decision to take actions to pursue growth is never a risk-free choice for firms to make. Indeed, effective firms carefully evaluate their growth options before committing firm resources to any of them. Because the diversified firm operates in several different and unique product markets and likely in several businesses, it forms two types of strategies: corporate level and business level. Corporate-level strategy is concerned with two key issues: in what product markets and businesses the firm should compete and how corporate headquarters should manage those businesses.

For the diversified corporation, a business-level strategy must be chosen for each of the businesses in which the firm has decided to compete. In this regard, each of Brinker's dining concepts or businesses uses a differentiation business-level strategy. As is the case with a business-level strategy, a corporate-level strategy is expected to help the firm earn above-average returns by creating value. Some suggest that few corporate-level strategies actually create value. This may have been the case at Morgan Stanley under former CEO Philip Purcell's leadership, as some analysts contend that the corporate-level strategy he put into place lacked coherence and was poorly implemented. In fact, the degree to which corporate-level strategies create value beyond the sums of the value created by all of a firm's business units remains an important research question. Evidence suggests that a corporate-level strategy's value is ultimately determined by the degree to which "the businesses in the portfolio are worth more under the management of the company than they would be under any other ownership." Thus, an effective corporate-level strategy creates, across all of a firm's businesses, aggregate returns that exceed what those returns would be without the strategy and contributes to the firm's strategic competitiveness and its ability to earn above-average returns. Product diversification, a primary form of corporate-level strategies, concerns the scope of the markets and industries in which the firm competes as well as "how managers buy, create and sell different businesses to match skills and strengths with opportunities presented to the firm."

Successful diversification is expected to reduce variability in the firm's profitability as earnings are generated from different businesses. Brinker International executives have this expectation, in that they believe that "even when market factors or internal challenges impact one or more concepts, the other restaurants in our portfolio are there to balance our overall performance." In another example, recent weakness in Boeing Co.'s defense business is being offset by increasing strength in its commercial plane business. Because firms incur development and monitoring costs when diversifying, the ideal portfolio of businesses balances diversification's costs and benefits. CEOs and their top-management teams are responsible for determining the ideal portfolio for their company. We begin this chapter by examining different levels of diversification.

After describing the different reasons firms diversify their operations, we focus on two types of related diversification. When properly used, these strategies help create value in the diversified firm, either through the sharing of resources or the transferring of core competencies across the firm's different businesses. We then discuss unrelated diversification, which is another corporate-level strategy that can create value. The chapter then shifts to the topic of incentives and resources that may stimulate diversification, although the effects of this type of diversification tend to be value neutral. However, managerial motives to diversify, the final topic in the chapter, can actually destroy some of the firm's value.

LEVELS OF DIVERSIFICATION

Diversified firms vary according to their level of diversification and the connections between and among their businesses. Five categories of businesses according to increasing levels of diversification. The single- and dominant-business categories denote relatively low levels of diversification; more fully diversified firms are classified into related and unrelated categories. A firm is related through its diversification when there are several links between its businesses; for example, businesses may share products, technologies, or distribution channels. The more links among businesses, the more "constrained" is the relatedness of diversification. Unrelatedness refers to the absence of direct links between businesses.

LOW LEVELS OF DIVERSIFICATION

A firm pursing a low level of diversification uses either a single- or a dominant-business corporate-level diversification strategy. A *single-business diversification strategy* is a corporate-level strategy wherein the firm generates 95 percent or more of its sales revenue from its core business area. For example, Wm. Wrigley Jr. Company, the world's largest producer of chewing and bubble gums, historically used a single-business strategy while operating in relatively few product markets. Wrigley's trademark chewing gum brands include Spearmint, Doublemint, and Juicy Fruit, although the firm produces other products as well. Sugar-free Extra, which holds the largest share of the U.S. chewing gum market, was introduced in 1984. Alpine is a "throat relief " gum and in 2005 remained the only gum of this type in the market. Wrigley is beginning to diversify its product portfolio to become an important player in the confectionery market. In 2005, Wrigley acquired certain confectionary assets from Kraft Foods Inc., including the well-known brands Life Savers and Altoids.

The purpose of this diversification is to weave the firm's "brands even deeper into the fabric of everyday life around the world." With increasing diversification of its product lines, Wrigley may soon begin using the dominantbusiness corporate-level strategy. With the *dominant-business diversification strategy,* the firm generates between 70 and 95 percent of its total revenue within a single business area. United Parcel Service uses this strategy. Recently UPS generated 74 percent of its revenue from its U.S. package delivery business and 17 percent from its international package business, with the remaining 9 percent coming from the firm's non-package business. Though the U.S. package delivery business currently generates the largest percentage of UPS's sales revenue, the firm anticipates that in the years to come its other two businesses will account for the majority of growth in revenues. This expectation suggests that UPS may become more diversified, both in terms of the goods and services it offers and the number of countries in which those goods and services are offered. If this were to happen, UPS would likely become a moderately diversified firm.

MODERATE AND HIGH LEVELS OF DIVERSIFICATION

A firm generating more than 30 percent of its revenue outside a dominant business and whose businesses are related to each other in some manner uses a related diversification corporate-level strategy. When the links between the diversified firm's businesses are rather direct, a *related constrained diversification strategy* is being used. Campbell Soup, Procter & Gamble, Kodak, and Merck & Company all use a related constrained strategy, as do some large cable companies. With a related constrained strategy, a firm shares resources and activities between its businesses. Cable firms such as Comcast and Time Warner Inc., for example, share technology-based resources and activities across their television programming, high-speed Internet connection, and phone service businesses. Currently, Comcast and Time Warner are seeking to add another related product offering, wireless services, to their portfolios of businesses. For each firm, adding wireless would provide another opportunity to share resources and activities to create more value for stakeholders.

The diversified company with a portfolio of businesses with only a few links between them is called a mixed related and unrelated firm and is using the *related linked diversification strategy*. Johnson & Johnson, General Electric and Cendant use this corporate-level diversification strategy. Compared with related constrained firms, related linked firms share fewer resources and assets between their businesses, concentrating instead on transferring knowledge and core competencies between the businesses. As with firms using each type of diversification strategy, companies implementing the related linked strategy constantly adjust the mix in their portfolio of businesses as well as make decisions about how to manage their businesses.

As explained in the Strategic Focus, GE recently reorganized its businesses in an effort to better manage them and to facilitate the firm's transition from an industrial firm to a more technology-driven company. GE is seeking to create value through its corporatelevel strategy both in terms of the choices made about the businesses in which the firm will compete and how to manage those businesses.

A highly diversified firm that has no relationships between its businesses follows an *unrelated diversification strategy*. United Technologies, Textron, Samsung, and Hutchison Whampoa Limited are examples of firms using this type of corporate-level strategy. Commonly, firms using this strategy are called *conglomerates*. HWL is a leading international corporation committed to innovation and technology with businesses spanning the globe. Ports and related services, telecommunications, property and hotels, retail and manufacturing, and energy and infrastructure are HWL's five core businesses. These businesses are not related to each other, and the firm makes no efforts to share activities or to transfer core competencies between or among them. Each of these five businesses is quite large; for example, the retailing arm of the retail and manufacturing business has more than 6,200 stores in 31 countries. Groceries, cosmetics, electronics, wine, and airline tickets are some of the product categories featured in these stores. This firm's size and diversity suggest the challenge of successfully managing the unrelated diversification strategy.

REASONS FOR DIVERSIFICATION

There are many reasons firms use a corporate-level diversification strategy. Typically, a diversification strategy is used to increase the firm's value by improving its overall performance. Value is created either through related diversification or through unrelated diversification when the strategy allows a company's businesses to increase revenues or reduce costs while implementing their business-level strategies.

Other reasons for using a diversification strategy may have nothing to do with increasing the firm's value; in fact, diversification can have neutral effects or even reduce a firm's value. Value-neutral reasons for diversification include those of a desire to match and thereby neutralize a competitor's market power. Decisions to expand a firm's portfolio of businesses to reduce managerial risk can have a negative effect on the firm's value. Greater amounts of diversification reduce managerial risk in that if one of the businesses in a diversified firm fails, the top executive of that business remains employed by the corporation. In addition, because diversification can increase a firm's size and thus managerial compensation, managers have motives to diversify a firm to a level that reduces its value. Diversification rationales that may have a neutral or negative effect on the firm's value are discussed later in the chapter.

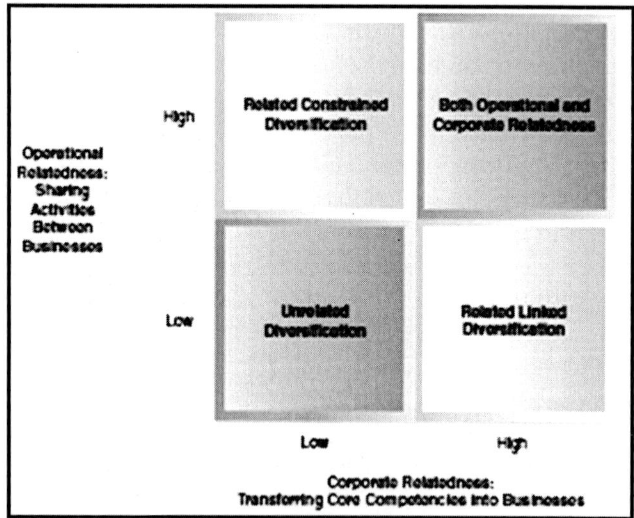

Fig. Value Creating Diversification Strategies: Operational and Corporate Relatedness

Operational relatedness and corporate relatedness are two ways diversification strategies can create value. Study of these independent relatedness dimensions shows the importance of resources and key competencies. The figure's vertical dimension depicts opportunities to share operational activities between businesses while the horizontal dimension suggests opportunities for transferring corporate-level core competencies. The firm with a strong capability in managing operational synergy, especially in sharing assets between its businesses, falls in the upper left quadrant, which also represents vertical sharing of assets through vertical integration. The lower right quadrant represents a highly developed corporate capability for transferring one or more core competencies across businesses. This capability is located primarily in the corporate headquarters office. Unrelated diversification is in the lower left quadrant. Financial economies, rather than either operational or corporate relatedness, are the source of value creation for firms using the unrelated diversification strategy.

VALUE-CREATING DIVERSIFICATION: RELATED CONSTRAINED AND RELATED LINKED DIVERSIFICATION

With the related diversification corporate-level strategy, the firm builds upon or extends its resources and capabilities to create value. The company using the related diversification strategy wants to develop and exploit economies of scope between its businesses. Available to companies operating in multiple product markets or industries, economies of scope are cost savings that the firm creates by successfully sharing some of its resources and capabilities or transferring one or more corporate-level core competencies that were developed in one of its businesses to another of its businesses. Firms seek to create value from economies of scope through two basic kinds of operational economies: sharing activities and transferring corporate-level core competencies. The difference between sharing activities and transferring competencies is based on how separate resources are jointly used to create economies of scope. To create economies of scope, tangible resources, such as plant and equipment or other business-unit physical assets, often must be shared. Less tangible resources, such as manufacturing know-how, also can be shared. However, know-how transferred between separate activities with no physical or tangible resource involved is a transfer of a corporate-level core competence, not an operational sharing of activities.

OPERATIONAL RELATEDNESS: SHARING ACTIVITIES

Firms can create operational relatedness by sharing either a primary activity or a support activity—see Chapter 3's discussion of the value chain. Firms using the related constrained diversification strategy share activities in order to create value. Procter & Gamble uses this corporate-level strategy. P&G's paper towel business and baby diaper business both use paper products as a primary input to the manufacturing process. The firm's paper production plant produces inputs for both businesses and is an example of a shared activity. In addition, because they both produce consumer products, these two businesses are likely to share distribution channels and sales networks. P&G recently acquired Gillette Co. Although the exact nature of the sharing of activities that will be possible after these firms combine their operations is to be determined, there is little doubt that the innovation capabilities of the two firms will be integrated to facilitate activity sharing. In one analyst's words, here is an example of what might happen: "P&G prides itself on what it calls its 'technology transfer' ability, mainly its drive to take technology from one brand and use it in another.

For example, it potentially could apply some of its Olay skin-care ability to Gillette's women's razors, since razors are increasingly trying to include skin-care features." Early reactions to the value-creating possibilities of the transaction between P&G and Gillette were quite favorable, with one analyst saying that that the combination of the two firms was "likely to be a match made in heaven." The ability to share technology from one part of the firm to another may be a cause of the analyst's optimism. If the newly formed P&G becomes more innovative, this is a positive outcome, in that increasingly, "innovation is the driving force behind value creation and competitive advantage." Firms expect activity sharing among units to result in increased strategic competitiveness and improved financial returns. For example, Fidelity Investments has established a money-management unit, called Pyramis Global Advisors. This unit of the giant financial services powerhouse is responsible for overseeing all of Fidelity's equity accounts for institutional investors. At the time of Pyramis's launching, Fidelity was a minor player in the market to manage money for large institutions. Although Pyramis is to operate separately from Fidelity's other businesses, some activities such as the work of financial analysts will be shared to reduce costs and to generate economies of scope.

Other issues affect the degree to which activity sharing creates positive outcomes. For example, managers of other businesses in the firm may feel that a newly created business is unfairly receiving assets. This could be the case at Fidelity where in the short run at least, Robert J. Haber will serve as the chief investment officer for the new business. The issue here is that Haber will also continue managing Fidelity's Focused Stock Fund, which was up 13 percent toward the end of the third quarter in 2005. Thus, analysts working in the successful Focused Stock Fund group may feel that Haber's simultaneously serving as the chief investment office for a newly formed business within Fidelity could reduce his effectiveness with their group. Activity sharing is also risky because ties among a firm's businesses create links between outcomes.

For instance, if demand for one business's product is reduced, there may not be sufficient revenues to cover the fixed costs required to operate the facilities being shared. Organizational difficulties such as these can reduce activity sharing success. Although activity sharing across business businesses isn't risk free, research shows that it can create value. For example, studies that examined acquisitions of firms in the same industry, such as the banking industry, have found that sharing resources and activities and thereby creating economies of scope contributed to postacquisition increases in performance and higher returns to shareholders. Additionally, firms that sold off related units in which resource sharing was a possible source of economies of scope have been found to produce lower returns than those that sold off businesses unrelated to the firm's core business. Still other research discovered that firms with very closely related businesses had lower risk. These results suggest that gaining economies of scope by sharing activities across a firm's businesses may be important in reducing risk and in creating value. Further, more attractive results are obtained through activity sharing when a strong corporate headquarters office facilitates it.

CORPORATE RELATEDNESS:TRANSFERRING OF CORE COMPETENCIES

Over time, the firm's intangible resources, such as its know-how, become the foundation of core competencies. Corporate-level core competencies are complex sets of resources and capabilities that link different businesses, primarily through managerial and technological knowledge, experience, and expertise. The ability to successfully price new products in all of the firm's businesses is an example of what research has shown to be a value-creating, corporate-level competence. Firms seeking to create value through corporate relatedness use the related linked diversification strategy.

There are at least two ways the related linked diversification strategy helps firms to create value. First, because the expense of developing a core competence has been incurred in one of the firm's businesses, transferring it to a second business eliminates the need for that second business to allocate resources to develop it. This is the case at Henkel KGaA, where the firm intends to transfer its competence in nanotechnology from its commercial adhesives business to its industrial adhesives business. Resource intangibility is a second source of value creation through corporate relatedness. Intangible resources are difficult for competitors to understand and imitate. Because of this difficulty, the unit receiving a transferred corporate-level competence often gains an immediate competitive advantage over its rivals. A number of firms have successfully transferred one or more corporate-level core competencies across their businesses.

Virgin Group Ltd. transfers its marketing core competence across travel, cosmetics, music, drinks, mobile phones, health clubs, and a number of other businesses. Thermo Electron uses its entrepreneurial core competence to start new ventures and maintain a new-venture network. Honda has developed and transferred its competence in engine design and manufacturing to its businesses making products such as motorcycles, lawnmowers, and cars and trucks. With respect to smaller engines, for example, these transfers of the corporate-level competence in terms of engine design and manufacturing have been very successful, in that company officials believe that "Honda has become known as the leader in creating fourstroke engines that are reliable, technologically advanced and easy to start." One way managers facilitate the transfer of corporate-level core competencies is by moving key people into new management positions.

However, the manager of an older business may be reluctant to transfer key people who have accumulated knowledge and experience critical to the business's success. Thus, managers with the ability to facilitate the transfer of a core competence may come at a premium, or the key people involved may not want to transfer. Additionally, the top-level managers from the transferring business may not want the competencies transferred to a new business to fulfill the firm's diversification objectives. This could be the case at Fidelity Investments, where managers of the firm's other businesses may not want one or more of their competencies transferred to the newly established Pyramis Global Advisors business. Research partly supports some hesitancy on managers' parts when it comes to transfers, in that those studying this activity have found that transferring expertise in manufacturing-based businesses often does not result in improved performance. Moreover, it seems that businesses in which performance does improve often demonstrate a corporate-wide passion for pursuing skill transfer and appropriate coordination mechanisms for realizing economies of scope.

MARKET POWER

Firms using a related diversification strategy may gain market power when successfully using their related constrained or related linked strategy. Market power exists when a firm is able to sell its products above the existing competitive level or to reduce the costs of its primary and support activities below the competitive level, or both. Federated Department Stores Inc. acquired May Department Stores Co. in part to give the combined company the clout it needs to reduce various costs such as purchasing and distribution below those of competitors. Having market power helps firms successfully use their related diversification strategy. As explained in the Strategic Focus, market power is one of the forces driving Whirlpool Corp.'s proposed acquisition of Maytag Corp.

The transaction between these two firms may face regulatory challenges, primarily because the combined company would have a large part of certain U.S. markets. If approved, though, Whirlpool and Maytag may have complementary resources and capabilities that, when integrated, could result in increased market power. The combined firm might have the clout to reduce costs and to increase product sales by using compatible design and innovation skills to crisply differentiate products from competitors' offerings. Achieving one or both outcomes would increase Whirlpool's market power relative to its competitors. However, increasing its market power is challenging, because competitors are not standing still.

China's Haier Group, for example, is seeking to establish a global brand name for its array of products. In addition to efforts to gain scale as a means of increasing market power, as Whirlpool is attempting to do by acquiring Maytag, firms can create market power through multipoint competition and vertical integration. Multipoint competition exists when two or more diversified firms simultaneously compete in the same product areas or geographic markets. The actions taken by United Parcel Service and FedEx in two markets, overnight delivery and ground shipping, illustrate multipoint competition. UPS has moved into overnight delivery, FedEx's stronghold; FedEx has been buying trucking and ground shipping assets to move into ground shipping, UPS's stronghold. Moreover, there is geographic competition for markets as DHL, the strongest shipping company in Europe, tries to move into the U.S. market. All three competitors are trying to move into large foreign markets to either gain a stake in a market or to expand their existing share of a market. For instance, because China was allowed into the World Trade Organization and government officials have declared the market more open to foreign competition, the battle for global market share among these three top shippers is raging in China and other countries throughout the world. If one of these firms successfully gains strong positions in several markets while competing against its rivals, its market power may increase.

Some firms using a related diversification strategy engage in vertical integration to gain market power. Vertical integration exists when a company produces its own inputs or owns its own source of output distribution. In some instances, firms partially integrate their operations, producing and selling their products by using company businesses as well as outside sources. Vertical integration is commonly used in the firm's core business to gain market power over rivals. Market power is gained as the firm develops the ability to save on its operations, avoid market costs, improve product quality, and, possibly, protect its technology from imitation by rivals. Market power also is created when firms have strong ties between their assets for which no market prices exist. Establishing a market price would result in high search and transaction costs, so firms seek to vertically integrate rather than remain separate businesses.

There are limits to vertical integration. For example, an outside supplier may produce the product at a lower cost. As a result, internal transactions from vertical integration may be expensive and reduce profitability relative to competitors. Also, bureaucratic costs may occur with vertical integration. And, because vertical integration can require substantial investments in specific technologies, it may reduce the firm's flexibility, especially when technology changes quickly. Finally, changes in demand create capacity balance and coordination problems. If one business is building a part for another internal business, but achieving economies of scale requires the first division to manufacture quantities that are beyond the capacity of the internal buyer to absorb, it would be necessary to sell the parts outside the firm as well as to the internal business. Thus, although vertical integration can create value, especially through market power over competitors, it is not without risks and costs.

For example, Merck, the pharmaceutical company, previously owned a pharmacybenefits management company called Medco Health. Medco acts as a middleman between patients, insurers, and drugmakers, which led to conflicts of interest with its parent company. By revenue, Medco was 50 percent larger than Merck, but had a much smaller profit margin. Because of the legal headaches caused by the conflicts of interest, as well as the small profit margin and a desire to focus more attention on its own underlying profitability, Merck spun off Medco in mid-2003. This decision indicates that the benefits Merck expected from vertical integration did not fully materialize. Many manufacturing firms no longer pursue vertical integration as a means of gaining market power. In fact, deintegration is the focus of most manufacturing firms, such as Intel and Dell, and even some large auto companies, such as Ford and General Motors, as they develop independent supplier networks. Solectron Corp., a contract manufacturer, represents a new breed of large contract manufacturers that is helping to foster this revolution in supply-chain management. Such firms often manage their customers' entire product lines and offer services ranging from inventory management to delivery and after-sales service. Conducting business through e-commerce also allows vertical integration to be changed into "virtual integration." Thus, closer relationships are possible with suppliers and customers through virtual integration or electronic means of integration, allowing firms to reduce the costs of processing transactions while improving their supply-chain management skills and tightening the control of their inventories. This evidence suggests that *virtual integration* rather than *vertical integration* may be a more common source of market power gains for today's firms.

SIMULTANEOUS OPERATIONAL RELATEDNESS AND CORPORATE RELATEDNESS

Some firms simultaneously seek operational and corporate relatedness to create economies of scope. Although difficult, the ability to simultaneously create economies of scope by sharing activities and transferring core competencies is very hard for competitors to understand and learn how to imitate. However, firms that fail in their efforts to simultaneously obtain operational and corporate relatedness may create the opposite of what they seek—namely, diseconomies of scope instead of economies of scope. Walt Disney Co. uses a related diversification strategy to simultaneously create economies of scope through operational and corporate relatedness. Within the firm's Studio Entertainment business, for example, Disney can gain economies of scope by sharing activities among its different movie distribution companies such as Touchstone Pictures, Hollywood Pictures, and Dimension Films, among others. Broad and deep knowledge about its customers is a capability on which Disney relies to develop corporate-level core competencies in terms of advertising and marketing. With these competencies, Disney is able to create economies of scope through corporate relatedness as it cross-sells products that are highlighted in its movies through the distribution channels that are part of its Parks and Resorts and Consumer Products businesses.

Thus, characters created in movies become figures that are marketed through Disney's retail stores. In addition, themes established in movies become the source of new rides in the firm's theme parks, which are part of the Parks and Resorts business. As we have described, Walt Disney Co. successfully uses related diversification as a corporate-level strategy through which it creates economies of scope by sharing some activities and by transferring core competencies. However, it is difficult for investors to actually observe the value created by a firm as it shares activities and transfers core competencies. Because of this, the value of the assets of a firm using a diversification strategy to create economies of scope in these manners tend to be discounted by investors. In general, the reason for this discount is that investors face a "lingering question whether multiple revenue streams will outpace multiple-platform overhead."

UNRELATED DIVERSIFICATION

Firms do not seek either operational relatedness or corporate relatedness when using the unrelated diversification corporate-level strategy. An unrelated diversification strategy can create value through two types of financial economies. Financial economies are cost savings realized through improved allocations of financial resources based on investments inside or outside the firm. Efficient internal capital allocations can lead to financial economies. Efficient internal capital allocations reduce risk among the firm's businesses—for example, by leading to the development of a portfolio of businesses with different risk profiles. The second type of financial economy concerns the purchasing of other corporations and then the restructuring of their assets. Here, the diversified firm buys another company, restructures that company's assets in ways that allow it to operate more profitably, and then sells the company for a profit in the external market. Next, we discuss the two types of financial economies in greater detail.

EFFICIENT INTERNAL CAPITAL MARKET ALLOCATION

In a market economy, capital markets are thought to efficiently allocate capital. Efficiency results as investors take equity positions with high expected future cash-flow values. Capital is also allocated through debt as shareholders and debtholders try to improve the value of their investments by taking stakes in businesses with high growth and profitability prospects. In large diversified firms, the corporate headquarters office distributes capital to its businesses to create value for the overall corporation. The nature of these distributions may generate gains from internal capital market allocations that exceed the gains that would accrue to shareholders as a result of capital being allocated by the external capital market.

This happens because while managing the firm's portfolio of businesses, those in a firm's corporate headquarters may gain access to detailed and accurate information regarding those businesses' actual and prospective performance. Compared with corporate office personnel, investors have relatively limited access to internal information and can only estimate the performances of individual businesses as well as their future prospects. Moreover, although businesses seeking capital must provide information to potential suppliers, firms with internal capital markets may have at least two informational advantages. First, information provided to capital markets through annual reports and other sources may not include negative information, instead emphasizing positive prospects and outcomes. External sources of capital have limited ability to understand the operational dynamics of large organizations.

Even external shareholders who have access to information have no guarantee of full and complete disclosure. Second, although a firm must disseminate information, that information also becomes simultaneously available to the firm's current and potential competitors. With insights gained by studying such information, competitors might attempt to duplicate a firm's value-creating strategy. Thus, an ability to efficiently allocate capital through an internal market may help the firm protect the competitive advantages it develops while using its corporatelevel strategy as well as its various business-unit level strategies. If intervention from outside the firm is required to make corrections to capital allocations, only significant changes are possible, such as forcing the firm into bankruptcy or changing the top management team. Alternatively, in an internal capital market, the corporate headquarters office can fine-tune its corrections, such as choosing to adjust managerial incentives or suggesting strategic changes in one of the firm's businesses. Thus, capital can be allocated according to more specific criteria than is possible with external market allocations.

Because it has less accurate information, the external capital market may fail to allocate resources adequately to high-potential investments. The corporate headquarters office of a diversified company can more effectively perform such tasks as disciplining underperforming management teams through resource allocations. Research suggests, however, that in efficient capital markets, the unrelated diversification strategy may be discounted. "For years, stock markets have applied a 'conglomerate discount': they value diversified manufacturing conglomerates at 20 percent less, on average, than the value of the sum of their parts. The discount still applies, in good economic times and bad. Extraordinary manufacturers can defy it for a while, but more ordinary ones cannot." One reason for this discount could be that firms sometimes substitute acquisitions for innovation. In these instances, too many resources are allocated to analyzing and completing acquisitions to further diversify a firm instead of allocating an appropriate amount of resources to nurture internal innovations. This happened for some Japanese drug firms between 1975 and 1995, a time period during which "corporate diversification was a strategic substitute for significant innovation." In spite of the challenges associated with it, a number of corporations continue to use the unrelated diversification strategy.

This is certainly the case in Europe, where the use of unrelated diversification is increasing, and in emerging markets as well. The Achilles' heel for firms using the unrelated diversification strategy in a developed economy is that competitors can imitate financial economies more easily than they can replicate the value gained from the economies of scope developed through operational relatedness and corporate relatedness. This is less of a problem in emerging economies, where the absence of a "soft infrastructure" supports and encourages use of the unrelated diversification strategy. In fact, in emerging economies such as those in India and Chile, diversification increases the performance of firms affiliated with large diversified business groups. The increasing skill levels of people working in corporations located in emerging markets may support the successful use of the unrelated diversification strategy.

RESTRUCTURING OF ASSETS

Financial economies can also be created when firms learn how to create value by buying, restructuring, and then selling other companies' assets in the external market. As in the real estate business, buying assets at low prices, restructuring them, and selling them at a price exceeding their cost generates a positive return on the firm's invested capital. In recent years, Blackstone Group, a private equity firm, has bought and restructured hotel assets. Blackstone acquired Wyndham International Inc. in 2005 with the intention of building the brand name as the foundation for positively restructuring the chain's assets. Previously, Blackstone bought and then restructured the assets of the 143-hotel AmeriSuites chain before profitably selling the chain to Hyatt Corp.

Creating financial economies by acquiring and restructuring other companies' assets requires an understanding of significant trade-offs. Success usually calls for a focus on mature, low-technology businesses because of the uncertainty of demand for high-technology products. In high-technology businesses, resource allocation decisions become too complex, creating information-processing overload on the small corporate headquarters offices that are common in unrelated diversified firms. High-technology businesses are often human-resource dependent; these people can leave or demand higher pay and thus appropriate or deplete the value of an acquired firm. Buying and then restructuring service-based assets so they can be profitably sold in the external market is also difficult. Here, sales often are a product of close personal relationships between a client and the representative of the firm being restructured. Thus, for both high-technology firms and service-based companies, relatively few tangible assets can be restructured to create value that can be profitably sold. It is difficult to restructure intangible assets such as human capital and effective relationships that have evolved over time between buyers and sellers.

VALUE-NEUTRAL DIVERSIFICATION: INCENTIVES AND RESOURCES

The objectives firms seek when using related diversification and unrelated diversification strategies all have the potential to help the firm create value by using a corporatelevel strategy. However, these strategies, as well as single- and dominant-business diversification strategies, are sometimes used with value-neutral rather than value-creating objectives in mind. As we discuss next, different incentives to diversify sometimes surface, and the quality of the firm's resources may permit only diversification that is value neutral rather than value creating.

INCENTIVES TO DIVERSIFY

Incentives to diversify come from both the external environment and a firm's internal environment. External incentives include antitrust regulations and tax laws. Internal incentives include low performance, uncertain future cash flows, and the pursuit of synergy and reduction of risk for the firm.

Antitrust Regulation and Tax Laws

Government antitrust policies and tax laws provided incentives for U.S. firms to diversify in the 1960s and 1970s. Antitrust laws prohibiting mergers that created increased market power were stringently enforced during that period. Merger activity that produced conglomerate diversification was encouraged primarily by the Celler-Kefauver Antimerger Act, which discouraged horizontal and vertical mergers. As a result, many of the mergers during the 1960s and 1970s were "conglomerate" in character, involving companies pursuing different lines of business. Between 1973 and 1977, 79.1 percent of all mergers were conglomerate. During the 1980s, antitrust enforcement lessened, resulting in more and larger horizontal mergers. In addition, investment bankers became more open to the kinds of mergers facilitated by regulation changes; as a consequence, takeovers increased to unprecedented numbers.

The conglomerates, or highly diversified firms, of the 1960s and 1970s became more "focused" in the 1980s and early 1990s as merger constraints were relaxed and restructuring was implemented. In the late 1990s and early 2000s, antitrust concerns emerged again with the large volume of mergers and acquisitions. Mergers are now receiving more scrutiny than they did in the 1980s and through the early 1990s. As we noted in a Strategic Focus, the proposed transaction between Whirlpool and Maytag is expected to be carefully examined by regulators. The tax effects of diversification stem not only from corporate tax changes but also from individual tax rates. Some companies generate more cash from their operations than they can reinvest profitably. Some argue that *free cash flows* should be redistributed to shareholders as dividends. However, in the 1960s and 1970s, dividends were taxed more heavily than were capital gains. As a result, before 1980, shareholders preferred that firms use free cash flows to buy and build companies in high-performance industries. If the firm's stock value appreciated over the long term, shareholders might receive a better return on those funds than if the funds had been redistributed as dividends, because returns from stock sales would be taxed more lightly than dividends would. Under the 1986 Tax Reform Act, however, the top individual ordinary income tax rate was reduced from 50 to 28 percent, and the special capital gains tax was changed to treat capital gains as ordinary income.

These changes created an incentive for shareholders to stop encouraging firms to retain funds for purposes of diversification. These tax law changes also influenced an increase in divestitures of unrelated business units after 1984. Thus, while individual tax rates for capital gains and dividends created a shareholder incentive to increase diversification before 1986, they encouraged less diversification after 1986, unless it was funded by tax-deductible debt. The elimination of personal interest deductions, as well as the lower attractiveness of retained earnings to shareholders, might prompt the use of more leverage by firms, for which interest expense is tax deductible. Corporate tax laws also affect diversification. Acquisitions typically increase a firm's depreciable asset allowances. Increased depreciation produces lower taxable income, thereby providing an additional incentive for acquisitions. Before 1986, acquisitions may have been the most attractive means for securing tax benefits, but the 1986 Tax Reform Act diminished some of the corporate tax advantages of diversification.

The recent changes recommended by the Financial Accounting Standards Board—eliminating the "pooling of interests" method for accounting for the acquired firm's assets and eliminating the write-off for research and development in process—reduce some of the incentives to make acquisitions, especially acquisitions in related high-technology industries. Although there was a loosening of federal regulations in the 1980s and a retightening in the late 1990s, a number of industries have experienced increased merger activity due to industry-specific deregulation activity, including banking, telecommunications, oil and gas, and electric utilities. Regulations changes have also affected convergence between media and telecommunications industries, which has allowed a number of mergers, such as the successive Time Warner and AOL Time Warner mergers. The Federal Communications Commission has made a highly contested ruling "allowing broadcasters to own TV stations that reach 45 percent of U.S. households, up from 35 percent, own three stations in the largest markets and own a TV station and newspaper in the same town."

Critics argued that the change in regulations would allow "an orgy of mergers and acquisitions" and that "it is a victory for free enterprise, but it is not a victory for free speech." Although the FCC has put forth new rules, those rule revisions were found to be substantially unjustified by Congress, which remanded them to the FCC for further deliberation. Also, Congress is considering legislation that may affect regulation of broadcasting, including ownership restrictions. Because of the impending regulatory change, a number of firms have considered potential acquisitions. For example, the FCC has allowed cable companies to get into local phone service. In Orange County, California, cable TV companies now provide 25 percent of local phone service. Phone companies have also been moving into selling TV service, although technology has been hindered until recently because high frequencies, which TV signals use, fade out on thin copper wires. At one point, to overcome this problem, SBC, a large local telephone operator, considered acquiring DirecTV, a satellite TV market leader. Thus, regulatory changes such as the ones we have described create incentives for diversification.

Low Performance

Some research shows that low returns are related to greater levels of diversification. If "high performance eliminates the need for greater diversification," then low performance may provide an incentive for diversification. Poor performance may lead to increased diversification, as it did with the formerly independent Sears, Roebuck and Co., especially if resources exist to do so. During the 1990s and early into the 21st century, Sears struggled and teetered on the edge of bankruptcy. During these times, Sears endured competitive threats from a number of fronts, including Home Depot and Lowe's strong movements into appliances. One of Sears' responses to the threats it faced was to diversify its operations. The purchase of Lands' End in 2002, for example, moved Sears into a different type of clothing. However, in total, the efforts Sears undertook to improve its performance, including diversification-related decisions, weren't successful. In November 2004, Sears and Kmart merged to form what the firms called "a major new retail company." The newly created firm, Sears Holdings Company, is widely diversified and is the third largest retailer in the United States. Time will tell if creating a widely diversified corporation will be the pathway to the strategic success that eluded both Sears and Kmart when they were independent companies.

Research evidence and the experience of a number of firms suggest that an overall curvilinear relationship may exist between diversification and performance. The German media company Bertelsmann was led by then CEO Thomas Middelhoff into a variety of new ventures, especially Internet ones, that have proved to be a drag on the company's resources and have provided very little return on investment. The current CEO, Gunter Thielen, is emphasizing a return to basics by getting rid of non-core businesses, such as the Internet ventures. "The course has been pretty clear since Middelhoff left," says a German consultant: "Focus on the businesses that they understand and dominate." These businesses include producing books, magazines, music, and TV shows. Under Thielen's leadership, Bertelsmann has regrouped and refocused on what it does best.

Uncertain Future Cash Flows

As a firm's product line matures or is threatened, diversification may be taken as an important defensive strategy. Small firms and companies in mature or maturing industries sometimes find it necessary to diversify for long-term survival. For example, uncertainty was one of the dominant reasons for diversification among railroad firms during the 1960s and 1970s. Railroads diversified primarily because the trucking industry was thought to have the capability to have substantially negative effects on the rail business. The trucking industry created uncertainty for railroad operators regarding the future levels of demand for their services. Diversifying into other product markets or into other businesses can reduce the uncertainty about a firm's future cash flows. Competing in five parts of the casual dining segment helps to reduce demand uncertainty for Brinker International, for example. In this instance, while the demand for one of Brinker's dining concepts might decline at a point in time, demand for one or more of its other concepts might increase at the same moment. The uncertainty of cash flows is one of the reasons Brinker has diversified into different parts of the casual dining segment of the restaurant industry.

Synergy and Firm Risk Reduction

Diversified firms pursuing economies of scope often have investments that are too inflexible to realize synergy between business units. As a result, a number of problems may arise. Synergy exists when the value created by business units working together exceeds the value that those same units create working independently. But as a firm increases its relatedness between business units, it also increases its risk of corporate failure, because synergy produces joint interdependence between businesses that constrains the firm's flexibility to respond. This threat may force two basic decisions. First, the firm may reduce its level of technological change by operating in environments that are more certain. This behavior may make the firm risk averse and thus uninterested in pursuing new product lines that have potential, but are not proven.

Alternatively, the firm may constrain its level of activity sharing and forgo synergy's potential benefits. Either or both decisions may lead to further diversification. The former would lead to related diversification into industries in which more certainty exists. The latter may produce additional, but unrelated, diversification. Research suggests that a firm using a related diversification strategy is more careful in bidding for new businesses, whereas a firm pursuing an unrelated diversification strategy may be more likely to overprice its bid, because an unrelated bidder may not have full information about the acquired firm. However, firms using either a related or an unrelated diversification strategy must understand the consequences of paying large premiums. For example, even though the P&G and Gillette transaction is being viewed positively, as we previously noted, the annual growth rate of Gillette's product lines in the newly created company will need to average 12.1 percent or more for P&G's shareholders to benefit financially from the additional diversification resulting from this merger.

RESOURCES AND DIVERSIFICATION

As we have discussed, there are several value-neutral incentives for firms to diversify as well as value-creating incentives. However, even when incentives to diversify exist, a firm must have the types and levels of resources and capabilities needed to successfully use a corporate-level diversification strategy. Although both tangible and intangible resources facilitate diversification, they vary in their ability to create value. Indeed, the degree to which resources are valuable, rare, difficult to imitate, and non-substitutable influence their ability to create value through diversification. For instance, free cash flows are a tangible, financial resource that may be used to diversify the firm.

However, compared with diversification that is grounded in intangible resources, diversification based on financial resources only is more visible to competitors and thus more imitable and less likely to create value on a long-term basis. Tangible resources usually include the plant and equipment necessary to produce a product and tend to be less-flexible assets. Any excess capacity often can be used only for closely related products, especially those requiring highly similar manufacturing technologies. Excess capacity of other tangible resources, such as a sales force, can be used to diversify more easily. Again, excess capacity in a sales force is more effective with related diversification, because it may be utilized to sell similar products. The sales force would be more knowledgeable about related-product characteristics, customers, and distribution channels. Tangible resources may create resource interrelationships in production, marketing, procurement, and technology, defined earlier as activity sharing. Intangible resources are more flexible than tangible physical assets in facilitating diversification. Although the sharing of tangible resources may induce diversification, intangible resources such as tacit knowledge could encourage even more diversification. Sometimes, however, the benefits expected from using resources to diversify the firm for either value-creating or value-neutral reasons are not gained. For example, Wendy's International decided to sell up to 18 percent of its Tim Horton's doughnut chain through an initial public offering that was to be completed by the end of the first quarter of 2006.

Influencing this decision was the fact that the doughnut chain had "posted break-even results over the past three years." Thus, Wendy's resources were being used for value-neutral purposes through its diversification into the doughnut business. Wendy's expected to use the resources generated through the IPO to focus on product development improvements in its core restaurants and perhaps to pursue other diversification possibilities that would create value rather than being only value neutral. Similarly, Sara Lee Corporation is "embarking on an aggressive strategic plan that will transform the entire enterprise into a tightly focused food, beverage and household products company." Through these efforts, Sara Lee intends to eliminate both the valuecreating and value-neutral diversification choices that were not helping the firm substantially improve its financial performance. Under the direction of the firm's new CEO, resources generated by selling off assets were to be redeployed toward strategic acquisitions and product innovation.

VALUE-REDUCING DIVERSIFICATION: MANAGERIAL MOTIVES TO DIVERSIFY

Managerial motives to diversify can exist independently of value-neutral reasons and value-creating reasons. The desire for increased compensation and reduced managerial risk are two motives for toplevel executives to diversify their firm beyond value-creating and value-neutral levels. In slightly different words, top-level executives may diversify a firm in order to diversify their own employment risk, as long as profitability does not suffer excessively. Diversification provides additional benefits to top-level managers that shareholders do not enjoy. Research evidence shows that diversification and firm size are highly correlated, and as firm size increases, so does executive compensation. Because large firms are complex, difficult-to-manage organizations, top-level managers commonly receive substantial levels of compensation to lead them.

Greater levels of diversification can increase a firm's complexity, resulting in still more compensation for executives to lead an increasingly diversified organization. Governance mechanisms, such as the board of directors, monitoring by owners, executive compensation practices, and the market for corporate control, may limit managerial tendencies to overdiversify. These mechanisms are discussed in more detail in Chapter 10. In some instances, though, a firm's governance mechanisms may not be strong, resulting in a situation in which executives may diversify the firm to the point that it fails to earn even average returns. The loss of adequate internal governance may result in poor relative performance, thereby triggering a threat of takeover. Although takeovers may improve efficiency by replacing ineffective managerial teams, managers may avoid takeovers through defensive tactics, such as "poison pills," or may reduce their own exposure with "golden parachute" agreements. Therefore, an external governance threat, although restraining managers, does not flawlessly control managerial motives for diversification.

Most large publicly held firms are profitable because the managers leading them are positive stewards of firm resources, and many of their strategic actions, including those related to selecting a corporate-level diversification strategy, contribute to the firm's success. As mentioned, governance mechanisms should be designed to deal with exceptions to the managerial norms of making decisions and taking actions that will increase the firm's ability to earn above-average returns. Thus, it is overly pessimistic to assume that managers usually act in their own self-interest as opposed to their firm's interest.

Top-level executives' diversification decisions may also be held in check by concerns for their reputation. If a positive reputation facilitates development and use of managerial power, a poor reputation may reduce it. Likewise, a strong external market for managerial talent may deter managers from pursuing inappropriate diversification. In addition, a diversified firm may police other firms by acquiring those that are poorly managed in order to restructure its own asset base. Knowing that their firms could be acquired if they are not managed successfully encourages executives to use value-creating, diversification strategies.

The level of diversification that can be expected to have the greatest positive effect on performance is based partly on how the interaction of resources, managerial motives, and incentives affects the adoption of particular diversification strategies. As indicated earlier, the greater the incentives and the more flexible the resources, the higher the level of expected diversification. Financial resources should have a stronger relationship to the extent of diversification than either tangible or intangible resources. Tangible resources are useful primarily for related diversification. As discussed in this chapter, firms can create more value by effectively using diversification strategies. However, diversification must be kept in check by corporate governance. Appropriate strategy implementation tools, such as organizational structures, are also important.

We have described corporate-level strategies in this chapter. In the next one, we discuss mergers and acquisitions as prominent means for firms to diversify and to grow profitably while doing so. These trends toward more diversification through acquisitions, which have been partially reversed due to restructuring, indicate that learning has taken place regarding corporate-level diversification strategies. Accordingly, firms that diversify should do so cautiously, choosing to focus on relatively few, rather than many, businesses. In fact, research suggests that although unrelated diversification has decreased, related diversification has increased, possibly due to the restructuring that continued into the 1990s and early 21st century.

This sequence of diversification followed by restructuring is now taking place in Europe and other places such as Korea, mirroring actions of firms in the United States and the United Kingdom. Firms can improve their strategic competitiveness when they pursue a level of diversification that is appropriate for their resources and core competencies and the opportunities and threats in their country's institutional and competitive environments.

4

Corporate Media

"Corporate media" is a term which refers to a system of mass media production, distribution, ownership, and funding which is dominated by corporations and their CEOs. It is owned by the capitalist imperatives of maximizing profits for investors, stockholders, and advertisers. It is sometimes used as a term of derision to indicate a media system which does not serve the public interest in place of the "mainstream media" or "MSM," which tends to be used by both the political left and the right as a derisive term.

Media critics such as Robert McChesney, Ben Bagdikian, Ralph Nader, Jim Hightower, Noam Chomsky and Amy Goodman suggest that such a media system, especially when allowed to dominate the mainstream media, inevitably will be manipulated by these same corporations to suit their own interests. These critics point out that the main national networks, NBC, CBS, and ABC, as well as most if not all of the smaller cable channels, are owned, funded, and controlled by an interconnected network of large corporate conglomerates and international banking interests, which they say manipulate and filter out news that does not fit their corporate agenda.

They also argue that the programming on these outlets clearly reflects the conservative views of its owners, most notably Fox News Channel, headed by Rupert Murdoch through his parent company News Corp., as well as Roger Ailes, the CEO of FOX News itself.

PROPAGANDA MODEL

Noam Chomsky and Edward S. Herman have established a propaganda model which purports to explain this bias. The common misinterpretation of this model is that all bias is conscious and centralized. The process however is hypothesized to be decentralized and operates as a confluence of factors that includes the overt pressure from owners and advertisers, but also by the gradual internalization of the biases and values of the corporate owners, leading to self-censorship.

Other factors include the tendency of journalists to avoid doing original research, instead obtaining news from the same few wire services, such as Reuters and Associated Press, which themselves tend to cover the same news under the same perspective. Due to the desire to reduce operation costs, the mainstream media favour news pieces that are pre-made by these news agencies instead of conducting their own reporting.

Impact of Public Relations on News and Public Affairs Programming

This same economic pressure makes media susceptible to manipulation by government and other corporate sources through the widespread use of press releases, often created by industry-funded public relations firms.

Impact of the Corporate Media Propaganda Model on World Events and Societies

The point of view and statements made by governments, officials, military, police, national security organizations (such as the FBI and CIA), as well as various other political offices are regularly reported as facts and are published without any (or very little) fact checking by the corporate media. Perhaps the most infamous current example of the impact of the propaganda model on world events and societies was during the two year period following September 11, 2001.

During this time, according to a five year in depth research project conducted by The Centre for Public Integrity; the President of the United States (George W. Bush) and seven high ranking officials in his administration made at least 935 or more false statements about the threat posed to the world and to American national security by Suddam Hussein. These false statements were virtually uncontested by the corporate media and presented as a sound rationale for both the invasion of (and war against) Iraq and "The War on Terror/ism".

The result was the "manufacturing of consent" for the invasion of Iraq and "The Global War on Terror/ism" in which hundreds of thousands of people have lost their lives to date. As an example Jessica Yellin on Anderson Cooper 360 admitted being pressured by corporate executives to present positive stories during the run up to the Iraq war.

Anderson Cooper 360 Transcript of Jessica Yellin

COOPER: Jessica, McClellan took press to task for not upholding their reputation. He writes: "The National Press Corps was probably too deferential to the White House and to the administration in regard to the most important decision facing the nation during my years in Washington, the choice over whether to go to war in Iraq.

The 'liberal media' — in quotes — didn't live up to its reputation. If it had, the country would have been better served." Dan Bartlett, former Bush adviser, called the allegation "total crap." What is your take? Did the press corps drop the ball? Jessica yellin, cnn congressional correspondent: I wouldn't go that far. I think the press corps dropped the ball at the beginning. When the lead-up to the war began, the press corps was under enormous pressure from corporate executives, frankly, to make sure that this was a war that was presented in a way that was consistent with the patriotic fever in the nation and the president's high approval ratings.

And my own experience at the White House was that, the higher the president's approval ratings, the more pressure I had from news executives — and I was not at this network at the time — but the more pressure I had from news executives to put on positive stories about the president. I think, over time.

Cooper: You had pressure from news executives to put on positive stories about the president?

Yellin: Not in that exact — they wouldn't say it in that way, but they would edit my pieces. They would push me in different directions. They would turn down stories that were more critical and try to put on pieces that were more positive, yes. That was my experience.

Factcheck.org, created by the Annenberg school of Public Policy at the University of Pennsylvania, found hundreds of misrepresentations in political ads that were never corrected by the mainstream media. Studies also show that those who rely on the media for their information have a poor understanding of the issues and are unable to discern misrepresentations in political advertising.

As documented by authors Sheldon Rampton and John Stauber, it is becoming increasingly common for video news releases (VNR) to be created by government and corporations, mimicking TV news story-format to be used straight into broadcasting in a newscast. Other factors include the cost of litigation. Large corporations tend to sue over any news that are against their interests, causing great expense for the news editors. Even if the litigation is lost, the cost of time and pressure will certainly bias a reporter towards avoiding such possibility.

WATCHDOG JOURNALISM

Watchdog journalism is a type of investigative journalism. It refers to forms of activist journalism aimed at holding accountable public personalities and institutions whose functions impact social and political life. The term lapdog journalism is sometimes used as a conceptual opposite to watchdog journalism.

Watchdog journalism is most commonly found in think tanks, alternative media, and citizen journalism such as blogs. It is occasionally found in mainstream media as well. Since independent media and think tanks are not profit-oriented, they have more latitude in which to adopt strong positions and cover a wide range of topics.

However, it is also more difficult to determine the backing of non-mainstream outlets so those are sometime subject to covert exploitation by well-funded interests. In recent history, a notable example of watchdog journalism was the exposure of Dan Rather's investigative segment which cast George W. Bush's military record in an unfavorable light. The segment was based on the Killian documents, which blogger journalists exposed as being insufficiently verifiable as authentic.

ALTERNATIVE MEDIA

Alternative media are media (newspapers, radio, television, movies, Internet, etc.) which are alternatives to the business or government-owned mass media. Proponents of alternative media argue that the mainstream media are biased. While sources of alternative media can also be biased (sometimes proudly so), proponents claim that the bias is significantly different than that of the mainstream media, hence these media provide an "alternative" viewpoint.

As such, advocacy journalism tends to be a component of many alternative outlets. Because the term "alternative" has connotations of self-marginalization, some media outlets now prefer the term "independent" over "alternative".

PROPAGANDA MODEL

The propaganda model is a theory advanced by Edward S. Herman and Noam Chomsky that alleges systemic biases in the mass media and seeks to explain them in terms of structural economic causes.

First presented in their 1988 book Manufacturing Consent: The Political Economy of the Mass Media, the "Propaganda model" views the private media as businesses interested in the sale of a product — readers and audiences — to other businesses (advertisers) rather than that of quality news to the public. Describing the media's "societal purpose", Chomsky writes, "... the study of institutions and how they function must be scrupulously ignored, apart from fringe elements or a relatively obscure scholarly literature". The theory postulates five general classes of "filters" that determine the type of news that is presented in news media.

These five classes are:

1. Ownership of the medium
2. Medium's funding sources
3. Sourcing
4. Flak
5. Anti-communist ideology

The first three are generally regarded by the authors as being the most important. Although the model was based mainly on the characterization of United States media, Chomsky and Herman believe the theory is equally applicable to any country that shares the basic economic structure and organizing principles which the model postulates as the cause of media biases.

THE FILTERS

Ownership

The sheer size, concentrated ownership, immense owner wealth, and profit-seeking imperative of the dominant media corporations could hardly yield any other result. It was not always thus. In the early nineteenth century, a radical British press had emerged which addressed the concerns of workers. But excessive stamp duties, designed to restrict newspaper ownership to the 'respectable' wealthy, began to change the face of the press. Nevertheless there remained a degree of diversity. In postwar Britain, radical or worker-friendly newspapers such as the Daily Herald, News Chronicle, Sunday Citizen (all since failed or absorbed into other publications) and the Daily Mirror (at least until the late 1970s) regularly published articles questioning the capitalist system.

Herman and Chomsky argue that since mainstream media outlets are either large corporations or part of conglomerates (*e.g.* Westinghouse or General Electric), the information presented to the public will be biased with respect to these interests. Such conglomerates frequently extend beyond traditional media fields, and thus have extensive financial interests that may be endangered when certain information is widely publicized. According to this reasoning, news items that most endanger the corporate financial interests of those who own the media will face the greatest bias and censorship.

It then follows that if to maximize profit means sacrificing news objectivity, then the news sources that ultimately survive must be fundamentally biased, with regard to news in which they have a conflict of interest.

Funding

The second filter of the propaganda model is advertising. Most newspapers have to attract and maintain a high proportion of advertising in order to cover the costs of production; without it, they would have to increase the price of their newspaper. There is fierce competition throughout the media to attract advertisers; a newspaper which gets less advertising than its competitors is put at a serious disadvantage. Lack of success in raising advertising revenue was another factor in the demise of the 'people's newspapers' of the nineteenth and twentieth centuries.

The product is composed of the affluent readers who buy the newspaper — who also comprise the educated decision-making sector of the population — while the audience includes the businesses that pay to advertise their goods. According to this filter, the news itself is nothing more than "filler" to get privileged readers to see the advertisements which makes up the real content, and will thus take whatever form is most conducive to attracting educated decision-makers. Stories that conflict with their "buying mood", it is argued, will tend to be marginalized or excluded, along with information that presents a picture of the world that collides with advertisers' interests. The theory argues that the people buying the newspaper are themselves the product which is sold to the businesses that buy advertising space; the news itself has only a marginal role as the product.

Sourcing

The third of Herman and Chomsky's five filters relates to the sourcing of mass media news: "The mass media are drawn into a symbiotic relationship with powerful sources of information by economic necessity and reciprocity of interest." Even large media corporations such as the BBC cannot afford to place reporters everywhere. They therefore concentrate their resources where major news stories are likely to happen: the White House, the Pentagon, 10 Downing Street, and other centralised news "terminals".

Although British newspapers may occasionally complain about the "spin-doctoring" of New Labour, for example, they are in fact highly dependent upon the pronouncements of "the Prime Minister's personal spokesperson" for government-related news.

Business corporations and trade organisations are also trusted sources of stories considered newsworthy. Editors and journalists who offend these powerful news sources, perhaps by questioning the veracity or bias of the furnished material, can be threatened with the denial of access to their media life-blood - fresh news. Thus, the media become reluctant to run articles that will harm corporate interests that provide them with the resources that the media depend upon.

This relationship also gives rise to a "moral division of labour", in which "officials have and give the facts," and "reporters merely get them". Journalists are then supposed to adopt an uncritical attitude that makes it possible for them to accept corporate values without experiencing cognitive dissonance.

Flak

The fourth filter is 'flak', described by Herman and Chomsky as 'negative responses to a media statement or [TV or radio] programme. It may take the form of letters, telegrams, phone calls, petitions, law-suits, speeches and Bills before Congress, and other modes of complaint, threat and punitive action'. Business organisations regularly come together to form flak machines.

Perhaps one of the most well-known of these is the US-based Global Climate Coalition (GCC) - comprising fossil fuel and automobile companies such as Exxon, Texaco and Ford. The GCC was started up by Burson-Marsteller, one of the world's largest public relations companies, to rubbish the credibility of climate scientists and 'scare stories' about global warming. For Chomsky and Herman "flak" refers to negative responses to a media statement or programme. The term "flak" has been used to describe what Chomsky and Herman see as targeted efforts to discredit organizations or individuals who disagree with or cast doubt on the prevailing assumptions which Chomsky and Herman view as favorable to established power (*e.g.*, "The Establishment"). Unlike the first three "filtering" mechanisms — which are derived from analysis of market mechanisms — flak is characterized by concerted and intentional efforts to manage public information.

Anti-ideologies; Substitutes for Anti-communism

The fifth and final news filter that Herman and Chomsky identified was 'anti-communism'. *Manufacturing Consent* was written during the Cold War. A more apt version of this filter is the customary western identification of 'the enemy' or an 'evil dictator' - Colonel Gaddafi, Saddam Hussein, or Slobodan Milosevic (recall the British tabloid headlines of 'Smash Saddam!' and 'Clobba Slobba!'.

The same extends to mainstream reporting of environmentalists as 'eco-terrorists'. *The Sunday Times* ran a series of articles in 1999 accusing activists from the non-violent direct action group Reclaim The Streets of stocking up on CS gas and stun guns. Anti-ideologies exploit public fear and hatred of groups that pose a potential threat, either real, exaggerated, or imagined. Communism once posed the primary threat according to the model. Communism and socialism were portrayed by their detractors as endangering freedoms of speech, movement, the press, *etc.* They argue that such a portrayal was often used as a means to silence voices critical of elite interests.

Empirical Support

Following the theoretical exposition of the propaganda model, Manufacturing Consent contains a large section where the authors seek to test their hypotheses. If the propaganda model is right and the filters do influence media content, a particular form of bias would be expected — one that systematically favors corporate interests.

They also looked at what they perceived as naturally-occurring "historical control groups" where two events, similar in their relevant properties but differing in the expected media attitude towards them, are contrasted using objective measures such as coverage of key events (measured in column inches) or editorials favoring a particular issue (measured in number).

Finally, the authors examine what points of view they believe are expressed in the media. In one case, the authors examined over fifty of Stephen Kinzer's articles about Nicaragua in the New York Times. They criticize Kinzer for failing to quote a single person in Nicaragua who is pro-Sandinista and contrast this with independent polls reporting only 9% support for all the opposition parties taken together. Chomsky states "The polls show that all of the opposition parties in Nicaragua combined had the support of only 9 per cent of the population, but they have 100 per cent of Stephen Kinzer. Based on this example and select others, the authors argue that such a persistent bias can only be explained by a model like the one they advocate.

APPLICATIONS

Since the publication of Manufacturing Consent, both Herman and Chomsky have adopted the theory and have given it a prominent role in their writings, lectures, and theoretical frameworks. Chomsky, in particular, has made extensive use of its explanative power to lend support to his own interpretations of mainstream media attitudes towards a wide array of events, including the following:

- Panama invasion (1989)
- Gulf War (1990)
- Iraq invasion (2003)
- *Ethanol as fuel*: energy balance, impact on world food prices and allegations of amazon rainforest depletion (2008)

Herman, seeking to build upon a more institutionalized framework to analyse mainstream media functioning, joined the media watchdog group Fairness and Accuracy in Reporting (FAIR), which has since 1986 attempted to expose media bias through critique, documentation, and statistical analysis. With the emergence of the World Wide Web as a cheap and potentially wide-ranging means of communication, a number of independent websites have surfaced which adopt the propaganda model to subject media to close scrutiny. Several examples of these are, Free Press, FAIR and Media Lens, a British-based site authored by David Edwards and David Cromwell.

In May, 2007, both Chomsky and Herman spoke at the University of Windsor in Canada summarizing developments and responding to criticisms related to the model. Both authors stated they felt the propaganda model is still applicable today (Herman said even more so than when it was originally introduced), although they did suggest a few areas where they believe it falls short and needs to be extended in light of recent developments.

Chomsky has commented in the "ChomskyChat Forum" on the applicability of the Propaganda Model to the media environment of other countries: "That's only rarely been done in any systematic way. There is work on the British media, by a good University of Glasgow media group. And interesting work on British Central America coverage by Mark Curtis in his book Ambiguities of Power. There is work on France, done in Belgium mostly, also a recent book by Serge Halimi (editor of Le Monde diplomatique). There is one very careful study by a Dutch graduate student, applying the methods Ed Herman used in studying US media reaction to elections (El Salvador, Nicaragua) to 14 major European newspapers.

CRITICISM

Inroads: A Journal of Opinion

Gareth Morley argues in an article in *Inroads: A Journal of Opinion* that widespread coverage of Israeli mistreatment of protesters as compared with little coverage of similar (or much worse) events in sub-Saharan Africa is poorly explained. Chomsky responded that when testing a model, examples should be carefully paired to avoid reasons for discrepancies not related to political bias.

For instance, general coverage of the two areas compared should be similar. In this case, according to Chomsky, they are not: news from Israel (in any form) is far more common than news from sub-Saharan Africa.

New York Times Review

Historian Walter LaFeber criticized the book *Manufacturing Consent* for overstating its case, in particular with regards to reporting on Nicaragua, and not adequately explaining how a powerful propaganda system would let military aid to the Contra rebels be blocked. Herman responded in a letter by stating that the system was not "all powerful" and that LaFaber did not address their main point regarding Nicaragua. LaFaber replied that:

Mr. Herman wants to have it both ways: to claim that leading American journals "mobilize bias," but object when I cite crucial examples that weaken the book's thesis. If the news media are so unqualifiedly bad, the book should at least explain why so many publications (including my own) can cite their stories to attack President Reagan's Central American policy.

MEDIA LENS

Media Lens is a media analysis website based in the United Kingdom. It was established in 2001 to highlight what its founders consider to be "serious examples of bias, omission or deception in British mainstream media", with a primary emphasis on media intended to be impartial (BBC, Channel 4 News) or generally thought of as liberal (*The Guardian, The Independent*), and to encourage members of the public to challenge the relevant journalist, editor, newspaper or broadcaster. It is run by editors David Cromwell and David Edwards. The editors encourage polite and constructive engagement with journalists and discourage abusive emails. The website is maintained by webmaster Oliver Maw, and is financed through voluntary subscription and donations from grant-funding bodies.

The Media Lens editors have collaborated on two books, Guardians of Power: The Myth of the Liberal Media and Newspeak in the 21st Century. In 2007, Media Lens was awarded the Gandhi International Peace Award. The award was presented by Denis Halliday, former United Nations Humanitarian Co-ordinator in Iraq, and himself a recipient of the award in 2003.

Criticism of Media Lens

Media Lens has been criticised by Peter Beaumont, foreign affairs editor of The Observer, as "controlling Politburo lefties who insist that the only acceptable version of the truth is theirs alone and that everybody else should march to the same step and sing the same (old party) song". Beaumont states the Media Lens does not engage in dialogue with the targets of their criticism, but rather exploits the media to create a virtual soap box for their views.

Beaumont accused the group of a campaign intended to silence John Sloboda and his Iraq Body Count project, because it produced a victim count lower than the academic surveys on the casualties during the Iraq War published in the The Lancet by academics from Johns Hopkins Bloomberg School of Public Health.

Media Lens and its methods have been regularly criticised by The Times commentator Oliver Kamm, who described the organisation as "a shrill group of malcontents who exploit the patience of practising journalists", and its practices as "pernicious and anti-journalistic". Kamm took issue with their criticism of a review of the film Flags of Our Fathers, published by The Independent. Kamm challenged Media Lens' editors' knowledge of source material relevant to the US atomic bombings of Hiroshima and Nagasaki and claimed this was "a subject wholly outwith Cromwell's competence." David Cromwell wrote further on the debate in January 2008.

Praise of Media Lens

- Peter Barron former Editor of the BBC's *Newsnight* and currently Head of PR in Europe for Google: "Another organisation that tries to influence our [*Newsnight's*] running orders is Medialens... In fact I rather like them. David Cromwell and David Edwards, who run the site, are unfailingly polite, their points are well-argued and sometimes they're plain right."
- Noam Chomsky, Professor Emeritus of Linguistics at the Massachusetts Institute of Technology: "Regular critical analysis of the media, filling crucial gaps and correcting the distortions of ideological prisms, has never been more important. Media Lens has performed a major public service by carrying out this task with energy, insight, and care."
- Edward S. Herman, Professor Emeritus of Finance at the Wharton School of the University of Pennsylvania: "Media Lens is doing an outstanding job of pressing the mainstream media to at least follow their own stated principles and meet their public service obligations."
- John Pilger, journalist and film-maker: "The creators of Media Lens, David Edwards and David Cromwell, assisted by their webmaster, Olly Maw, have had such an extraordinary influence since they set

up the site in 2001 that, without their meticulous and humane analysis, the full gravity of the debacles of Iraq and Afghanistan might have been consigned to bad journalism's first draft of bad history."

INDEPENDENT MEDIA CENTRE

The Independent Media Centre (aka Indymedia or IMC) is a global participatory network of journalists that report on political and social issues. It originated during the anti-WTO protests worldwide in 1999 and remains closely associated with the global justice movement, which criticizes neo-liberalism and its associated institutions. Indymedia uses an open publishing and democratic media process that allows anybody to contribute. According to its homepage, "Indymedia is a collective of independent media organizations and hundreds of journalists offering grassroots, non-corporate coverage.

Indymedia is a democratic media outlet for the creation of radical, accurate, and passionate tellings of truth." Indymedia was founded as an alternative to government and corporate media, and seeks to facilitate people being able to publish their media as directly as possible.

The first Indymedia project was started in late November 1999 to report on protests against the WTO meeting that took place in Seattle, Washington, and to act as an alternative media source. This followed a successful experiment in June that year, reporting the events of the Carnival Against Capitalism in London, UK.

The Media team there used software and unmediated reports from protest participants. The open publishing script was first developed by video activists in Sydney, Australia.

After Seattle the idea and network spread rapidly. By 2002, there were 89 Indymedia websites covering 31 countries (and the Palestinian territories), growing to over 150 by January 2006. Indymedia websites publish in a number of languages, including English, Spanish, German, Italian, Portuguese, French, Russian, Arabic and Hebrew.

IMC collectives distribute print, audio, photo, and video media, but are most well known for their open publishing newswires, sites where anyone with internet access can publish news from their own perspective. The content of an IMC is determined by its participants, both the users who post content, and members of the local Indymedia collective who administer the site.

While Indymedias worldwide are run autonomously and differ according to the concerns of their users, they share a commitment to provide copyleft content. The general rule is that content on Indymedia sites can be freely reproduced for non-commercial purposes. Indymedia sites run on a number of free software platforms, many developed especially for the purpose; these include DadaIMC, Mir, Oscait, Active, SF-Active, Activismo, Drupal and Plone.

CONTENT AND FOCUS

The origins of IMCs themselves came out of protests against the concentrated ownership and perceived biases in corporate media reporting. The first IMC node, attached as it was to the Seattle anti-corporate globalization protests, was seen by activists as an alternative news source to that of the corporate media, which they accused of only showing violence and confrontation, and portraying all protesters negatively.

As a result, between 1999 and 2001, IMC newswires tended to be focused on up-to-the-minute coverage of protests, from local demonstrations to summits where anti-globalization movement protests were occurring. In 2007, this was still the case, but some IMCs are attempting to broaden their coverage to include more of what "traditional" journalism ignores.

Print Projects

There have been a number of print-based projects under the Indymedia banner, including short-run papers and longer-running newspapers. New York City IMC has produced The Indypendent, a bi-weekly "free paper for free people" for over five years. Winner of numerous awards from the Independent Press Association for original writing, photography, design and art, the Indypendent is currently the most widely circulated underground paper in North America.

During the 2004 Republican National Convention in New York City, the Indypendent printed hundreds of thousands of copies and briefly attained a mass circulation. Contentious issues have included consistent editorial practices, commercial advertising and a diversity of perspectives rare among radical publications.

Short-run papers for protests have included the Unconvention during the Philadelphia "R2K" protests during the Republican National Convention in 2000. Other newspapers include the Bay Area's Fault Lines, and papers in Connecticut, Maine, Baltimore and St. Louis in the United States, as well as in Wellington, New Zealand.

Radio projects: They have a global radio project, which aggregates audio RSS feeds from around the world.

Video project: They produce a regular DVD magazine, called newsreal. As well as the American one there is a European one and an Australian one. Some of their footage has been used in evidence in several court cases, eg Genoa.

ORGANIZATIONAL STRUCTURE

Local

Local IMC collectives are expected to be open and inclusive of individuals from a variety of different local anti-capitalist points of view, whether or not these have any definite political philosophy, so that even those without internet access can participate in both content creation and in content consumption. Editorial policies, locally chosen by any Indymedia collective, generally involve removing articles which the Indymedia editors believe promote racism, sexism, hate speech, and homophobia. All Indymedia collectives are expected to have a locally chosen, thoroughly discussed and clearly stated editorial policy for posts to their website.

Global

The overall Indymedia network is decentralized to the extent that the local IMCs operate independently once they are authenticated into the IMC network. The process of admission into the IMC network is somewhat centralized but is relatively relaxed and transparent compared to the occasionally contentious disputes within local IMCs and has not generated a great deal of criticism.

Local IMC collectives vary widely in their openness, editorial policies and tolerance of different viewpoints. Along with the locally-organised collectives are IMC websites dealing with particular topics (such as biotechnology) or for different media (such as video). Along with contributing their own media, core organizers maintain IMC's open publishing infrastructure, enabling different people throughout the internet to publish their news. IMC editing is done by a system of layered admin which contributors apply to join for each site, by participating on open email lists and attending open meetings.

As an example of different models for collective internal organizing, the DC IMC (one of the older IMCs in the network) became a Coop with dues with a workshop/office, now closed. In contrast, other IMC local collectives are without any formally-defined membership and have minimal organizational structure. Some IMC memberships require its members to sign a mission statement – not every IMC has a formalized policy. Some collectives do ban members for repeated rules violations. Some feel that membership includes only those actively doing organizing or other IMC work, while some feel that it actually extends to every IMC contributor.

Funding

IMCs tend to be funded solely by donations of money and equipment from individuals. In maintaining its independence and anti-corporate stance, Indymedia has had struggles with funding issues.

For example, in September 2002, the Ford Foundation proposed funding for an Indymedia regional meeting. This was ultimately refused because many volunteers, especially some from IMC Argentina, were uncomfortable with accepting money from the Foundation, which some believe to be linked to the CIA.

REPUTATION

Indymedia has a variable reputation, both among its users and outside critics. While some criticize Indymedia for adopting a position hostile to the interests of capital, others believe that this is the purpose of the media.

Still others believe that its editorial policy on feature selection and hiding or deletion of articles is overly biased in certain topic areas, such as the Israeli-Palestinian conflict. Some critics argue that since anyone can publish with little to no editorial process, unsubstantiated allegations and conspiracy theories are often published as fact, along with inaccurate articles and content that can offend.In its favour, others argue Indymedia is a viable or preferable alternative to corporate media.

Its operations are conducted by activists around the world, who, though they may be lacking in journalistic training and corporate funding, tend to make up for this with enthusiasm for reporting issues of social justice and unique related events, which in their view, the corporate media under-reports or censors. For example, the Bolivian Gas War in 2003 was virtually unheard of in the US media, while it received extensive worldwide and multilingual reporting through Indymedia. Another example is the February 15, 2003 anti-war protest in many US and European cities, which received detailed coverage written by its participants. While Indymedia has global aspirations, the vast majority of IMCs are in North America, Latin America and Europe. Although the Middle East is an area of considerable interest to Indymedia, there are only three IMCs in the region, located in Beirut, Lebanon; Cyprus and Israel, although there was a Palestine IMC in Jerusalem between 2001 and 2003. The Lebanon centre is one of three IMCs in Muslim nations; the other two are in Jakarta, Indonesia and Istanbul, Turkey.

Temporary Removal from Google News searches

In early May 2003, after receiving numerous complaints about newswire stories that referred to the Israeli military (IDF) as "Zionazi forces" or to Israelis as "Zionazis", Google temporarily stopped including some IMCs in Google News searches (many non-English IMCs remained in the search).

Google News described the term "Zionazi" as a "degrading, hateful slur" and refused to index the Bay Area IMC because it had appeared there; SF Bay Area Indymedia agreed that it "could be considered hate speech". This spawned a petition which sought to promise that content the Indymedia community finds offensive will be moderated from the front page as a matter of editorial policy. IMCs were still included in normal Google web searches.

CONTROVERSY AND CRITICISM

Hate Speech

Open publishing has left some IMCs in Europe vulnerable to legal action or threats of legal action related to questions of libel or hate speech. In some such cases, local IMC collectives took autonomous decisions to temporarily suspend the site while the different activist groups reorganized to find a consensual, constructive method of dealing with these problems and to increase openness and non-authoritarian organizing methods.

FBI Investigation

In March 2006, the Los Angeles Times alleged that Indymedia had appeared with Food Not Bombs and the Communist Party of Texas on an FBI terrorist watchlist, revealed at a presentation at the University of Texas School of Law. A reference to the 2005 IndyConference was made at the same presentation.

Editorial Policy

Although attempts have been made to formalize global editorial standards, the autonomous and independent nature of Indymedia has meant that many IMCs prefer their own local policies. As a result, many deal with similar issues and complaints, particularly around matters of distinguishing between criticism and hateful comments ("hate speech"); and the criteria for selecting issues and authors for the websites' "featured articles". While freedom of speech is valued by Indymedia collectives, it is rarely the overriding principle guiding editorial policy.

Many IMCs now routinely remove from the front page "newswire" articles copied from corporate-run or state-run press sources. This policy (where implemented) is intended by those IMCs to keep Indymedia as an independent news source, rather than a blog of articles from existing news sources. There is generally an editorial electronic mailing list, to which questions and complaints may be directed.

SERVERS SEIZURES

Seizure of Servers by the FBI

On October 7, 2004, the FBI took possession of several server hard drives used by a number of IMCs and hosted by US-based Rackspace Managed Hosting. The servers in question were located in the United Kingdom and managed by the British arm of Rackspace, but some 20 mainly European IMC websites were affected, and several unrelated websites were affected (including the website of a Linux distribution). No reasons were given at first by the FBI and Rackspace for the seizure, in particular IMC was not informed.

Rackspace claimed that it was banned from giving further information about the incident. Some (but not all) of the legal documents relating to the confiscation of the servers were unsealed by a Texas district court in August 2005, following legal action by the Electronic Frontier Foundation.

The documents revealed that the government never officially demanded the computer servers—the subpoena to Rackspace only requested server log files. This contradicted previous statements by the web host that it took the servers offline because the government had demanded the hardware. Thus, it is unclear whether it is correct to say the servers were seized by the FBI.

The documents also contradicted Rackspace's claim that it had been ordered by the court not to discuss publicly the government's demand. The seized servers were returned on October 13, 2004.

A statement by Rackspace stated that the company had been forced to comply with a court order under the procedures laid out by the Mutual Legal Assistance Treaty, which governs international police co-operation on "international terrorism, kidnapping and money laundering". The investigation that led to the court order was said to have arisen outside of the U.S. Rackspace stated that they were prohibited on giving further detail. Agence France-Presse reported FBI spokesman Joe Parris, who said the incident was not an FBI operation, but that the subpoena had been issued at the request of the Italian and the Swiss governments. Again, no further details on specific allegations were given. UK involvement was denied in an answer given to a parliamentary question posed by Richard Allan, Liberal Democrat MP.

Indymedia pointed out that they were not contacted by the FBI and that no specific information was released on the reasons of seizing the servers. Indymedia also sees the incident in the context of "numerous attacks on independent media by the US Federal Government", including a subpoena to obtain IP logs from Indymedia at the occasion of the Republican National Conference, the shut-down of several community radio stations in the US by the FCC, and a request by the FBI to remove a post on Nantes IMC containing a photograph of alleged undercover Swiss police.

The move was condemned by the International Federation of Journalists, who stated that "The way this has been done smacks more of intimidation of legitimate journalistic inquiry than crime-busting" and called for an investigation. Criticism was also voiced by European civil liberties organisation Statewatch and the World Association of Community Radio Broadcasters (AMARC).

In Italy, the federal prosecutor of Bologna Marina Plazzi confirmed that an investigation against Indymedia had been opened because of suspected "support of terrorism", in the context of Italian troops in the Iraqi city of Nasiriyah. The Italian minister of justice, Roberto Castelli, has refused further details. In November 2003, 17 members of parliament belonging to the right-wing Alleanza Nazionale, including Alessandra Mussolini demanded that Indymedia be shut down. A senior AN member and government official had announced the co-operation with US authorities (AN was a member of the Italian coalition government), and AN spokesman Mario Landolfi welcomed the FBI's seizure of the Indymedia servers. Left-wing Italian politicians denounced the move and called for an investigation.

Bristol Server Seizure

Not long after the Rackspace affair another server in the UK was seized by police in June 2005. An anonymous post on the Bristol Indymedia server, came to police attention for suggesting an "action" against a freight train carrying new cars as part of a protest against cars and climate change in the run up to that year's Gleneagles G8 summit. The police claimed that the poster broke the law by "incitement to criminal damage", and sought access logs from the server operators. Despite being warned by lawyers that the servers were "journalistic equipment" and subject to special laws, the police proceeded with the seizure and a member of the Bristol Indymedia group was arrested. Indymedia was supported in this matter by the National Union of Journalists, Liberty and Privacy International, along with others. This incident ended several months later with no charges being brought by the police and the equipment returned.

Other legal actions - IMC UK

In 2005, Indymedia UK was threatened with a libel action by the US arms company EDO Corporation, for publishing articles accusing their UK branch EDO (UK) of EDO MBM Technology Ltd (who supply the US, UK, and Israel armed forces) of being 'warmongers'. Their lawyers ultimately withdrew the writ.

EDO MBM then launched a further High Court lawsuit against the protest group Smash EDO in April 2005, under anti-stalker laws, presenting as evidence articles that had been posted anonymously on Indymedia UK. Although a controversial interim injunction was imposed on this evidence, the suit collapsed without reaching a trial in early 2006.

Other Legal Actions - IMC US

On January 30, 2009, one of the system administrators of the server that hosts indymedia.us received a grand jury subpoena from the Southern District of Indiana federal court. The subpoena asked the administrator to provide all "IP addresses, times, and any other identifying information" for every visitor to the site on June 25, 2008. The subpoena also included a gag order that stated that the recipient is "not to disclose the existence of this request unless authorized by the Assistant U.S. Attorney." The administrator of indymedia.us could not have provided the information because Indymedia sites generally do not keep IP address logs. The Electronic Frontier Foundation determined that there was no legal basis for the gag order, and that the subpoena request "violated the SCA's restrictions on what types of data the government could obtain using a subpoena." Under Justice Department guidelines, subpoenas to news media must have the authorization of the attorney general. According to a CBS News blog, the subpoena of indymedia.us was never submitted for review by the attorney general. On February 25, 2009, a United States Attorney sent a letter to an attorney with the Electronic Frontier Foundation stating that the subpoena had been withdrawn.

ASSAULTS ON JOURNALISTS

On August 15, 2000, The Los Angeles Police Department temporarily shut down the satellite uplink and production studio of the Los Angeles Independent Media Centre on its first night of Democratic National Convention coverage, claiming explosives were in a van in the adjacent parking lot. No explosives were ever found.

In July, 2001 at the 27th G8 summit in Genoa, Indymedia journalists claim to have been seriously assaulted at the Diaz school where Indymedia had set up a temporary journalism centre and radio station. In an ongoing trial, twenty-nine Italian police officers were indicted for grievous bodily harm, planting evidence and wrongful arrest during a night-time raid on the Diaz School, of which thirteen were convicted. A further 45 state officials, including police officers, prison guards and doctors, were charged with physically and mentally abusing demonstrators and journalists held in a detention centre in the nearby town of Bolzaneto. Video evidence from Indymedia and from the video activist group Undercurrents, is being used as key evidence for the prosecution.

On June 1, 2003, Indymedia journalist Guy Smallman was seriously injured by a police grenade in Geneva. He was covering protests against the G8 summit in nearby Evian for Indymedia and Image Sans Frontière.

On June 9, 2003, Alejandro Goldín, a photographer for Indymedia Argentina claims to have been assaulted by Federal Police officers while covering an incident between police and factory workers at the Brukman textile factory in Buenos Aires.Goldín claims that although he identified himself as press and showed his credentials, police tried to smash his equipment. Goldín claims that he was beaten on the head with a shotgun, shoved to the ground and kicked repeatedly by officers.

On May 19, 2005, two videographers were roughed up by the Houston Police Department's Mounted Patrol during the Halliburton Shareholders Meeting - both videographers were contributors to Houston Indymedia. Both videographers were charged with assault on a police officer, but the charges were dropped after mainstream media from KTRK-TV (ABC13), KPRC-TV (Local 2 Houston), and KHOU-TV (Channel 11 Houston) provided the Harris County District Attorney's office with video footage that exonerated the journalists.

5

Corporate Media Planning

SMALL BUSINESS MANAGEMENT

This guide discusses Advertising Media Planning. A wise man once said, "The person who saves money by not advertising is like the man who stops the clock to save time." In today's fast-paced, high-tech age, businesses have to use some form of advertising to make prospects aware of their products and services. Even a famous company like Coca-Cola continually spends money on media advertising to support recognition of their products. Last year Coca-Cola spent more than $150 million to keep its name in the forefront of the public's eye. So the question isn't whether or not you can afford to advertise, you simply must if you want your business to succeed.

Some questions you should consider before buying ads are (Small Business Advertising Marketing Media):

- What marketing media is the best to use?
- How important is creativity?
- Is there a way to buy space and time that will stretch my advertising budget?

When it comes to advertising, a lot of people really don't know what they want, where to get it or what to do with it after they have it. This guide will help you learn to determine what type of advertising media is best for you, and learn to identify guidelines you can use to obtain the advertising exposure you need.

It will help you identify ways to make your advertising more cost efficient. Advertising is an investment in your business's future. And like any investment, it's import-ant to find out as much as you can before you make a decision. You'll be able to use this guide as a reliable reference tool often in the months and years to come.

NEWSPAPER MEDIA ADVERTISING

Every advertising medium has characteristics that give it natural advantages and limitations. As you look through your newspaper(s), you'll notice some businesses that advertise regularly. Observe who they are and how they advertise their products and services. More than likely, their advertising investment is working if it's selling!

Some Advantages in Newspaper Media Advertising

Almost every home receives a newspaper, either by newsstand or home delivery. Reading the newspaper is a habit for most families. And, there is something for everybody: sports, comics, crosswords, news, classifieds, etc. You can reach certain types of people by placing your ad in different sections of the paper. People expect advertising in the newspaper. In fact, many people buy the paper just to read the ads from the supermarket, movies or department stores.

Unlike advertising on TV and radio, advertising in the newspaper can be examined at your leisure. A newspaper ad can contain details, such as prices and telephone numbers or coupons. There are many advantages to advertising in the newspaper. From the advertiser's point-of-view, newspaper advertising can be convenient because production changes can be made quickly, if necessary, and you can often insert a new advertisement on short notice.

Another advantage is the large variety of ad sizes newspaper advertising offers. Even though you may not have a lot of money in your budget, you can still place a series of small ads, without making a sacrifice.

Some Disadvantages with Newspaper Advertising

Advertising in the newspaper offers many advantages, but it is not without its inherent disadvantages, such as:

- Newspapers usually are read once and stay in the house for just a day.
- The print quality of newspapers isn't always the best, especially for photographs. So use simple artwork and line drawings for best results.
- The page size of a newspaper is fairly large and small ads can look minuscule.
- Your ad has to compete with other ads for the reader's attention.
- You're not assured that every person who gets the newspaper will read your ad. They may not read the section you advertised in, or they may simply have skipped the page because there wasn't any interesting news on it.

Newspaper Representative

Every newspaper has its own sales staff, and you're normally appointed your personal newspaper "Sales Representative." A newspaper sales rep can be very helpful. He or she can keep you posted on special sections or promotions that may apply to your business, but always keep in mind it is the sales rep's job to sell you advertising. Your sales rep might say that the newspaper can layout any of your ads, pre-prepared or not.

But these ads are assembly line products and are not often very creative or eye-catching. Consider using an artist or agency for your ads. In addition, your sales rep can sometimes be instrumental in making sure your story or upcoming announcement "finds" the right reporter because the relationship between the advertising and editorial staff is chummier than most people think, even though they claim total anonymity.

BUYING NEWSPAPER MARKETING MEDIA SPACE

Newspaper Marketing Media Space advertising is sold by column and inch. You can determine the size ad you want just by looking in the newspaper in which you want to advertise. If you can't locate an ad that's the size you want, just measure the columns across and the inches down. For example, an ad that measures 3 columns across and 7 inches down would be a 21 inch ad. If the inch rate is $45.67, your ad would cost $959.07. In case your newspaper is still on the line rate system, remember there are 14 lines to an inch. So, if the line rate is $3.75, multiply it by 14 and you will have the cost of an inch rate. (the rate would be $45.50 an inch.)

Here are some other things to remember:

- Newspaper circulation drops on Saturdays and increases on Sundays, which is also the day a newspaper is read most thoroughly.
- Position is important, so specify in what section you want your ad to appear. Sometimes there's a surcharge for exact position...but don't be afraid to pay for it if you need it.
- Request an outside position for ads that have coupons. That makes them easier to cut out.
- If a newspaper is delivered twice daily (morning/evening), it often offers "combination" rates or discounts for advertising in both papers, You usually can reach more readers, so this kind of advertising may be something to consider.

Other important tips to remember are:

- Before you advertise, have in mind a definite plan for what it is you want to sell.
- Create short, descriptive copy for your ad. Include prices if applicable. Consider using a copywriter or ask your newspaper for free copy assistance.
- Face your products toward the inside of the ad. If the product you want to use faces right, change your copy layout to the left.
- Be sure to include your company name and logo, address and telephone number in the ad.

- Neat, uncluttered and orderly ads encourage readership. Don't try to crowd everything you can in the layout space. If the newspaper helps you with the layout, be sure to request a proof of the final version so you can approve it or make changes before it is printed.

Always make sure you are satisfied with what your advertising says and how it looks before it goes to print.

MAGAZINE MARKETING MEDIA

Many of the same "print" type principles which apply to newspaper advertising also apply to magazine advertising.

The biggest differences are:

- Magazines are usually weekly or monthly publicat-ions instead of daily.
- Advertising messages are more image-oriented and less price-oriented.
- The quality of the pictures and paper are superior to newsprint.
- Advertisements involve colour more often.

The general rule that you can run the same ad 3-5 times within a campaign period before its appeal lessens applies to magazine advertising as well, even with a monthly publication. So it makes sense to spend extra time and money to prepare a worthwhile ad that can be successfully repeated. Over long terms such as these, however, be aware that the client (you) often tire of the ad before the audience does.

Because ads in magazines are not immediate, they take more planning. Often, an ad for a monthly magazine must be prepared at least a month in advance of publication, so ads detailing prices and items have to be carefully crafted to insure accuracy. Since the quality of the magazines are superior, the advertising that you generate must be superior as well. Negatives are usually required instead of prints or "PMTs" (photo-mechanical transfers). Consider getting assistance from a graphic artist or an advertising agency.

There are two categories of magazines: trade magazines and consumer magazines. Trade magazines are publications that go to certain types of businesses, services and industries. Consumer magazines are generally the kind you find on the average news stand. Investigate which type would do your business the most good. An agency can also purchase the magazine space for you, often at no charge, because the magazine pays the agency a commission directly. If you wish to purchase the advertising yourself, contact the magazine directly and ask for an "Ad Kit" or "Media Package." They will send you a folder that includes demographic information, reach information, a current rate card and a sample of the publication.

Although most magazines are national in nature, many have regional advertising sections that allow your business to look like it purchased a national ad when it only went to a certain geographical area. This can be especially useful if your product or service is regional in nature as well and could not benefit from the magazine's complete readership. Each magazine does this differently, so contact the one(s) you are interested in and ask them about their geographic editions. Some sophisticated magazines even have demographic editions available, which might also be advantageous.

RADIO ADVERTISING MEDIA

Since its inception, radio has become an integral part of our culture. In some way, it touches the lives of almost everyone, every day. Radio, as a medium, offers a form of entertainment that attracts listeners while they are working, traveling, relaxing or doing almost anything.

A farmer, for example, may listen to the radio while he is having breakfast or plowing his field. People driving to work often listen to the radio. Radio offers information such as: news, weather reports, traffic conditions, advertising and music for your listening pleasure.

Good Things About Radio

Radio media advertising is a relatively inexpensive way of reaching people. It has often been called the "theater of the mind" because voices or sounds can be used to create moods or images that if crested by visual effects would be impossible to afford. You can also negotiate rates for your commercials, or even barter. Stations are often looking for prizes they can give away to listeners, so it's possible to get full commercial credit for the product or service you offer.

Advantages to radio advertising media include:

- The ability to easily change and update scripts are paramount to radio broadcasting, since news stories can and often do happen live.
- Radio is a personal advertising medium. Station personalities have a good rapport with their listeners. If a radio personality announces your commercial, it's almost an implied endorsement.
- Radio is also a way to support your printed advertising. You can say in your commercial, "See our ad in the Sunday Times," which makes your message twice as effective.

Limitations to Radio Advertising Media

Radio advertising is not without its disadvantages too, such as:

- You can't review a radio commercial. Once it plays, it's gone. If you didn't catch all the message, you can't go back and hear it again.
- Since there are a lot of radio stations, the total listening audience for any one station is just a piece of a much larger whole. That's why it's important to know what stations your customers and prospects probably listen to. Therefore, most of the time, you'll have to buy time on several radio stations to reach the market you are after.

- People don't listen to the radio all the time...only during certain times of day. So, it's important to know when your customers or prospects are listening. For example, if you want to reach a large portion of your audience by advertising during the morning farm report, you'll have to specify that time period to the radio station when you buy the time.

One of the most popular times to reach people is during Drive Times (from 6 a.m. to 10 a.m. and 3 p.m. to 7 p.m.) It's called that because most people are going to or from work during this period, and because most people listen to their radio when they drive. Unfortunately, radio stations know that this is a favourite time to advertise, so commercial costs are much higher during this time.

- Radio as a broadcasting medium, can effectively sell an image...or one or two ideas at the most. It is not, however, a detailed medium...and is a poor place for prices and telephone numbers.
- Radio listeners increase in the spring and summer, contrary to television audiences which increase in the fall and winter and decrease in the summer. This is an important aspect to consider when you are choosing advertising media.

Buy Time on the Radio

Like a newspaper, each radio station has its own advertising staff. Each wants you to believe that their station is the absolute best buy for your money...and many will go to great lengths to prove it. But if you've done your research, or you are using an advertising agency, you probably have a good idea of the station you want to buy time on and when.

If you don't know which stations you want to use, ask each station for its own research, that is, the type of programming, musical format, geographic reach, number of listeners and station ratings. By getting the station ratings and the number of people it reaches, you can figure out the cost-per-thousand people (CPM) by simply dividing the cost of a commercial by the thousands of people you are reaching.

Example:

- Cost of commercial = $35.00, Audience reached =45,000 people.
- Cost of commercial per 1000 people = 35/45 = $0.78 per 1000.

Without getting complicated, here are two cardinal rules for radio advertising:

- It's better to advertise when people are listening than when they are not.
- It's better to bunch your commercials together than to spread them apart.

A lot of radio sales reps will try to talk you out of advertising during specific times. They'll offer you a reduced rate called TAP (Total Audience Plan) that splits your advertising time into 1/3 drive, 1/3 mid-day and 1/3 night. This may sound like a good deal, but airing commercials during times when your audience isn't listening is bad advertising. If however, you are sponsoring a show such as Paul Harvey or the Morning Farm Report, it makes sense to advertise once or twice a day on a regular basis, since those programs have regular listenership.

Frequency is a vital element for effective radio advertising. Since you can't automatically recall the radio commercial and hear it again, you may have to hear the same commercial two, four, or maybe six times before the message sinks in. If you missed the address the first time, you consciously or subconsciously are hoping the commercial will be aired again so you can get the information you need. That's the way radio advertising works. And that's also the way you buy it.

Most of the time, radio advertising should be bought in chunks. High frequency over a short period of time is much more effective than low frequency over a longer period of time. It's important for your audience to hear your spot again to get more information out of it.

For example, if you wanted to advertise a two week campaign and you could afford 42 radio commercials, the following buy would serve you well: On Tuesdays, Wednesdays and Thursdays, place three spots between 7-9 a.m. and four spots between 3-6 p.m. for two weeks. Notice that both day and hour periods are concentrated.

By advertising in concentrated areas in tight day groups, you seem larger than you really are. And people hearing your concentrated campaign for two or three days will think you're on all the time. The radio sales reps may try to sell you three spots everyday on the station for 14 days (a total of 42 spots). But your campaign won't be nearly as effective.

Tips to Plan Commercials

- If you're including your address in the commercial, simplify it. Instead of "134525 East Pines," say "at the corner of First & Pines, next to Gumbies." It's easier to remember.
- Don't use phone numbers in your commercial. If you have to mention your phone number, refer to the Yellow Pages in the local phone book.
- Radio works better when you combine it with other advertising media.
- Check out the price differences between 60-second and 30-second commercials. Normally, 30-second commercials are only 1/3 less than 60's, which makes a 60-second commercial a better buy.
- Be creative with your radio advertising, too. If it sounds like all the rest of the commercials, it won't stand out. Your message won't be heard nearly as well. Advertising agencies are usually quite good at producing creative radio commercials.

If you decide to write your own radio scripts, remember these basic copy writing rules:

- Get your listener's attention immediately.
- Write in conversational style.
- Avoid using buzz words or jargon.
- Repeat your important points.
- Make your ending strong and positive with call-to-action for response.

TELEVISION MARKETING MEDIA

Television is often called "king" of the advertising media, since a majority of people spend more hours watching TV per day than any other medium. It combines the use of sight, colour, sound and motion...and it works. TV has proven its persuasive power in influencing human behaviour time and time again. But it's also the "king" of advertising costs.

Advantages in Television Advertising Media

Television reaches very large audiences-audiences that are usually larger than the audience your city's newspaper reaches. The area that a television station's broadcast signal covers is called A.D.I., which stands for "Area of Dominant Influence."

Some advantages of television advertising include the following:

- Advertising on television can give a product or service instant validity and prominence.
- You can easily reach the audiences you have targeted by advertising on TV. Children can be reached during cartoon programming, farmers during the morning agricultural reports and housewives during the afternoon soap operas. A special documentary on energy sources for heating homes and business will also attract viewers interested in heating alternatives.
- TV offers the greatest possibility for creative advertising. With a camera, you can take your audience anywhere and show them almost anything.
- Since there are fewer television stations than radio stations in a given area, each TV audience is divided into much larger segments, which enables you to reach a larger, yet, more diverse audience.

Disadvantages in Television Advertising Media

Because TV has such a larger A.D.I., the stations can charge more for commercials based on the larger number of viewers reached.

The cost of television commercial time is based on two variables:

1. The number of viewers who watch the programme.
2. The time during the day the programme airs.

One 30 second television commercial during prime time viewing (8 p.m. to 11 p.m.) can cost 10 to 30 times more than one radio spot during drive time (which is considered prime listening time). While the newspaper may cover the city's general metropolitan area, TV may cover a good portion of the state where you live. If such a coverage blankets most of your sales territory, TV advertising may be the best advertising alternative for your business. Producing a commercial is also an important variable to consider. On the whole, television audiences have become more sophisticated and have come to expect quality commercials.

A poorly produced commercial could severely limit the effectiveness of your message, and may even create a bad image in your customer's mind. Advertising agencies or TV commercial production facilities are the best organizations for creating a commercial that will be effective for the goods or service you are offering. But the cost of a well-produced commercial is often more expensive than people think.

Some TV stations will claim they can put together commercials for "almost nothing." Before agreeing to this, find out what "almost nothing" means. Then, determine if the commercial quality and content they are proposing will represent your firm's image. Many companies use the station's commercial production facilities for creating "tag lines" on pre-produced commercials. Often, the station will help you personalize the spot for little or no cost...if you advertise with them. Remember, more than anything else, when it comes to making a TV commercial, you get what you pay for. And when you're buying commercial time, it makes sense to have the best sales presentation possible. Remember, like radio, the message comes and goes...and that's it. The viewer doesn't see your commercial again unless you buy more placements.

VITAL ELEMENT

When you advertise on TV, your commercial is not only competing with other commercials, it's also competing with the other elements in the viewer's environment as well. The viewer may choose to get a snack during the commercial break, go to the bathroom or have a conversation about what they just saw on the show they were viewing.

Even if your commercial is being aired, viewers may never see it unless it is creative enough to capture their attention. That's why it's so important to consider the kind of commercial you are going to create...and how you want your audience to be affected. Spending money on a good commercial in the beginning will pay dividends in the end.

Don't Use TV Unless Your Budget Allows

Attempting to use TV advertising by using a poorly-produced commercial; buying inexpensive late night commercial time that few people watch; or just placing your commercial a couple times on the air will guarantee disappointing results.

To obtain positive results from TV advertising you must have enough money in your budget to:

- Pay for the cost of producing a good TV commercial.
- Pay for effective commercial time that will reach your viewer at least 5-7 times.

Properly done, television advertising is the most effective medium there is. But it is big league advertising...and you shouldn't attempt it unless you have enough money in your budget to do it right. If you're still attracted to TV, it's a good idea to call in an advertising agency for production and media buying estimates. Then, figure out what sales results you can expect. With such data, you should be able to reach a logical advertising decision.

Buying Television Advertising Media Time

There are many things to know and consider before buying a TV programming schedule. That's why, in most cases, using an advertising agency or a media buying service is recommended when advertising on TV. If these services are unavailable, find a TV representative that you can trust. Your agency or representative can help you select the programs you should advertise on in order to reach your market. Also, ask about "fringe" time, adjacencies and package plans.

When you are engineering your schedule, remember that repetition (or frequency) is a very important ingredient to use. Make sure your audience sees your commercial with the context of the programs you're buying. Ask for a commercial affidavit. Normally, it doesn't cost any more and the station will provide you with a list of the exact times your commercial was run.

Other Considerations

For an effective and inexpensive way to get your message on the TV screen, consider using pre-prepared TV commercials that may be available to you through a manufacture or distributor you deal with. You can add your name and logo to the end of the commercial for little or no cost. Look at cooperative advertising too. Many companies offer prepared advertising materials you can use and at the same time may pay for a portion of the advertising schedule.

Cable Advertising

Cable advertising is a lower cost alternative to advertising on broadcast television. It has many of the same qualities as broadcast television, and in fact, since it offers more programming, it's even easier to reach a designated audience. The trouble with cable is it doesn't reach everyone in the market area, since the signal has to be wired instead of broadcast, and also because not everyone subscribes to cable. If cable does reach a large part of your market, have an advertising agency investigate its cost or call the cable company's advertising sales department. Chances are the commercial time will be 10 to 20 per cent of the costs of regular broadcast time.

Yellow Pages

Telephone book advertising is another way to reach your market area. It allows you to place your business listing or ad in selected classifications within the book, with the theory being that when people need your product or service, they look up the classification and contact you. Much of the "sell" copy for a product or service, therefore, does not have to be in your ad content, since the people who have looked up your classification are already in the market to buy. The thing to be aware of when you write the ad is the other firms' ads within your classification. In other words, why should the reader select your firm over your competition? That is the crucial question — and your ad should provide the answer. Telephone Yellow Pages salespeople often employ the technique of selling as large of ad as they can to one company, then showing the other companies in the same classification what the one company is doing so that they can match it or beat it. This is not the best criteria for determining ad size, but is definitely good for the ad salesperson.

To determine the size you should use, consider the following:

- Your ad should be large enough to incorporate the vital information the reader needs to make a contact decision.
- Remember your lessons in print advertising. Keep your ad clean, creative and eye-appealing. Even though the phone company will "design your ad for free," some firms employ graphic artists and advertising agencies to create a Yellow Pages ad that really stands out.
- Give yourself a budget to work with. Figure out how much you want to spend on Yellow Pages advertising for the entire year, then divide it by 12. That will give you the payment that is automatically attached to your phone bill every month.
- Do something unique or different. If no one else is using colour, use colour. Even shades of gray can make an ad look better and more appealing.

Advantages of Yellow Pages Advertising

- One ad works all year long.
- Gives your prospect a method of easily locating and contacting your business, even if they didn't initially know your name.
- Can help you describe the differences between you and your competition.
- You pay by the month instead of one large payment.

Disadvantages of Yellow Pages Advertising

- You must commit to an entire year of advertising.
- You are immediately placed with a group of your competitors, making it easy for the prospect to comparison shop.
- Some classifications are so cluttered with advertising, your ad is buried and ineffective.
- It is only effective when a prospect looks you up in the correct classification, assuming the prospect knows what classification to look for in the first place.

If you require more than one classification, your Yellow Pages representative often has packages and programs that can save you some money. In addition, the same is often true if you need to be advertising in more than one city or market.

Yellow Pages advertising is an important medium to consider in our fast-paced, information-hungry society. People really do let their "fingers do the walking" instead of driving around blindly. Make sure your Yellow Pages ad is attractive and informative enough to be the one or two businesses the prospect actually does select to call. And then make sure you have the resources to deal with the inquiry. After all, there is nothing more annoying than being put "on-hold" by a busy checker or being served by an uninterested or unknowledge-able employee.

Outdoor Advertising Media

When people think of Outdoor Advertising, they usually think of the colorful billboards along our streets and highways. Included in the "outdoor" classification, however, are benches, posters, signs and transit advertising (the advertising on buses, subways, taxicabs and trains). They are all share similar advertising rules and methods.

Outdoor advertising reaches its audience as an element of the environment. Unlike newspaper, radio or TV, it doesn't have to be invited into the home. And it doesn't provide entertainment to sustain its audience.

Some Outdoor Advantages

- Since it is in the public domain, Outdoor Advertising assuredly reaches its audience. People can't "switch it off" or "throw it out." People are exposed to it whether they like it or not. In this sense, outdoor advertising truly has a "captured audience."
- It's messages work on the advertising principle of "frequency." Since most messages stay in the same place for a period of a month or more, people who drive by or walk past see the same message a number of times.
- Particular locations can be acquired for certain purposes. A billboard located a block in front of your business can direct people to your

showroom. Or you can reach rural areas efficiently by placing a billboard in each small town.

- Outdoor advertising is an excellent adjunct to other types of advertising you are doing. In fact, it is most effective when coupled with other media.

Some Outdoor Disadvantages

- Outdoor advertising is a glance medium. At best, it only draws 2-3 seconds of a reader's time.
- Messages must be brief to fit in that 2-3 second time frame. Ninety-five per cent of the time, either the message or the audience is in motion.
- The nature of the way you have to buy outdoor advertising (usually a three month commitment) is not conducive to a very short, week-long campaign.

When you buy outdoor advertising, remember that location is everything. High traffic areas are ideal. A billboard in an undesirable area will do you little good. Keep your message concise (use only five to seven words) and make it creatively appealing to attract readership. Few words, large illustrations (or photos), bold colors and simple backgrounds will create the most effective outdoor advertising messages.

DIRECT MAIL

What makes "direct" mail different than regular mail? Nothing. It's just a way the advertising world describes a promotional message that circumvents traditional media (newspaper, radio, TV) and appeals directly to an individual consumer. Usually through the mail, but other carriers also participate.

Direct mail may be used more than you think. Studies indicate that it is the third largest media expenditure behind television and newspaper.

Rules to Remember

- *Define your audience*: Figure out who you want to reach before developing your direct mail programme. This allows you to specifically target your message to fit common needs. It is the best advertising medium for "tailoring" your appeal.
- *Locate the right mailing list*: You can either build a "house list" by doing the research yourself and compiling the information on a computer - or you can purchase an "outside list" from a list house or mailing organization already pre-prepared and ready to go.
- *There are many ways to purchase lists*: You can buy them demographically (by age, profession, habits or business), or geographically (by location, or zip code). Or you can by a list with both qualities. More than likely, there is a mailing list company in

your area that would happy to consult with you on your needs. If not, there are a number of national mailing lists available.

- For assembly, addressing and mailing your project, you also have the choice of doing it yourself or locating a mailing service company to do it for you. As the numbers of your direct mail pieces increase, the more practical it is for you to enlist such an organization for assistance. They also are very good at getting you the lowest postal rates.
- Consider using a self-addressed reply card or envelope to strengthen return. Use a Business Reply Postage Number on the envelope and you'll only pay for the cards which are sent back to you.

The blessing (or curse) of direct mail is that there are no set rules for form or content. The task of deciding what your mailing should have as content, its design and its message(s) is up to you. However, remember to attract the reader's attention with colour and creativity. Use clear, comfortable writing and make your appeal easy to respond. And of course, coordinate the mailing with other advertising media if you are also using them in the same campaign. It can significantly increase the potential return.

SPECIALTY ADVERTISING

"Giveaways" — the pencils, pens, buttons, calendars and refrigerator magnets you see everyday — are called "Specialty Advertising" in the advertising business. Chances are, you have some specialty advertising items right at your desk. Businesses imprint their name on items and give them away (or sometimes sell them at very low cost) in order that:

- You notice their name enough times on the item to build "top-of-the-mind" awareness. So when you need a restaurant, for instance, you think of their name first.
- You appreciate the goodwill of the company giving you the item and eventually return the favour by giving them some business.

These are both long-term advertising investments that can take months or years to turn into actual sales.

First, select the best item that would tell your story most effectively. While an accountant can give away an inexpensive calculator, the same item may not be ideal for a hairdresser. A comb or brush might be more appropriate in that case.

Second, decide what you are going to say on the item. A company slogan? Address directions? Since you have a relatively small area, you must be very concise and direct.

Third, figure out your method of distribution. Are you going to send them to each customer through the mail? If so, how much will that cost? Will you have them in a big bowl that says "take one"? Distribution is just as important to consider as buying the item. Just as there are many reputable specialty advertising professionals in your area, the industry is notorious with a lot of high-pressure telephone and mail solicitors who often give specialty advertising a bad name. Don't buy specialty advertising through the mail without checking the quality and prices with trusted local representatives first. And, buying specialty advertising over the telephone is not recommended at all.

Specialty advertising is a unique way to generate goodwill and put your name on items that people remember. But don't do it unless you have an item and distribution plan that will benefit your business. There is no one - sure-fire - best way to advertise your product or service. It is important to explore the various advertising media and select those which will most effectively convey your message to your customers in a cost-efficient manner. Always remember, advertising is an investment in the future of your business.

6

Corporate Communication

Most tangibly, corporate communication is a separate function within a company. The function has close ties to, or includes, investor relations, employee communication, government relations, corporate advertising, corporate philanthropy, business policy, CSR, public relations and media relations. One European Chief Communication Officer described the function as "furthering the strategic goals of the company and removing obstacles to those goals." With historical roots in public relations, the most dramatic change in the corporate communication function has been its changing role from responsibility for "in house" external communication to aligning internal and external messages engaging the company's stakeholders.

At the same time, communicating "the company story" has become a key role of the general manager, not just the responsibility of corporate communication and the CEO. What is really implied by communicating to fully engaging a company's stakeholders?

Corporate communication can also be thought of as the continuous communications that take place within a corporation. Are these communications a help or a distraction? When does communication improve productivity? What kinds of interactions—official and informal— are necessary for people to connect with their work, to feel a sense of purpose? Although business schools teach corporate communication under the umbrella of "management communication," communication for managers can be best understood within the context of an individual organization or industry. Graduate students do not need to be told how quickly and dramatically communication in business is changing, or how difficult it is to predict what will happen in the next few years. Still, a set of trends can be identified. Taken together, this course suggests the following terms describe a "rhetoric" of corporate communication—the factors that make up the ways in which organizations persuade.

IDENTITY

An individual manager is said to be communicating effectively when they are acting "naturally" or being "themselves". So too, an organization's messages are most effective when they relate to substantive attributes of the organization, its heritage, and demonstrable behaviour. Johnson and Johnson, for example, is regularly a "most admired" company because managerial decisions can be connected to its credo.

IBM changed its identity from "big blue" to a "solutions" company by changing its business model and communicating the change. At one time, corporate identity was simply a firm's visual identity. But identity has become a strategic starting point, as well as a way to capture symbolic meaning for stakeholders. Some researchers connect conceptions of individual identity and corporate identity. Do organizations have a personality?

BRAND

Leveraging the corporate brand might be a sustainable strategy for a one company but not for another. The "brand-power" of a company like Virgin is at once obvious and "intangible". Brand is plainly related to identity and corporate history. Proctor and Gamble in the U.S. or Unilever in the U.K. are examples of "endorsed identity." The firm's product brands connect to consumers more than the corporate brand. For Coke, product and corporate brand have long been seen as co-terminus. Mitsubishi has a "monolithic" identity although it makes televisions and trucks. Some corporations, like Samsung, have taken on adventurous corporate branding strategies describing what the brand does.

Alfred Sloane of GM invented "endorsed identity," but his company's brand has been struggling to reconnect with American consumers. The phrase "a brand is a promise" to its customers is a familiar one.

Corporate brand extends this notion to mean that a company delivers on the values the brand stands for. This could include: financial performance: treatment of employees: commitment to community: environmental sustainability. What are the similarities and differences between corporate and product brands, their measurement? When is a strong corporate brand a competitive advantage?

REPUTATION

For some executives, the corporate brand is a key building block for reputation, for others, an end in itself. Investment banks, for example, are dependent on their reputations, on the trust of investors. With each cycle of financial scandals since the mid-20th century, trust has eroded. Reputations take a long time to build and, as we have tragically seen, can vanish in a day. Reputation management has become a major factor in corporate communication.

Attempts to accurately measure an organization's reputation have advanced a good deal in the last ten years. Polls like *Fortune's* "Most Admired Companies" have taken on a life of their own. Paradoxically, trust in big business is at all time lows, while business is increasingly expected to solve social problems from education to saving the planet. This was not the original purpose of the corporation. What is the role of the corporation in civil society today?

CRISIS

Crisis communication is the most widely-known aspect of corporate communication. In a crisis the organization must speak with one voice and speak quickly. Hardly a day passes when a corporate crisis does not prominently appear in the national newspapers. Business is arguable the dominant "fact" of our time, and so always newsworthy. Cable news shows and the web have drastically shortened the time managers have to respond to a crisis. Since the famous Tylenol and Exxon crises, an extensive literature on crisis management has developed. Sensible "rules" about managing crises can be found, but most crises are particular to themselves, if also related to similar precedents. New kinds of crises (and issues management) have emerged with the growth of Non Governmental Organizations and the web. Concern over social issues from foods safety to the cost of health care has grown in intensity. How can crises be prevented, risk minimized?

For our purposes, a second set of terms significantly influence the first four:

1. *Technology and Social Media*: It is difficult to imagine that a relatively short time ago Royal Dutch Shell and Intel were taken by surprise by the power of the web. Greenpeace streamed video of protests against the sinking of the Brent Spar oil rig, images that made the front page of the next day's *Financial Times*. Intel thought a flaw in a complex calculation would not matter to consumers. Following the "Pentium bug crisis", Andy Grove coined the term "inflection point." Companies today wrestle with guidelines for employee blogs. Corporate communication managers become members of product-related chat rooms. Converse posted short films by costumers in a twist on BMW's "The Driver" soon after they were acquired by Nike. New kinds of electronic communication result in new kinds of communities of trust (Face Book and so on) and pose new risks. Some companies have been remarkably adroit at incorporating social media as internal ways to build trust and identity. Can social media be managed?
2. *Blurred Boundaries and shifting stakeholders*: A primary, if not the primary, role of corporate communication has become aligning strategic messages to internal and external stakeholders. Yet, it is increasingly clear that stakeholders are no longer made up of stable or discreet groups. An employee may be, for example, a customer and a member of an environmental group. CSR will increasingly play a role in corporations. As the millennial generation enters the

workplace, some companies strive to make the media environment at work mirror the media environment at home. Are we in a "global village" or should companies still seek to conform to local circumstances? Globalization further blurs boundaries. The Ford Firestone crisis was an exercise in frustration when executives tried to explain arcane technical issues as well as cross-cultural factors in a sound-bite world. How can aligning stakeholders create value?

3. *Trust and Authenticity*: The collapse of trust in legendary institutions that we have just witnessed is still unfolding. But executives like Warren Buffett have long acknowledged that reputation is a company's most valuable asset. How could so many firms lose their bearings on this crucial point? To be sure, recent events are highly complex; yet, it is difficult not to think, or wish, that the council of communication executives could have had some affect at turning points where taking on excessive threatened the reputation of the firm. Authenticity, like transparency, has become something of a "buzzword". What roles do transparency and authenticity play for communication in today's wired world?
4. The origins of modern management can be traced to F.W. Taylor's *Scientific Management*. If business remains in many ways a science, it is one deeply entwined with intangible factors as well as popular culture, that most unpredictable of contexts. How can business best interact with this phenomenon?

Corporate communication is the communication issued by a corporate/ organization/ body/ institute to all its public(s). Publics here can be both internal (employees, stakeholders, i.e. - share and stock holders) and external (agencies, channel partners, media, government, industry bodies and institutes, educational institutes and general public).

An organization needs to talk the same message to all of its stakeholders, in order to transmit coherence, credibility and ethic. If one of these points is broken, the whole community can make this organization disappear.

The Corporate Communication area will help this organization to build its message, combining its vision, mission and values and will also support the organization by communicating its message, activities and practices to all of its stakeholders. According to the book *Essentials of Corporate Communication* by Cees van Riel and Charles Fombrun the term *Corporate Communication* can be defined as the set of activities involved in managing and orchestrating all internal and external communications aimed at creating favorable starting points with stakeholders on which the company depends.

Corporate communication consists of the dissemination of information by a variety of specialists and generalists in an organization, with the common goal of enhancing the organization's ability to retain its license to operate. As Jackson (1987) remarks: Note that it is corporate communication — without a final "s". Tired of being called on to fix the company switchboard, recommend an answering machine or meet a computer salesman, I long ago adopted this form as being more accurate and left communications to the telecommunications specialists. It's a small point but another attempt to bring clarity out of confusion. Corporate communication serves as the liaison between an organization and its publics.Organizations can strategically communicate to their audiences through public relations and advertising. This may involve an employee newsletter or video, crisis management with the news media, special events planning, building product value and communicating with stockholders, clients or donors.

CORPORATE COMMUNICATION ENCODES AND PROMOTES

- Strong corporate culture
- Coherent corporate identity
- Reasonable corporate philosophy
- Genuine sense of corporate citizenship
- An appropriate and professional relationship with the press, including quick, responsible ways of commun-icating in a crisis
- Understanding of communication tools and techno-logies
- Sophisticated approaches to global communications

How an organization communicates with its employees, its extended audiences, the press and its customers brings its values to life. Corporate communications is all about managing perceptions and ensuring:

- Effective and timely dissemination of information
- Positive corporate image
- Smooth and affirmative relationship with all stakeholders

Be it a corporate body, company, organization, institution, non-governmental organization, governmental body, all of them need to have a respectable image and reputation. In today's day and age of increasing competition, easy access to information and the media explosion, reputation management has gained even more importance.

Therefore, corporate communications as a role has become significant and professional in nature.Gone are the days when corporate communication merely meant 'wining and dining the client' - it has now emerged as a science and art of perception management.

Key Tasks of Corporate Communication

The responsibilities of corporate communication are therefore:

- To flesh out the profile of the "company behind the brand" (corporate branding)
- To develop initiatives that minimize discrepancies between the company's desired identity and brand features;

- To indicate who should perform which tasks in the field of communication;
- To formulate and execute effective procedures in order to facilitate decision making about matters concerning communication;
- To mobilize internal and external support behind corporate objectives.
- To co ordinate with international business firms

Tools of Corporate Communication

Integrated communication can be achieved in various ways.

The main four practices are:

1. Application of visual identity systems (sometimes referred to as "house style")
2. Use of integrated marketing communications;
3. Reliance on coordinating teams;
4. Adoption of a centralized planning system.

The communication Agenda: To Build Reputation

Corporate communication helps an organization to create distictive and appealing images with its stakeholder groups, build a strong corporate brand, and develop reputation capital. To achieve those ends, all forms of communication must be orchestrated into a coherent whole, and success criteria developed that enable measuring the effects of the organization's communication on its reputation and value.

External Communication

This involves building and maintaining a positive relationship with the media (television, print, web,). This inclu-des, but is not limited to, drafting and dissemination of press releases, organizing press conferences and meeting with media professionals and organizing events for the media as a group.

External Events

Could involve vendor/ supplier/ distributor meets, channel partner meetings, events related to product launches, important initiatives, et cetera.

Company/Spokesperson Profiling

Ensuring that the company/organization spokesperson is in the public limelight, is well-known and considered as an authority in the respective sector/field.

- Managing content of corporate websites and/or other external touch points
- Managing corporate publications - for the external world
- Managing print media

Brand Management

- Development and upkeep of the corporate identity to ensure adherence to corporate brand guidelines

To improve overall business communications so as to clearly and effectively communicate the essence of the company.

Corporate Identity/Organizational Identity

There are two approaches for Identity, respectively Corporate Identity and Organizational Identity.

- "Corporate identity is the reality and uniqueness of an organization, which is integrally related to its external and internal image and reputation through corporate communication"
- "Organizational Identity comprises those characteri-stics of an organization that its members believe are central, distinctive and enduring. That is, organiza-tional identity consists of those attributes that members feel are fundamental to (central) and uniquely descriptive of (distinctive) the organization and that persist within the organization over time (enduring)".

CORPORATE REPUTATION

Reputations are overall assessments of organizations by their stakeholders. They are aggregate perceptions by stakeholders of an organizaitons's ability to fulfil their expectations, whether these stakeholders are interested in buying the company's products, working for the company, or investing in the company's shares.

In 2000, the US based Council of PR Firms identified seven programs that were developed by either media organizations or market research firms, and that were being used by companies to assess or benchmark their corporate reputations. Of these only three are conducted regularly and have broad visibility:

- "America's Most Admired Companies" by Fortune Magazine;
- The "Brand Asset Valuator" by Young & Rubicam;
- "RepTrak" by Reputation Institute.

Crisis communications

Crisis has four defining characteristics. Seeger, Sellnow and Ulmer explain that a crises are "specific, unexpected, and non-routine events or series of events that [create] high levels of uncertainty and threat or perceived threat to an organization's high priority goals."

Thus the first three characteristics are that the event is:

1. Unexpected (i.e., a surprise),
2. Creates uncertainty,
3. Is seen as a threat to important goals.

Venette argues that "crisis is a process of transformation where the old system can no longer be maintained." Therefore the fourth defining quality is the need for change. If change is not needed, the event could more accurately be described as a failure.

Crisis communication can be broadly defined as the exchange of information before, during, or after a crisis event. Crisis communication is sometimes considered a sub-specialty of the public relations profession that is designed to protect and defend an individual, company, or organization facing a public challenge to its reputation. These challenges may come in the form of an investigation from a government agency, a criminal allegation, a media inquiry, a shareholders lawsuit, a violation of environmental regulations, or any of a number of other scenarios involving the legal, ethical, or financial standing of the entity.

Crisis communication professionals preach that an organization's reputation is often its most valuable asset. When that reputation comes under attack, protecting and defending it becomes the highest priority. This is particularly true in today's 24 hour news cycle, fuelled by government investigations, Congressional or parliamentary hearings, lawsuits, and "gotcha journalism". When events like these happen, the media firestorm can quickly overwhelm the ability of the entity to effectively respond to the demands of the crisis. To emerge with its reputation intact, an organization must anticipate every move and respond immediately and with confidence. Companies facing such a threat will often bring in experienced crisis communications specialists to help prepare and guide them through the process.

Effectively responding to the challenges of a crisis requires more than the typical skills of the public relations professional, requiring instead experience at the highest levels of the field, such as investigative reporting, politics, and the White House. Crisis communication can include crafting thorough and compelling statements, known as "messages," often tested by research and polling. A rapid response capability—pioneered by the 1992 Clinton-Gore campaign operatives and refined during Bill Clinton's eight years under attack by his political adversaries while in the White House, has also become an essential element of crisis communication.

Additional tactics may include proactive media outreach to get messages and context to the media, identifying and recruiting credible third-party allies who can attest to the company's side of the story, and striking first, not waiting to be hit. Crisis communication is a part of larger process referred to as crisis management though it may well be a major tool of handling a crisis situation in government, organization or business. Crisis Communication is also sometimes considered a sub-speciality of the Business Continuity area of modern business. The aim of crisis communication in this context is to assist organisations to achieve continuity of critical business processes and information flows under crisis, disaster or event driven circumstances.

Responding quickly, efficiently, effectively and in a premeditated way are the primary objectives of an effective crisis communication strategy and/or solution. Harnassing technology and people to ensure a rapid and co-ordinated response to a range of potentially crippling scenarios distinguishes a well thought out and executed plan from a poorly or ill-considered one. The inherent lag time in marshalling responses to a crisis can result in considerable losses to company revenues, reputation as well as substantially impacting on costs.

Effective crisis communication strategies will typically consider achieving most, if not all, of the following objectives:

- Maintain connectivity
- Be readily accessible to the news media
- Show empathy for the people involved
- Allow distributed access
- Streamline communication processes
- Maintain information security
- Ensure uninterrupted audit trails
- Deliver high volume communications
- Support multi-channel communications
- Remove dependencies on paper based processes

By definition a crisis is an unexpected and detrimental situation or event. Crisis communication can play a significant role by transforming the unexpected into the anticipated and responding accordingly.

Some of the most effective recent examples of crisis communication include Richard Branson's (Virgin) and John Armitt's (Network Rail) dignified press conference after the Grayrigg rail disaster of 2007 and US Airways handling of the media after their crashlanding on the Hudson river.

Employee communication:

- Sharing information with employees, building employer pride, managing employee issues, et cetera.
- Manage the Intranet and other internal web portals

Organizational communication: Encourage and enable the employees to plan for new ideas and effectively implement them.

Internal communication:

- Managing corporate publications for employees and partners
- Organising internal events for staff

Corporate Communication Officers

Recent research on the corporate communication function reports that corporate communication officers (CCOs) in Global Fortune 500 companies tend to have average tenures of about 4.5 years and that nearly one-half (48 per cent) report to the Chief Executive Officer. CCOs say that approximately 42 per cent of their job is strategic and 58 per cent is tactical. Over the next year, they will be focusing more on social responsibility, social media and reputation. The research done by Weber Shandwick and Spencer Stuart found distinct differences between CCOs in Most Admired companies versus Contender companies.

CORPORATE VIDEO

Corporate video production refers to audio-visual corporate communications material (such as DVD, High-definition video, streaming video or other media) commissioned primarily for a use by a company, corporation or organisation.

A corporate video is often intended for a specific purpose in a corporate or B2B environment and viewed only by a limited or targeted audience. This may include product, service or company promotional videos, training videos and information videos·Corporate video production is frequently the responsibility of a company marketing or corporate communications manager. Examples of corporate video include staff training and safety videos, promotional/brand films, and financial results videos.With the growth of digital technology, there is now often convergence between corporate video and other forms of media communications, such as broadcast television and TV advertising.

For example, a company might feature a promotional video on their website' and is then potentially available to a much wider audience. Also, a corporate video may be produced using the same production techniques and style as a broadcast television programme (such as using outside broadcasting facilities)—as a way of engaging audiences who are used to viewing popular media, a corporate video might even be themed on a well-known television series. A corporate video production company may typically take the client brief, develop a script or treatment (and sometimes a storyboard), liaise with the client, and agree on a production schedule and delivery date.

The time and scale of a corporate video production can vary greatly. Some videos may use only minimal crew and basic equipment, whilst some large scale corporate videos may have similar (or often higher) budgets and level of production than a broadcast television programme or TV commercial.

The corporate video production process will frequently involve the following stages:

- Pre-Production, including script writing and storyboarding. The budget will also be agreed at this stage between the production company and client.
- Production, including location filming with a camera crew and director. This may also include other elements, such as actors and presenters.
- Post-production and video editing - the filmed (live action) footage is edited together. This may also include recording an audio voice-

over, adding graphics, composing a music score or soundtrack, and including 2D/3D animation sequences with the finished video.

Types and Usage

- Staff training/induction and safety videos
- Investor relations/ financial results
- Company promotional/brand videos
- Video role play (often with actors)
- Client and customer testimonial videos
- Corporate event filming (for example, a new product launch or conference)
- Live and on-demand webcasting
- Technology and product demonstration videos
- Business television

CORPORATE IMAGE

A corporate image refers to how a corporation is perceived. It is a generally accepted image of what a company stands for. Marketing experts who use public relations and other forms of promotion to suggest a mental picture to the public.

Typically, a corporate image is designed to be appealing to the public, so that the company can spark an interest among consumers, create share of mind, generate brand equity, and thus facilitate product sales. A corporation's image is not solely created by the company: Other contributors to a company's image could include news media, journalists, labour unions, environmental organizations, and other NGOs. Corporations are not the only form of organization that create these types of images. Governments, charitable organizations, criminal organizations, religious organizations, political organizations, and educational organizations all tend to have a unique image, an image that is partially deliberate and partially accidental, partially self-created and partially exogenous.

CORPORATE PROPAGANDA

Corporate propaganda are propagandist claims made by a corporation (or corporations), nearly always for the purpose of manipulating market opinion to the benefit of their product or to divide public opinion with regard to controversial issues related to that corporation, and its associated business dealings.

Corporate propaganda is distinct from advocacy. Advocacy presents product and service information fully, fairly, and without exploitation of consumer emotions. Just as the use of these products and services can provide pluses which outweigh the minuses to society and individuals, their advocacy may function more positively than negatively. The most common forms of corporate propaganda are advertising and public relations.

Examples

- Decision Earth Procter & Gamble propaganda materials distributed to schools, to influence young children with pseudoscientific notions.
- Bechtel Corporation
- Tobacco industry Long history of advertising and litigation wherein practices of manipulation and deception are common.
- Captain Planet
- Walt Disney's Production of Propaganda for the US Government During World War II

Marketing Speak

Marketing speak refers to particular patterns of language often used to promote a product or service to a wide audience by seeking to create the impression that the vendors of the service possess a high level of sophistication, skill, and technical knowledge. Such language is often used in marketing press releases, advertising copy, and prepared statements read by executives and politicians. Marketing speak is characterized by its heavy use of buzzwords, neologisms, and terms appropriated from specialized technical fields which are eventually rendered almost meaningless through heavy repeated use in inappropriate contexts.

Examples:

- Unique selling proposition (USP)
- Low hanging fruit (LHF)
- Pushing the envelope
- *Lean forward* and *Lean back* media
- Deep-dive

ORGANIZATIONAL COMMUNICATION

Organizational communication is a subfield of the larger discipline of communication studies. Organizational communication, as a field, is the consideration, analysis, and criticism of the role of communication in organizational contexts. The field traces its lineage through business information, business communication, and early mass communication studies published in the 1930s through the 1950s. Until then, organizational communication as a discipline consisted of a few professors within speech departments who had a particular interest in speaking and writing in business settings.

The current field is well established with its own theories and empirical concerns distinct from other communication subfields and other approaches to organizations. Several seminal publications stand out as works broadening the scope and recognizing the importance of communication in the organizing process, and in using the term "organizational communication". Nobel Laureate Herbert Simon wrote in 1947 about "organization communications systems", saying communication is "absolutely essential to organizations". In the 1950s, organizational communication focused largely on the role of communication in improving organizational life and organizational output. In the 1980s, the field turned away from a business-oriented approach to communication and became concerned more with the constitutive role of communication in organizing. In the 1990s, critical theory influence on the field was felt as organizational communication scholars focused more on communication's possibilities to oppress and liberate organizational members.

EARLY ORGANIZATIONAL COMMUNICATION

Some of the main assumptions underlying much of the early organizational communication research were.

- *Humans act rationally*: Sane people behave in rational ways, they generally have access to all of the information needed to make rational decisions they could articulate, and therefore will make rational decisions, unless there is some breakdown in the communication process.
- Formal logic and empirically verifiable data ought to be the foundation upon which any theory should rest. All we really need to understand communication in organizations is:
  - Observable and replicable behaviors that can be transformed into variables by some form of measurement,
  - Formally replicable syllogisms that can extend theory from observed data to other groups and settings
- Communication is primarily a mechanical process, in which a message is constructed and encoded by a sender, transmitted through some channel, then received and decoded by a receiver. Distortion, represented as any differences between the original and the received messages, can and ought to be identified and reduced or eliminated.
- Organizations are mechanical things, in which the parts (including employees functioning in defined roles) are interchangeable. What works in one organization will work in another similar organi-zation. Individual differences can be minimized or even eliminated with careful management tech-niques.
- Organizations function as a container within which communication takes place. Any differences in form or function of communication between that occurring in an organization and in another setting can be identified and studied as factors affecting the communicative activity.

Herbert Simon introduced the concept of bounded rationality which challenged assumptions about the perfect rationality of communication participants. He maintained that people making decisions in organizations seldom had complete information, and that even if more information was available, they tended to pick the first acceptable option, rather than exploring further to pick the optimal solution.

Through the 1960s, 1970s and 1980s the field expanded greatly in parallel with several other academic disciplines, looking at communication as more than an intentional act designed to transfer an idea. Research expanded beyond the issue of "how to make people understand what I am saying" to tackle questions such as "how does the act of communicating change, or even define, who I am?", "why do organizations that seem to be saying similar things achieve very different results?" and "to what extent are my relationships with others affected by our various organizational contexts?"

In the early 1990s Peter Senge developed a new theories on Organizational Communication. These theories were learning organization and systems thinking. These have been well received and are now a mainstay in current beliefs toward organizational communications.

Communications Networks

Networks are another aspect of direction and flow of communication. Bavelas has shown that communication patterns, or networks, influence groups in several important ways. Communication networks may affect the group's completion of the assigned task on time, the position of the de facto leader in the group, or they may affect the group members' satisfaction from occupying certain positions in the network. Although these findings are based on laboratory experiments, they have important implications for the dynamics of communication in formal organizations.

There are several patterns of communication:

- "Chain",
- "Wheel",
- "Star",
- "All-Channel" network,
- "Circle".

The Chain can readily be seen to represent the hierarchical pattern that characterizes strictly formal information flow, "from the top down," in military and some types of business organizations. The Wheel can be compared with a typical autocratic organization, meaning one-man rule and limited employee participation.

The Star is similar to the basic formal structure of many organizations. The All-Channel network, which is an elaboration of Bavelas's Circle used by Guetzkow, is analogous to the free-flow of communication in a group that encourages all of its members to become involved in group decision processes. The All-Channel network may also be compared to some of the informal communication networks.

If it's assumed that messages may move in both directions between stations in the networks, it is easy to see that some individuals occupy key positions with regard to the number of messages they handle and the degree to which they exercise control over the flow of information.

For example, the person represented by the central dot in the "Star" handles all messages in the group. In contrast, individuals who occupy stations at the edges of the pattern handle fewer messages and have little or no control over the flow of information.These "peripheral" individuals can communicate with only one or two other persons and must depend entirely on others to relay their messages if they wish to extend their range.

In reporting the results of experiments involving the Circle, Wheel, and Star configurations, Bavelas came to the following tentative conclusions. In patterns with positions located centrally, such as the Wheel and the Star, an organization quickly develops around the people occupying these central positions. In such patterns, the organization is more stable and errors in performance are lower than in patterns having a lower degree of centrality, such as the Circle. However, he also found that the morale of members in high centrality patterns is relatively low. Bavelas speculated that this lower morale could, in the long run, lower the accuracy and speed of such networks. In problem solving requiring the pooling of data and judgments, or "insight," Bavelas suggested that the ability to evaluate partial results, to look at alternatives, and to restructure problems fell off rapidly when one person was able to assume a more central (that is, more controlling) position in the information flow.

For example, insight into a problem requiring change would be less in the Wheel and the Star than in the Circle or the Chain because of the "bottlenecking" effect of data control by central members. It may be concluded from these laboratory results that the structure of communications within an organization will have a significant influence on the accuracy of decisions, the speed with which they can be reached, and the satisfaction of the people involved. Consequently, in networks in which the responsibility for initiating and passing along messages is shared more evenly among the members, the better the group's morale in the long run.

DIRECTION OF COMMUNICATION

If it's considered formal communications as they occur in traditional military organizations, messages have a "one-way" directional characteristic. In the military organization, the formal communication proceeds from superior to subordinate, and its content is presumably clear because it originates at a higher level of expertise and experience. Military communications also carry the additional assumption that the superior is responsible for making his communication clear and understandable to his subordinates.

This type of organization assumes that there is little need for two-way exchanges between organizational levels except as they are initiated by a higher level. Because messages from superiors are considered to be more important than those from subordinates, the implicit rule is that communication channels, except for prescribed information flows, should not be cluttered by messages from subordinates but should remain open and free for messages moving down the chain of command. "Juniors should be seen and not heard," is still an unwritten, if not explicit, law of military protocol. Vestiges of one-way flows of communication still exist in many formal organizations outside the military, and for many of the same reasons as described above.

Although management recognizes that prescribed information must flow both downward and upward, managers may not always be convinced that two-wayness should be encouraged. For example, to what extent is a subordinate free to communicate to his superior that he understands or does not understand a message? Is it possible for him to question the superior, ask for clarification, suggest modifications to instructions he has received, or transmit unsolicited messages to his superior, which are not prescribed by the rules? To what extent does the one-way rule of direction affect the efficiency of communication in the organization, in addition to the morale and motivation of subordinates?

These are not merely procedural matters but include questions about the organizational climate, pr psychological atmosphere in which communication takes place. Harold Leavitt has suggested a simple experiment that helps answer some of these questions. À group is assigned the task of re-creating on paper a set of rectangular figures, first as they are described by the leader under one-way conditions, and second as they are described by the leader under two-way conditions. A different configuration of rectangles is used in the second trial. In the one-way trial, the leader's back is turned to the group. He describes the rectangles as he sees them. No one in the group is allowed to ask questions and no one may indicate by any audible or visible sign his understanding or his frustration as he attempts to follow the leader's directions.

In the two-way trial, the leader faces the group. In this case, the group may ask for clarifications on his description of the rectangles and he can not only see but also can feel and respond to the emotional reactions of group members as they try to re-create his instructions on paper. On the basis of a number of experimental trials similar to the one described above, Leavitt formed these conclusions.

- One-way communication is faster than two-way communication.
- Two-way communication is more accurate than one-way communication.
- Receivers are more sure of themselves and make more correct judgments of how right or wrong they are in the two-way system.

- The sender feels psychologically under attack in the two-way system, because his receivers pick up his mistakes and oversights and point them out to him.
- The two-way method is relatively noisier and looks more disorderly. The one-way method, on the other hand, appears neat and efficient to an outside observer.

Thus, if speed is necessary, if a businesslike appearance is important, if a manager does not want his mistakes recognized, and if he wants to protect his power, then one-way communication seems preferable. In contrast, if the manager wants to get his message across, or if he is concerned about his receivers' feeling that they are participating and are making a contribution, the two-way system is better.

Interpersonal Communication

Another facet of communication in the organization is the process of face-to-face, interpersonal communication, between individuals. Such communication may take several forms. Messages may be verbal (that is, expressed in words), or they may not involve words at all but consist of gestures, facial expressions, and certain postures ("body language"). Nonverbal messages may even stem from silence.

Managers do not need answers to operate a successful business; they need questions. Answers can come from anyone, anytime, anywhere in the world thanks to the benefits of all the electronic communication tools at our disposal. This has turned the real job of management into determining what it is the business needs to know, along with the who/what/where/when and how of learning it. To effectively solve problems, seize opportunities, and achieve objectives, questions need to be asked by managers—these are the people responsible for the operation of the enterprise as a whole.

Ideally, the meanings sent are the meanings received. This is most often the case when the messages concern something that can be verified objectively. For example, "This piece of pipe fits the threads on the coupling." In this case, the receiver of the message can check the sender's words by actual trial, if necessary. However, when the sender's words describe a feeling or an opinion about something that cannot be checked objectively, meanings can be very unclear. "This work is too hard" or "Watergate was politically justified" are examples of opinions or feelings that cannot be verified. Thus they are subject to interpretation and hence to distorted meanings. The receiver's background of experience and learning may differ enough from that of the sender to cause significantly different perceptions and evaluations of the topic under discussion. Nonverbal content always accompanies the verbal content of messages. This is reasonably clear in the case of face-to-face communication. As Virginia Satir has pointed out, people cannot help but communicate symbolically (for example, through their clothing or possessions) or through some form of body language. In messages that are conveyed by the telephone, a messenger, or a letter, the situation or context in which the message is sent becomes part of its non-verbal content. For example, if the company has been losing money, and in a letter to the production division, the front office orders a reorganization of the shipping and receiving departments, this could be construed to mean that some people were going to lose their jobs — unless it were made explicitly clear that this would not occur.

A number of variables influence the effectiveness of communication. Some are found in the environment in which communication takes place, some in the personalities of the sender and the receiver, and some in the relationship that exists between sender and receiver. These different variables suggest some of the difficulties of communicating with understanding between two people. The sender wants to formulate an idea and communicate it to the receiver. This desire to communicate may arise from his thoughts or feelings or it may have been triggered by something in the environment.

The communication may also be influenced or distorted by the relationship between the sender and the receiver, such as status differences, a staff-line relationship, or a learner-teacher relationship. Whatever its origin, information travels through a series of filters, both in the sender and in the receiver, before the idea can be transmitted and re-created in the receiver's mind. Physical capacities to see, hear, smell, taste, and touch vary between people, so that the image of reality may be distorted even before the mind goes to work. In addition to physical or sense filters, cognitive filters, or the way in which an individual's mind interprets the world around him, will influence his assumptions and feelings.

These filters will determine what the sender of a message says, how he says it, and with what purpose. Filters are present also in the receiver, creating a double complexity that once led Robert Louis Stevenson to say that human communication is "doubly relative". It takes one person to say something and another to decide what he said.

Physical and cognitive, including semantic filters (which decide the meaning of words) combine to form a part of our memory system that helps us respond to reality. In this sense, March and Simon compare a person to a data processing system. Behaviour results from an interaction between a person's internal state and environmental stimuli.

What we have learned through past experience becomes an inventory, or data bank, consisting of values or goals, sets of expectations and preconceptions about the consequences of acting one way or another, and a variety of possible ways of responding to the situation. This memory system determines what things we will notice and respond to in the environment. At the same time, stimuli in the environment help to determine what parts of the memory system will be activated. Hence, the memory and the environment form an interactive system that causes our behaviour. As this interactive system responds to new experiences, new learnings occur which feed back into memory and gradually change its content. This process is how people adapt to a changing world.

Communication Approaches in an Organization

Informal and Formal Communication are used in an organization. Informal communication: Informal communi-cation, generally associated with interpersonal, horizontal communication, was primarily seen as a potential hindrance to effective organizational performance. This is no longer the case. Informal communication has become more important to ensuring the effective conduct of work in modern organizations. *Top-down approach*: This is also known as downward communication. This approach is used by the Top Level Management to communicate to the lower levels. This is used to implement policies, gudelines, etc. In this type of organizational communication, distortion of the actual information occurs. This could be made effective by feedbacks.

Research in Organizational Communication

Research Methodologies

Historically, organizational communication was driven primarily by quantitative research methodologies. Included in functional organizational communication research are statistical analyses (such as surveys, text indexing, network mapping and behaviour modeling). In the early 1980s, the interpretive revolution took place in organizational communication.

In Putnam and Pacanowsky's 1983 text Communication and Organizations: An Interpretive Approach. they argued for opening up methodological space for qualitative approaches such as narrative analyses, participant-observation, interviewing, rhetoric and textual approaches readings) and philosophic inquiries. During the 1980s and 1990s critical organizational scholarship began to gain prominence with a focus on issues of gender, race, class, and power/ knowledge. In its current state, the study of organizational communication is open methodologically, with research from post-positive, interpretive, critical, postmodern, and discursive paradigms being published regularly.

Organizational communication scholarship appears in a number of communication journals including but not limited to Management Communication Quarterly, Journal of Applied Communication Research, Communication Monographs, Academy of Management Journal, Communication Studies, and Southern Communication Journal.

Current Research Topics in Organizational Communication

The field of organizational communication has moved from acceptance of mechanistic models (e.g., information moving from a sender to a receiver) to a study of the persistent, hegemonic and taken-for-granted ways in which we not only use communication to accomplish certain tasks within organizational settings (e.g., public speaking) but also how the organizations in which we participate affect us.

These approaches include "postmodern", "critical", "participatory", "feminist", "power/political", "organic", etc. and adds to disciplines as wide-ranging as sociology, philosophy, theology, psychology, business, business administration, institutional management, medicine (health communication), neurology (neural nets), semiotics, anthropology, international relations, and music.

Currently, some topics of research and theory in the field are:

- Constitution
- Narrative
- Identity
- Interrelatedness
- Power

Constitution

- How communicative behaviors construct or modify organizing processes or products.
- How the organizations within which we interact affect our communicative behaviors, and through these, our own identities.
- Structures other than organizations which might be constituted through our communicative activity (e.g., markets, cooperatives, tribes, political parties, social movements).
- When does something "become" an organization? When does an organization become (an)other thing(s)? Can one organization "house" another? Is the organization still a useful entity/thing/concept, or has the social/political environment changed so much that what we now call "organization" is so different from the organization of even a few decades ago that it cannot be usefully tagged with the same word—"organization"?

Narrative

- How do group members employ narrative to acculturate/initiate/indoctrinate new members?
- Do organizational stories act on different levels? Are different narratives purposively invoked to achieve specific outcomes, or are there specific roles of "organizational storyteller"? If so, are stories told by the storyteller received differently than those told by others in the organization?
- In what ways does the organization attempt to influence storytelling

about the organization? under what conditions does the organization appear to be more or less effective in obtaining a desired outcome?

- When these stories conflict with one another or with official rules/ policies, how are the conflicts worked out? in situations in which alternative accounts are available, who or how or why are some accepted and others rejected?

Identity

- Who do we see ourselves to be, in terms of our organizational affiliations?
- Do communicative behaviors or occurrences in one or more of the organizations in which we participate effect changes in us? To what extent do we consist of the organizations to which we belong?
- Is it possible for individuals to successfully resist organizational identity? what would that look like?
- Do people who define themselves by their work-organizational membership communicate differently within the organizational setting than people who define themselves more by an avocational (non-vocational) set of relationships?
- For example, researchers have studied how human service workers and firefighters use humor at their jobs as a way to affirm their identity in the face of various challenges Tracy, S.J.; K. K. Myers; C. W. Scott. Others have examined the identities of police organizations, prison guards, and professional women workers.

Interrelatedness of Organizational Experiences

- How do our communicative interactions in one organizational setting affect our communicative actions in other organizational settings?
- How do the phenomenological experiences of participants in a particular organizational setting effect changes in other areas of their lives?
- When the organizational status of a member is significantly changed (e.g., by promotion or expuls-ion) how are their other organizational memberships affected?
- What kind of future relationship between business and society does organizational communication seem to predict?

Power

- How does the use of particular communicative practices within an organizational setting reinforce or alter the various interrelated power relationships within the setting? Are the potential responses of those within or around these organizational settings constrained by factors or processes either within or outside of the organization—(assuming there is an "outside"?

- do taken-for-granted organizational practices work to fortify the dominant hegemonic narrative? Do iDndividuals resist/confront these practices, through what actions/agencies, and to what effects?
- Do status changes in an organization (e.g., promotions, demotions, restructuring, financial/social strata changes) change communicative behaviour? Are there criteria employed by organizational members to differentiate between "legitimate" (i.e., endorsed by the formal organizational structure) and "illegitimate" (i.e., opposed by or unknown to the formal power structure)? Are behaviors? When are they successful, and what do we even there "pretenders" or "usurpers" who employ these communicativemean by "successful?"

COMMUNICATION STUDIES

Communication studies is an academic field that deals with processes of communication, commonly defined as the sharing of symbols over distances in space and time. Hence, communication studies encompasses a wide range of topics and contexts ranging from face-to-face conversation to speeches to mass media outlets such as television broadcasting. Communication studies, as a discipline, is also often interested in how audiences interpret information and the political, cultural, economic, and social dimensions of speech and language in context.

The field is institutionalized under many different names at different universities and in various countries, including "communications", "communication studies", "speech communication", "rhetorical studies", "communications science", "media studies", "communication arts", "mass communication", "media ecology," and sometimes even "mediology" although this latter is a different area of study. Communication studies often overlaps with academic programs in journalism, film and cinema, radio and television, advertising and public relations and performance studies. Recently, institutions have migrated towards the common term of "communication studies" to encapsulate and cohere the vast depth and breadth of the field.

In the United States, the National Communication Associ-ation (NCA) recognizes nine distinct but often overlapping sub-disciplines within the broader communi-cation discipline: Communication & Technology, Critical-Cultural, Health, Intercultural-International, Inter-personal-Small Group, Mass Communication, Organizational, Political, and Rhetorical.

The International Communication Association (ICA) recognizes a much larger and evolving list of sections, including among others Communication History; Commun-ication Law and Policy; Ethnicity and Race in Communication; Feminist Scholarship; Gay, Lesbian, Bisexual and Transgender Studies; Global Communication and Social Change; Informa-tion Systems; Instructional/Developmental Communication; Journalism Studies; Language and Social Interaction; Organizational Communication; Philosophy of Communi-cation; Political Communication; Popular Communication; Public Relations; and Visual Communication Studies.

Communication studies is often considered a part of both the social sciences and the humanities, drawing heavily on fields such as sociology, psychology, anthropology, political science, and economics as well as rhetoric, literary studies, linguistics, and semiotics. The field can incorporate and overlap with the work of other disciplines as well, however, including engineering, architecture, mathematics, computer science, gender and sexuality studies. The vast breadth and interdisciplinary nature of commun-ication studies has understandably made it difficult for both students and institutions to place it within the broader educational system. Despite intellectual incoherence, the field attracts and sustains large numbers of students, scholarly journals, professional associations, and lively discussions across the academy for researchers, educators, lawmakers, businesses, and reformers.

Broadly understood, the contemporary study of communication per se interfaces and overlaps with areas such as business, organizational development, philosophy, languages, composition, theatre, debate (often called "forensics"), literary criticism, sociology, psychology, history, anthropology, semiotics, international policy, economics and political science, among others. The breadth and the primacy of communication in many areas of life is responsible for the ubiquity of communication studies, as well as for the resulting confusion about what does and does not constitute communication. Ongoing debates rage whether commun-ication studies can best be understood as a discipline, a field, or simply a topic.

Most U.S. graduate programs in Communication today trace their history through speech to ancient rhetoric. Programs in Communication, Communication Arts or Communication Sciences often include Organizational Communication, Interpersonal Communication, Speech Communication (or Rhetoric), Mass Communication, and sometimes Journalism, Film criticism, Theatre, Political science (e.g., political campaign strategies, public speaking, effects of media on elections), or Radio, Television or Film production.

Graduates of formal communication programs can be found in a wide range of fields working as university professors, marketing researchers, media editors and designers, speech therapists, journalists, human resources managers, corporate trainers, public relations practitioners, and media managers and consultants in a variety of fields including, media production, life coaching, public speaking, organizational, political campaign/issue management and public policy.

Communication is often recognized as a cornerstone of modern society—it would be hard to conceive of modern life without it. However, communication as an English-language field of study and a subject of social thought took off only in the first part of the twentieth century, and is thus a relatively recent and thus unsettled discovery. In what is sometimes called the "transmission" view, communication is a process by which messages are sent, transmitted, filtered, and received. At core, the transmission view maps closely onto information theory inspired by Shannon's 1948 "a Mathematical Theory of Communication." A more recent "ritual" view, proposed by the late James W. Carey, holds that communication partakes in central daily rituals that forge meaningful human relationships and communities. While transmission proposes a model of communication as transportation (across space, in one time), the ritual model proposes that meaning can be constituted in repeated media events (across times, in one space). The newspaper, for instance, does not only transmit messages to the reader through text, but reminds and reassures the reader through repeated and meaningful events, such as its morning appearance on the doorstep and a familiar page layout. A fuller conceptualization of communication activity, many scholars contend, lies somewhere between and beyond these two views.

History, pre-20th Century

Various aspects of communication have long been the subject of human study. In ancient Greece and Rome, the study of rhetoric, the art of oratory and persuasion, was a vital subject for students. One significant ongoing debate was whether one could be an effective speaker in a base cause (Sophists) or whether excellent rhetoric came from the excellence of the orator's character (Socrates, Plato, Cicero). Through the European Middle Ages and Renaissance grammar, rhetoric, and logic constituted the entire trivium, the base of the system of classical learning in Europe.

History, North America

1900s–1920s

Though the study of communication reaches back to antiquity and beyond, early twentieth-century work by Charles Horton Cooley, Walter Lippmann, and John Dewey has been of particular importance for the academic discipline as it stands today in the United States. In his 1909 *Social Organization: a Study of the Larger Mind,* Cooley defines communication as "the mechanism through which human relations exist and develop—all the symbols of the mind, together with the means of conveying them through space and preserving them in time."

This view, which has subsequently been largely marginalized in sociology, gave processes of communication a central and constitutive place in the study of social relations. *Public Opinion,* published in 1922 by Walter Lippmann, couples this view of the constitutive importance of communication with a fear that the rise of new technologies and institutions of mass communication allowed for the manufacture of consent and generated dissonance between what he called 'the world outside and the pictures in our heads' on a scale that made democracy as classically conceived almost impossible to realise.

John Dewey's 1927 The Public and its Problems drew on the same view of communications, but coupled it instead with an optimistic progressive and democratic reform agenda, arguing famously "communication can alone create a great community". Cooley, Lippmann, and Dewey capture themes like the central importance of communication in social life, the rise of large and potentially powerful media institutions and the development of new communications technologies in societies undergoing rapid transformation, and questions regarding the relationship between communication, democracy, and community.

All these remain central to the discipline of communication studies. Many of these concerns are also central to the work of writers such as Gabriel Tarde and Theodor W. Adorno, which has been central to the development of communication studies elsewhere. The first decades of the twentieth century also saw the development of parallel currents of cultural criticism that drew less on the social sciences and more on the humanities. Though trained as a sociologist, the work of W. E. B. Du Bois on art and spirituals stands out here.

The study of American public address began during this time frame. In 1925, Herbert A. Wichelns published the essay "The Literary Criticism of Oratory" in the book *Studies in Rhetoric and Public Speaking in Honour of James Albert Winans.* ' Wicheln's essay attempted to "put rhetorical studies on par with literary studies as an area of academic interest and research." Wichelns wrote that oratory should be taken as seriously as literature, and therefore, it should be subject to criticism and analysis. Although the essay is now standard reading in most rhetorical criticism courses, it had little immediate impact on the field of rhetorical studies.

1930s–1950s

The institutionalization of communication studies in U.S. higher education and research has often been traced to Columbia University, the University of Chicago, and the University of Illinois Urbana-Champaign, where early pioneers and institutionalizers like Paul F. Lazarsfeld, Harold Lasswell, and Wilbur Schramm worked.

The Bureau of Applied Social Research was established in 1944 at Columbia University by Paul F. Lazarsfeld. It was a continuation of the Rockefeller Foundation-funded Radio Project that he had led at various institutions from 1937, which had been at Columbia as the Office of Radio Research since 1939. In its various incarnations, the Radio Project had involved Lazarsfeld himself, and people like Adorno, Hadley Cantril, Gordon Allport, and Frank Stanton (who went on to be president of CBS). Lazarsfeld and the Bureau mobilized substantial sums for research, and produced, with various co-authors, a series of books and edited volumes that helped define the discipline, such as *Personal Influence* which remains a classic in what is called the 'media effects'-tradition. At Columbia, communications studies have traditionally been closely aligned with sociology, and people like Robert Merton and others from the sociology programme were at times involved. The university did only recently, in the 1990s, establish an actual degree-granting graduate programme in communications, illustrating how much important research on communications continues to take place outside the discipline that carries the name. The Bureau, and Lazarsfeld's research more generally, exemplifies the close relations that have sometimes existed between communication studies and the media industries.

From the 1940s and onwards, the University of Chicago was home to several temporary but important committees and commissions on communications, programs that also educated several leading communication scholars. In contrast to what took place at Columbia, these programs explicitly claimed the name 'communications' for themselves. The Committee on Communication and Public Opinion, also funded by the Rockefeller Foundation, was staffed with, in addition to Lasswell, people such as Douglas Waples, Samuel A. Stouffer, Louis Wirth, and Herbert Blumer, all of whom held positions elsewhere at the university.

They formed a committee that essentially served as a scholarly and educational extension of the federal government's increasing interest in communications during times of war, and was in particular closely linked to the Office of War Information. The committee is a reminder of connection as important as the Bureau's with the industry, namely the connection between communication studies and government interests and funding.

Chicago later provided an institutional home for The Hutchins Commission on the Freedom of the Press and the Committee on Communication. The latter was a degree-granting programme that counted Elihu Katz, Bernard Berelson, Edward Shils, and David Riesman amongst its faculty, and produced graduates like Herbert J. Gans and Michael Gurevitch. The committee also produced publications like Berelson and Janowitz' *Public Opinion and Communication* and the journal *Studies in Public Communication*. The Institute for Communications Research was founded at the University of Illinois at Urbana-Champaign in 1947 by Wilbur Schramm, who was a key figure in the post-war institutionalization of communication studies in the U.S. Like the various Chicago committees, the Illinois programme claimed the name 'communications' and granted graduate degrees in the subject. Schramm, who, in contrast to the more social science-inspired figures at Columbia and Chicago, had a background in English literature, developed communication studies partly by merging existing programs in speech communication, rhetoric, and, especially, journalism under the aegis of communication. He also edited a textbook *The Process and Effects of Mass*

Communication that helped define the field, partly by claiming the Lazarsfeld, Lasswell, Carl Hovland, and Kurt Lewin as its founding fathers.

He also wrote several other manifestos for the discipline, including *The Science of Human Communication* 1963. Schramm and the Institute moved on to Stanford University in 1955. Many of Schramm's students, such as Everett Rogers, went on to make important contributions of their own.

1950s–1960s

From the 1950s onwards, communications studies branched out in several new and often very different directions. Numerous new programs opened up at various universities, and new journals were established. The work of what has been called 'medium theorists', arguably defined by Harold Innis' (1950) *Empire and Communications* grew increasingly important, and was popularized by Marshall McLuhan in his *Understanding Media*. This perspective informs the later work of Joshua Meyrowitz.

Two developments in the 1940s shifted the paradigm of communication studies in the 1950s and thereafter toward a more-quantitative orientation, or at least the inescapable need to consider such an orientation. One was cybernetics, as formulated by Norbert Wiener in his *Cybernetics: Or the Control and Communication in the Animal and the Machine.*

The other was information theory, as recast in quantitative terms by Claude E. Shannon and Warren Weaver in their *Mathematical Theory of Communication.* These works were widely appropriated to, and offered for some the prospect of, a general theory of society. The tradition of critical theory associated with the Frankfurt School was, as in Europe, an important source of influence for many researchers. While done out of sociology departments, the work of Jürgen Habermas, the US-based Leo Löwenthal, Herbert Marcuse, and Siegfried Kracauer, as well as earlier figures like Adorno and Max Horkheimer continued to inform a whole tradition of cultural criticism that often focused both empirically and theoretically on the culture industry.

In 1953, to address growing needs in industry, Rensselaer Polytechnic Institute began offering a master of science degree in technical writing. In the 1960s, partly because of the need to represent that the degree incorporated training in oral and audiovisual communication, the degree title became technical communication. It was the brainchild of longtime RPI professor and administrator Jay R. Gould.

1960s–1970s

In the 1960s Gould and his colleagues experienced increasing demand for doctoral-level studies in technical and business communication. As result, in 1965 RPI began its Ph.D. programme in communication and rhetoric. This Ph.D. degree programme became a prototype for other technologically oriented Ph.D. communication programs in the United States and other industrialized countries. The 1960s and 1970s saw the development of cultivation theory, pioneered by George Gerbner at the Annenberg School for Communication at the University of Pennsylvania. This approach shifted emphasis from the short-term effects that had been the central interest of many earlier works on the media, and instead tried to track the effect of exposure to, for instance, television over time on viewers' perceptions of reality.

1970s–1980s

Neil Postman founded the media ecology programme at New York University in 1971. Media ecologists draw on a wide range of inspirations in their attempts to study entire media environments in an even broader and more cultural fashion than the work done in the Canadian medium theory tradition. This perspective is the basis of a separate professional association, the Media Ecology Association.

In 1972, Maxwell McCombs and Donald Shaw published a path-breaking article that offered an agenda-setting theory of media effects that gave new ways of conceptualizing the short-term media effects that earlier work had generally deemed limited. This approach, organized around additional ideas such as framing, priming, and gatekeeping, has been highly influential, especially in the study of political communication and news coverage.

The 1970s also saw the development of what became known as uses and gratifications research, developed by scholars such as Elihu Katz, Jay G. Blumler, and Michael Gurevitch. Instead of looking at communications processes simply as a one-way flow from senders to receivers, this approach began scrutinizing what audiences get out of communications, what they do with it, why they engage with it—especially with mass media.

History, Germany

Communication studies in Germany has a rich hermeneutic heritage in philology, textual interpretation, and historical studies. The post-world war II era, however, has seen the rise of a number of new paradigms. Elisabeth Noelle-Neumann pioneered work on the spiral of silence in a tradition that has been widely influential across the world and has proven to be easily compatible with the dominant paradigms in, for instance, the United States.

In the 1970s, Karl Deutsch came to West Germany, and his cybernetics inspired work has been widely influential there as elsewhere. The work of the Frankfurt School has been a cornerstone of much German work on communication, in addition to Horkheimer, Adorno, and Habermas, figures like Oskar Negt and Alexander Kluge has been important in the development of this strand of thought. An important competing paradigm has been the systems theory developed by Niklas Luhmann and his students, such as Dirk Baecker and others. Finally, from the 1980s and onwards, people like Friedrich

Kittler has led the development of a 'new German medium theory', aligned partly with the Canadian medium theory of Innis and McLuhan and partly with post-structuralism.

Professional Associations

- National Communication Association (NCA): The main national professional organization covering many of the areas of communication studies in the U.S.
- International Communication Association is the main international association for communication studies, which combines an older focus on quantitatively based social science studies with newer critical and cultural studies of communicative phenomena.
- Association for Education in Journalism and Mass Communication.
- Association for Business Communication (ABC).
- International Association of Business Communicators (IABC).
- Society for Technical Communication (STC).
- Public Relations Society of America (PRSA).
- European Communication Research and Education Association (ECREA) is the main European association for communication studies.
- European Association for the Teaching of Academic Writing (EATAW) is the main European association for writing studies.
- Association for Teachers of Technical Writing (ATTW).
- International Association for Media and Communi-cations Research (IAMCR) is also a large international association for communication studies.
- IEEE Professional Communication Society.

ASSOCIATION FOR BUSINESS COMMUNICATION

The Association for Business Communication (ABC) is the primary academic organization for the field of business communication scholarship, research, education and practice. The mission statement on its website reflects this: "The Association for Business Communication (ABC) is an international organization committed to fostering excellence in business communication scholarship, research, education, and practice." Much of the strength of the organization rests in its interdisciplinary nature. Members belong to such varied academic fields as Management, Marketing, English, Foreign Languages, Speech, Communication, Linguistics, and Information Systems. Additionally the organization brings together university academicians, business practitioners, and business consultants.

Organizational Structure

ABC is an international organization, divided into eight regional divisions, each with its own separate academic conferences. The regions are

Europe, Asia and Pacific Rim, Caribbean and Central America, and five North American regions (Canada plus Eastern, Midwest, Southeast, and Southwest United States).

Each year the entire membership meets at the International Convention in October or November. Midyear, two regional conferences are held—one in the European region and the other in one of the North American regions. The Asia and Pacific Rim region holds a conference every two years. At the International Convention and at the regional conferences, members come together to share research in business communication, participate in workshops, and network. A Board of Directors and an Executive Committee lead the ABC. The Board of Directors is directly elected with a Vice President elected from each of 8 regions and 12 directors at large, with staggered terms. The executive committee consists of a permanent position of Executive Director and four officers of the Association. The members of the executive committee serve for four years in rotating capacity, beginning as second vice president in the first year, then first vice president the next, president the next, and past president the last year on the committee.

The organization as a whole elects the second vice president position from among candidates on the Board of Directors.The current Executive Director of the ABC is Dr. Betty S. Johnson of (Stephen F. Austin State University). She took office in 2007, succeeding Robert J. Myers of Baruch College in that position. When she took office, the headquarters of the ABC moved with her from New York City to Nacogdoches, Texas where Stephen F. Austin State University is located. For 2007-2008 the Executive Committee consists of President Dr. Roger Conaway, First Vice President Dr. James Dubinsky (Virginia Tech), Second Vice President, Deborah Valentine (Emory University, Atlanta, Georgia, USA), and Immediate Past President Dr. Jackie Harrison (AUT University, Auckland, New Zealand).

Journal of Business Communication

JBC was founded in 1963. At the time (and for several decades) it remained the only journal devoted solely to business communication theory. In its own words on the ABC website *JBC* "publishes manuscripts that contribute to knowledge and theory of business communication as a distinct, multifaceted field approached through the administrative disciplines, the liberal arts, and the social sciences."

JBC summarizes its research focus as devoted to articles which contribute to knowledge and theory of business communication as a distinct, multifaceted field approached through the administrative disciplines, the liberal arts, and the social sciences. Accordingly, JBC seeks manuscripts that address all areas of business communication including but not limited to business composition/ technical writing, information systems, international business communication, management commu-nication, and organizational and corporate communication. In addition, JBC welcomes submissions concerning the role of written, verbal, nonverbal and electronic communi-cation in the creation, maintenance, and performance of profit and not for profit business. The current editor-in-chief of the *JBC* is Dr. Margaret Baker Graham of Iowa State University. The last several editors-in-chief of *JBC* have been in Iowa State University's English Department, which also devotes office space and resources to *JBC* and to the *Journal of Business and Technical Communication.*

Business Communication Quarterly

Business Communication Quarterly was founded in 1937. In its earlier years, *BCQ* was known as the *Bulletin of the ABCA* and later the *Bulletin of the ABC*. It took on its present name in 1994. In its own words on the ABC website, *BCQ* is "devoted to the teaching of business communication, which is a broad, interdisciplinary field.

" *BCQ summarizes the focus of its articles as*:

- Discussions of issues and methods for teaching business communication in a variety of settings: two–year college, technical institute, four-year college, university, corporate or agency training programme, and the like
- Case studies of specific classroom techniques
- Tutorials on business communication processes or products, especially innovations in electronic technology that need to be introduced into the classroom
- Research on classroom teaching or assessment
- Summary reviews of literature on teaching business communication
- Book reviews—reviews of both textbooks and other items of interest to teachers
- Reports on strategies for programme development

The current editor of *BCQ* is Dr. Kathryn Riley of Illinois Institute of Technology.

Standing Committees, Ad Hoc Committees and Interest Groups

The ABC has 17 standing committees, as follow:

1. Association to Advance Collegiate Schools of Business (AACSB) Liaison
2. Business Practices Committee
3. Community College Committee
4. Convention Procedures Committee
5. Diversity Initiative Committee
6. Employment Opportunities Committee
7. Intercultural Communication Committee
8. International Issues Committee

9. Modern Language Association (MLA) Liaison Committee
10. Nominations Committee
11. Publications Board
12. Research Committee
13. Review of the Executive Director Committee
14. Student Competition Committee
15. Teaching Committee 16. Undergraduate Studies Committee
17. Web Board

The ABC has Ad Hoc Committees for interests that have not yet warranted a Standing Committee, but may in the future become so. Many of the Standing Committees began as Ad Hoc Committees. In 2006 has four Ad Hoc Committees:

- Marketing of ABC
- Non-Tenure Track Faculty
- Professional Ethics
- Retired Members

Additionally, ABC members pursue a number of professional objectives through voluntary interest groups. Interest group may be convened by the First Vice President or by members' current interest groups. In 2006, the ABC had the following five Interest Groups:

- MBA Consortium
- Business Practices
- Consultants' Interest Group
- Intercultural Communication
- Rhetoric Special Interest Group

ABC was founded in 1936, beginning with a modest membership of 72 members, all but one from the United States (the only exception being from Canada).

The organization, based at the University of Illinois, was then named the "Association of College Teachers of Business Writers." The next year, 1937, that name changed to the "American Business Writing Association."

By the 1960s, the field had grown considerably and became heavily interested in areas well beyond business writing (such as oral presentations, negotiations, and nonverbal communication among others). In 1967, the Board of Directors voted to change the name of the organization to the "American Business Communication Association" to reflect this change.

By the late 1970s, as the membership of the organization grew to include more member from outside the Americas and as the focus of research expanded heavily into the fields of intercultural communication and cross-cultural business communication practice, the term "American" became increasingly inaccurate of both the membership and focus of the organization. In 1985, the Board of Directors voted to change the name to its current "Association for Business Communication."

International Association of Business Communicators

The International Association of Business Communicators (IABC) is a leading association for business communication professionals. IABC has approximately 16,000 members in more than 100 chapters in 70 countries.

IABC members hold positions in a variety of communication professions, including: public relations, media relations, corporate communications, employee communi-cations, public affairs, investor relations, government relations, marketing communication, community relations, writing, editing, advertising, graphic design, human resources and teaching. IABC's headquarters are located in San Francisco, California, United States. IABC was founded in 1970 from a merger of the American Association of Industrial Editors and the International Council of Industrial Editors. Its initial focus was on internal communication. However, IABC expanded its mission after research showed that members would leave after being promoted into positions with wider public relations responsibilities.

Accreditation

IABC members can seek accreditation as Accredited Business Communicators (post-nominal ABC). Accreditation is offered as an IABC professional development programme. It offers communicators a way of demonstrating their ability to think and plan strategically and to successfully manage those skills essential to effective organizational communi-cation, which could include internal communications, media relations, crisis communications and external relations.

To receive accreditation, applicants must meet education and experience requirements, submit a portfolio that includes work samples with measurable outcomes, and pass both written and oral examinations. Accreditation recognizes communicators who have reached a standard of knowledge and proficiency that is globally accepted among the communication profession.

Code of Ethics

The organization has a code of ethics for those professionals in public relations. The themes of its values are that business communications must be "legal... ethical, and... in good taste". Members are required to follow the IABC Code of Ethics. However, it has been observed that there is not an enforcement programme in place that can realistically punish breaches of its code.

Research Foundation

Founded in 1982, IABC Research Foundation serves as the research and development arm of the International Association of Business Communicators. The Foundation supports and advances the practice of organizational communication by providing IABC members with research that bridges the divide between communication theory and practice by offering in-depth knowledge and tools that improve organizational communication performance and strengthen the commun-ication profession as a whole.

Awards Programs

Every year, IABC sponsors three levels of communication awards programs for members and nonmembers: Bronze Quill awards, Silver Quill awards, and Gold Quill awards.. Communicators can choose to enter their best professional work produced during the prior year in these Quill communications contests. The specific divisions and categories for each contest can vary, but typical categories include marketing communi-cations, member/ employee communi-cations, media relations, crisis communications, social responsibility, writing, graphic design, publication design, social media, interactive/web design, and photography.

Bronze Quill (BQ) awards programs are hosted by local IABC chapters. The respective chapter's board of directors plans and executes a BQ communications contest open to business communicators working with a specific city and/or a small region of a state/province. Silver Quill is sponsored by regional divisions, such as IABC's Heritage and Pacific Plains regions, and are open to communicators in the respective geographic area.

Open to all communicators worldwide, Gold Quill typically receives entries from over 25 countries. The programme aims to cross communication disciplines and reviews entries from professional communicators, ranging from strategists to tacticians. All Gold Quill Awards winners receive international recognition in IABC's magazine, Communication World; are eligible to participate in an awards ceremony at IABC's annual international conference, are mentioned on the IABC website, and are considered for publication in IABC's resource materials. In 2008, the programme attracted over 1,000 entries across 26 categories.

IABC awards programs are open to both members and non-members of the organization. Global Leadership Awards include the Fellow Award and the Chairman's Award. The IABC Fellow designation is the highest honour IABC can bestow on an individual and acknowledges outstanding leadership, professional accomplishment and service to IABC and the communication profession.

Criteria for the Fellow Award include contribution to the organizational communication field and profession; career achievement; authorship, speaking and lecturing; contribu-tions to IABC; and other professional recognition such as community activities and other business-related activities. The Chairman's Award recognizes IABC members who have made selfless contributions and worked behind the scenes at the international level to enhance the association's image, facilitate member development and benefit the communication profession.

Annual Conference and Networking Opportunities

IABC holds a world conference each year. In 2006, the host city was Vancouver, Canada. In 2007, the host city was New Orleans, Louisiana and IABC partnered with Wells Fargo to volunteer and provide financial support to build homes through Habitat for Humanity for the city's hurricane-damaged Ninth Ward. The 2008 conference was in New York City, and the 2009 event will be held in San Francisco from June 7 to June 10, 2009. Eurocomm 2009 will be held in Lugano, Switzerland February 9 - 10, 2009

IABC's world conference is open to communicators, regardless of membership. As a professional association, IABC offers networking opportunities for students and other people entering the industry. As the United States Department of Labour notes, IABC "provides an opportunity for students to exchange views with public relations specialists and to make professional contacts that may help them find a full-time job in the field."

THE EVOLUTION OF CORPORATE COMMUNICATIONS

Trying to get a message across to every employee in an organization is a lot like trying to control kids in a school bus: some will listen; some will hear but misunderstand the message; and some will ignore the message altogether and later complain, "But nobody told me."

Communicating to hundreds, sometimes thousands, of employees within an organization is no small feat. This challenge is further complicated in organizations with a global presence, where corporate headquarters is responsible for delivering the same message to satellite offices in geographically dispersed locations. But it's not enough to just create the message. Effective corporate communication involves not only the message itself, but also the medium that carries and delivers it. It's these two components of a communication that dictate whether employees will receive and understand it. But don't fool yourself in thinking that there's some long process of deliberation when they receive one of these messages. Most corporate communications will grab the attention of an employee for no more than a few seconds — if at all. It's within that very narrow window of opportunity that they will decide whether to read something or toss it aside.

Employees are processing more information than ever before — information dealing with their projects, their clients, and their industry as a whole. With all this information competing for employees' attention, does a single corporate communication stand a chance of making it through?

EFFECTIVE COMMUNICATION

Organizations have struggled to find the best way to get company communications to their employees for years. These communications can range from notices of service interruptions to announcements of corporate events. But is anyone really listening? Communication is a two-way street; it requires a sender and a receiver. If no one is listening, you're just a crazy person talking to yourself.

Anyone involved with corporate communications needs to be aware of their receivers' habits and idiosyncrasies before deciding on message and medium. It wouldn't make sense to use technology-based communications with an audience who's not tech-savvy without first providing them with adequate training; or to post an important announcement on a bulletin board when most users rely solely on their intranet for news. An understanding of the audience will help determine the best medium to use in order to get your message across.

Communication mediums can be classified into two methods: the sender pushes the message to the receiver (e.g., sending an e-mail) or the receiver pulls the message from a source (e.g., reading an intranet post). In the '90s, the IT industry was abuzz with the concept of push technology, a method of delivering content to users' desktop without requiring them to actively seek it out. The technology, however, never lived up to its hype and communications fell back to old stalwarts: the intranet and e-mail. But they have their problems too.

Posting corporate communications on an intranet requires employees to access the system repeatedly because they won't know when new information will be posted. There's a good chance that some employees will miss an important announcement because they were busy with other things and don't get the chance to check when the communication was posted. E-mail has the ability to alert every employee once a communication is sent, but there are uncontrollable factors that hinder its effectiveness as a corporate communications medium. E-mail failed through no fault of its own, and was perhaps a victim of its own success.

E-Mail

The advent of e-mail changed the way organizations communicated with their employees in a big way. Rather than post and send out large quantities of paper-based announcements, a single e-mail message could be sent to all employees at the same time, regardless of their geographic location. At the time, e-mail was the biggest advancement in corporate communication — until users just stopped reading them. So what happened?

Has e-mail outlived its usefulness as an internal corporate communications medium? The answer is yes and no. It's still a big part of corporate communication, but it's lost a lot of its effectiveness. There's perhaps no bigger contributor to this decline than spam. E-mail has been contaminated by so much junk that it's difficult to get an important message across. Users might give a company announcement a cursory glance and pass it by thinking it's just more unsolicited mail; or they might set-up e-mail filters so restrictive that the message never even makes it through. With the sheer volume of e-mail that comes pouring in daily, employees may simply treat these types of internal communications as white noise and ignore them. And with the time-sensitive nature of corporate communications, it might be too late when users finally discover the message.

RSS, the New E-mail

Many news Web sites and bloggers are already using RSS feeds to "broadcast" their content. Even marketers and advertisers are realizing the advantages of RSS as a means to attract potential customers. It's an easy, unintrusive way to syndicate frequently changing Web content such as daily blog entries or news headlines.

Momentum is also growing in the corporate environment for RSS. Organizations are beginning to see that RSS can be used to pick up where e-mail left off (or, some would say, failed) as an internal corporate communicator. One of the problems with corporate-wide e-mail announcements is that they can't be categorized. An important announcement concerning network downtime will end up in users' inbox, sandwiched between joke mail and spam. There's no context to e-mail messages short of the subject header, which is not always easily noticeable. RSS, however, offers more communication control on the part of both the sender and the receiver.

Senders can create topical RSS feeds based on different types of corporate communications, and receivers have the choice of which feeds they subscribe to. This ensures that employees only receive content that's relevant to them. It's up to organizations to decide how to best categorize its RSS feeds, but some examples might include:

- *Important announcements*: Crucial, time-sensitive information requiring immediate attention such as scheduled downtimes for IT and facility infrastruc-tures
- *Executive communications*: Messages from manage-ment.
- *Corporate events listings*: Details of special events such as company sponsored fundraisers, family days, and holiday parties.
- *Intranet changes and upgrades*: Announcements of new features and changes to the corporate intranet.
- *Corporate policy changes*: Updates to internal corporate policies such as flex hours, Internet usage and etiquette, and employee benefits.
- *Personnel changes*: Announcements of promotions, departmental transfers, and retirements.

Migrating to RSS is also a relatively simple proposition when compared to other types of IT implementations. It's not necessary to install standalone RSS readers (known as aggregators) throughout the company. RSS readers are becoming standard features in many e-mail clients and Web browsers, or they can be installed as plug-ins to existing applications that don't already have them. This allows employees to get the benefits of RSS without having to learn a whole new interface.

Advantages of RSS Over E-mail for Corporate Communication

- RSS separates important internal communications from all the "chatter" that can pollute e-mail: spam, jokes from friends, and newsletter subscriptions.
- RSS doesn't overwhelm users. RSS presents users with a headline and a short synopsis so they can decide if it's worth following the link to the full message stored on the corporate intranet. Many RSS readers will also give users the option of viewing only this summary information or the entire document.
- Unlike corporate-wide e-mail, RSS is completely opt-in. If you're not interested in hearing about the company's special events, you simply don't subscribe to that feed.
- RSS feeds won't be blocked by any filters so the message is sure to get through.
- RSS feeds don't compete with hundreds of e-mail messages for the users' attention. RSS has a singular focus so important announcements will stand out more clearly than an e-mail that's buried in a list of other messages.
- RSS standardizes the formating and display of the internal communications since it's stored on the intranet (Some users don't like to receive HTML-based e-mail so organizations had to develop both a formatted message and a text-only message to cover all its employees).

PODCASTING AND VODCASTING

Podcasting (audio) and vodcasting (video) are other methods that can be used for corporate communications, although they haven't been widely adopted yet. Contrary to popular misconception, podcasting and vodcasting are not simply multimedia files stored on a server for users to download.

Like RSS, they're based on a subscription model. Users subscribe to podcast and vodcast feeds through similar aggregator software that can be set-up to automatically download new content when it's available. But instead of reading the message, they listen to it or watch it. Podcasting and vodcasting are ideal ways to get messages — especially lengthy messages — across to large corporate audiences since it presents them with a much more convenient (and some would say, more natural) form of communication.

It's far more convenient to listen to an audio podcast of a CEO's quarterly results presentation on a portable media player while going to work than it is to sit at a desk reading through the twenty page equivalent. But there might be an annoyance factor when it comes to using a multimedia approach to corporate communications. Users who decide to listen to podcasts or watch vodcasts at their desks without the use of headphones might irritate their neighbors. What's worse is if several people were to access a podcast or vodcast at the same time, raising the noise pollution and tempers of the office.

CLOSING THOUGHTS

There's no perfect solution when it comes to corporate communications. You'll never be able to reach every employee all the time because even if the solution is rock solid, there will always be someone who just doesn't bother — regardless of the medium used. It's the responsibility of the organization to inform its employees, and to provide the means by which it gets its communications across easily and efficiently. But as the sender, organizations can only do so much. They can only make sure that it's not the message and the medium that fails the user community. The receiver of the communication also has a part to play. Each individual employee must be receptive to the message when it arrives. This is their responsibility. If they continually disregard corporate communications and claim, "But nobody told me," perhaps the response to that should be, "Why didn't you listen?"

INTERNAL COMMUNICATIONS STRATEGY

There are 12 essential elements of a successful internal communications strategy:

1. *Effective employee-directed communications must be led from the top*: Effective communications require the active commitment and endorsement of senior managers. It is not enough simply to develop a 'vision statement' or formulate in general terms the values by which the company lives. Behaviour is what counts. Managers must be seen to behave in a manner that is consistent with the ethos they are promoting.
2. *The essence of good communications is consistency*: At all costs, avoid following fashion and tinkering. If you try to improve communications and then fail—because your messages are inconsistent or are 'good news only'—things will not quietly settle back into the way they used to be. You will inevitably have created expectations, and may have to live with the consequences of having disappointed those expectations.
3. Successful employee communications owe as much to consistency, careful planning and attention to detail as they do to charisma or natural gifts: We might not all be another Zig Ziglar, Tony Robbins or Bill Clinton. But even such communication 'giants' slip up if they fail to plan, fail to pay attention to detail and fail to project a consistent message.

4. *Communication via the line manager is most effective:*' Line Manager to employee' communication is an opportunity for people to ask questions and check that they have understood the issues correctly. However, be aware that business urgency and reality may dictate the need, on many occasions, to inform employees directly rather than relying entirely on the cascade process. (Though managers will still need to answer people's questions and listen to their views.)
5. *Employee communications are not optional extras, they are part of business as usual and should be planned and budgeted for as such:* An employee communications plan—key themes, targets, objectives and resources—provides a context in which to deliver initiatives that arise at short notice.
6. *There must be integration between internal and external communications:* There must be a fit between what you are telling your people and what you are telling your customers, shareholders and public. (By the same token, there must be a fit between what you are telling your people, and what the external media are telling them.)
7. *Timing is critical*: However clearly expressed and well-presented your message may be, if it arrives at the wrong time you might as well not have bothered. Old news is often worse than no news. Consequently, it is important to ensure that the channels you use can really deliver at the time you need them to.
8. *Tone is important*: Expressing overly-gushing enthusiasm about a technical change of little real significance to your staff or public at large is scarcely calculated to make people take your message to heart. If they don't take that message to heart, why would they take the rest of what you say to their bosoms?
9. *Never lose sight of the 'what's in it for me?' factor*: We are self-interested creatures. I may have invented the most amazing gadget ever, but unless I get you emotionally involved you are never likely to listen to my message about it. But if I can show you how my gadget will revolutionise your life, add dollars to your wallet, free up your time, fix your smelly feet, wash your car for you, stop your kids arguing with you, bring peace with your spouse, bring world peace...
10. *Communication is a two-way process*: Employee communications are NOT a one-way information dump. Capturing feedback is of critical importance, and if you are not seen to be listening and acting on what you are told, why should people bother telling you?
11. *A single key theme or a couple of key themes is a means of giving coherence to a range of diverse employee communications initiatives:* In recent years, the overriding theme of many corporate employee communications has been the impact on the business of competition, regulation and economic forces. Many messages and initiatives can therefore be

evaluated according to the light they shed on one or more of these key themes.

12. *Set your standards and stick to them*: Determine which channels should be mandatory and which should be optional; establish quality standards for all channels and review these at least annually.

Whether you are working for a small business, large corporation, or are a student, there are numerous sources that you can turn to for help with writing. Businesses need to be able to effectively communicate with their customers, their employees and their potential customers. Effective verbal communication is equally important, but nonverbal communication in the form of copy writing, article writing, press release writing, and more requires a certain level of expertise and experience.

The typical small business wants to focus their efforts on their core business activities without spending too much time on projects that can easily be outsourced to consultants or freelance professionals. Many small businesses turn to freelancers to help them save time and money.

For example, a certified public accountant opened his own accounting practice after working in another accounting firm for the last ten years. One of the ways he decided to search for new clients was to embark on an advertising and promotional campaign. Although some of his previous clients followed him to his new practice, he wanted to increase the number of accounts he currently handled. These accounts included various individuals and small businesses from around the town. Rather than hire new employees or handle the projects himself, he decided to hire a consultant through a freelance web site to work on copy writing for a local newspaper ad campaign as well as to help with press releases and company news distribution. By outsourcing these non-core business activities to an independent consultant, he is able to save himself time and money and also gets the expertise of an established professional who specializes in the types of writing that he needs assistance with.

He decides to list his writing projects in a freelance marketplace and receives bids from independent consultants and freelance writers. He was able to choose a service provider based on factors related to cost, the service provider experience, references, and previous feedback from clients.

All small businesses have a decision to make about whether to outsource certain projects or to complete the work in house. Using economics as a deciding factor, it makes sense economically for businesses to outsource writing projects when the projects are non-core business activities that do not contribute to the company bottom line.

Small businesses also need to be able to effectively communicate with their current customers. Some of the more effective ways to get help writing effective communication for current customers involve using tools such as newsletters, email lists, and articles written by outsourced consultants.

Newsletters are very effective ways to keep customers informed of current events and happenings within the company. They also offer you the opportunity to gain new clients as the newsletter gets passed around and is often seen by more than one person during its life cycle. It makes sense and is a smart move to outsource corporate communications instead of keeping it in-house. Hiring a separate professional will save your business money and time.

For less than the cost of hiring a full time employee, and because it will contribute to allowing more concentration on the activities that will earn your business money, contracting with a consultant or freelancer for your corporate communications (writing of press releases to distribute company news, getting publicity through pieces in newspapers and magazines, and getting help writing newsletters or articles) simply makes sense. An expert in the field who has amassed many years of experience with business writing, persuasive writing, and copy writing in addition to having experience writing press releases, articles, essays, and possibly academic or technical research and term papers will have a lot to offer you and your business.

Large corporations use writing to effectively communicate on all levels of business. Business writing and corporate communications are essential elements that keep the public informed and give companies their corporate image. A company image, or its publicly perceived notion of credibility and reliability is extremely important to its bottom line. For example, upon its introduction many years ago an American car company introduced a car known as the "Nova".

After some time, it was discovered that the car was not selling well in many Spanish speaking countries. Because in Spanish, "No va" translates to "doesn't go", the car sales in these countries were dismal. Effective corporate communication can have far reaching effect. Ineffective corporate communication can result in lower sales as shown in the car sales example.

Large corporations also need to be effective communi-cators with their current employees. Internal corporate communications are equally important and keep your employees abreast of company accomplishments, events and human resource issues. Finally, students also need to be able to write effectively as well. Writing assignments can include writing essays, writing term papers, report writing, and thesis writing not to mention having to demonstrate writing ability in other subjects outside of English class.

For example, law students need to be able to write not only persuasive but argumentative writing as well. Foreign language students need to be able to translate into their native language and then back again. Science and technology students need to be able to demonstrate scientific writing ability. Taking writing tips from college professors that teach correct formatting and usage, including APA style, and improving your proofreading and editing skills will result in quality writing assignments. For the student that is looking for writing help and homework assistance for their assignments, freelance marketplaces that allow you to hire a consultant or tutor could be a productive and time saving solution. From a freelance or independent consultant's standpoint, marketing writing skills to potential service buyers is important to keeping any consulting business thriving. Registering with freelance marketplaces will enable you to showcase your writing skills, talents and abilities. Previous experience with all kinds of writing ranging from grant writing, fiction writing and interactive writing to writing short stories, articles and ebooks or even technical pieces, in addition to all forms of business writing will enable you to prove your varied background and skills.

All of which can be showcased in your freelance marketplace profile. Creating and managing a profile is important to make you stand out from the crowd of freelance writers competing for new writing projects. All in all, those looking for writing help can find a vast array of resources in the form of consultants who are more than willing to lend a helping hand.

The Nature of Corporate Communication

This article looks at the way organisations communicate with their employees, drawing parallels with the highly sophisticated means of communication that nature has developed, to see if these can be applied in business. It is argued that few organisations currently communicate effectively and by adopting some of nature's techniques many could get closer to achieving 'corporate homeostasis'.

Ensuring that communication within an organisation is as efficient as possible is the key to its success. Maintaining staff satisfaction and empowering people to feel informed and confident in their work should lead to smoother running, better customer experience and, in turn, increased activity. Therefore it is vital for management to understand how this can be implemented to best effect. Areas for discussion and improvement are identified in this article as: adapting organi-sations to suit the environment, communicating clearly and effectively with staff, making adjustments to find the right balance, knowing the limits of productivity and responding to threats. Focusing on these areas, suggestions are made as to how businesses can adopt specific communication techniques to improve operations.

It is potentially easier for organisations to look at current communication methods in place and compare to examples from nature than to those of competitors. By looking at their fundamental needs and how these are best met through natural means, businesses should avoid the unnecessary complications and complexities that come from the corporate environment.

Techniques for Effective Corporate Communication

Corporate communication today is the result of phenomenal progress in the electronic technology. Gadgetry such as the mobile phone and the Internet connectivity have harnessed the boon of electronic communication for the employer as well as the employee. The success of corporate workplace communication largely depends on the speed at which important information is disseminated, the accuracy of vocabulary, proper use of business etiquette and that of communication and of course, optimum use of technological development available at hand.

Even though most corporate communication is in-house, among the employees and between associates and affiliates among the executives, effective communication plays a critical role in the response generated. Effective communication skills are developed over a period of time and/or learned extensively at dedicated corporate training workshops and as a part of business management. However, they are expected to be tweaked within the work environment.

Depending on the organizational culture developed and observed within work stations and the business premised at large, communication styles differ. There are many work environs that prefer the informal communication style, while some are strictly formal. This way or that, at grass root level the core components remain the same. At all times and within all preferred communication styles, effective communication skills need to be regularly updated and upgraded because in the modern corporate world there is no scope for stagnancy. To keep up with the rest of the work force, establish a strong corporate identity and harness the ever-evolving corporate communication techniques, you need to consider applying the paradigm shifts as you adhere to the basic essentials that have stood the test of time. Effective corporate communication helps to address the need to span across physical boundaries and deliver vital information at a click, as a part of the business growth strategy. The technology is a part of every work station today, but are you using it to capacity?

Techniques for Effective Corporate Communication

Timelines

It is crucial to remember that your business interests and business relationships may be spanning the continents and hence, respecting timelines and calculating deadlines are of utmost importance. You need to devise a technique to try out and confirm to the best communication 'space' that works for you. Always focus on saving time and ensuring timely execution of important strategies and business plans. In order to save time and meet organizational goals amidst the workforce in one physical arena as well as across the globe, you should capitalize on the communication media like efax and internet telephone at hand.

Protocol

Formal, as well as informal work environs demand respect for protocol. It is very important to follow the same when communicating too and ensure that the chosen communication technique or techniques are designed to meet specifications. Irrespective of whether you are personally communicating at a presentation or using some form of communication media, acknowledging seniors within the hierarchy chart over those on lower rungs ensures that you don't rub sore shoulders. If this strategy is applied all the time, you will notice easier follow-through and much more clarity in the delegation and execution of work within the community.

Technology

Make the most of corporate communication mediums available at your disposal to build strong business relationships. You should optimize the use of online publications, Ezines and even automated responses to make your presence felt within the business community. This highly effective corporate communication technique or strategy helps you to literally 'be' at two or more places at the same time! Businesses around the world today, capitalize on the efficiency of electronic communication and internet technology. Don't be left behind.

Techniques for good corporate communication have a number of tangible and intangible benefits including optimized increased revenue, improved customer retention and service and lead examples of corporate leadership to colleagues and new recruits. As you sway between the frustration and by-the-minute exerted stress of responsibilities, focusing on a positive mental attitude and keeping the tried and tested techniques for successful corporate communication in mind helps a lot.

Communication in Corporate Affairs

Globalization of economy is the basic trend of 21st century. Most of the academic discussions concentrating on corporate communication which is important in the application of marketing techniques in the industry. The relevance of successful and coordinated corporate communication is unquestionable. Theoretically supported corporate communications are effective in the successful business and its effects identified by the leading companies. It is equally important as technology since application of technology need to communicate effectively in the corporate world. With out effective communication corporate relationship will be impossible. Proper communication will enable the business growth in an organization.

Now a days Information Technology and management are the recent trend in the career field. Most of the company is looking for the people who are able to make some changes. Communication skill is an essential element in this new generation job. Also employees should be able to take new challenges and to perform the job responsibility effectively. In this competitive world, employees should be able to understand the situation and to communicate the meaningful information in time.

The purpose of communication management is the accessibility of information flow from top management to bottom. It will be effective only when officials are communi-cating information effectively to all the employees. Thus all parties should be communicate and transfer the necessary information meaningfully and resourcefully. The development of the organization depends on its commun-ication process.

Since each and every business process communication is inevitable. It is an exchange of information and knowledge with the internal groups as well as stakeholders who have direct relationship with the organization, which will enhance the growth of the organization.

Corporate communication is the strong and consistent message which is influencing and motivating its employees and stakeholders and also it aims to attain business development success. If there is any change or business crisis, corporate communication plays a very vital role to handle it effectively. Every body is looking forward how will the change or crisis affect the organization and how it handled by the authorities.

They also have the curiosity to know how a company tackles the situations even after the event is over. In corporate life it is very indispensable; you need to put into words what ever you did. Moreover you need to communicate confidently. Communication is the cornerstone function of every organization to buildup its status in the corporate world as well as its stakeholders. Their work is very concerned with internal communications management from the standpoint of sharing knowledge and decisions from the enterprise with employees, suppliers, investors and partners. Communications is one of the most important link between an organization and the public.

Major companies are considered communication as an effective tool to intensifying its scope and rationalizing its service. They have renewed their communication strategy to expand their branches in various parts of the country. Organization interaction with the community, its stakeholders, staff and other interested groups always channel its progress. Leading organizations have their own communication team with efficient communicators who are responsible for communication function with various national and international organizations.

Each communication department has its own Communi-cators and communications director is the head of the board. They have communication teams and department has its own right. Certain other organizations communications happen in the areas of public involvement, clients and the corporate affairs department. Communication can be a part of someone's job. Time demands are not concerned in the case of important communications. Communications professional's role is different based on their seniority and designation. It may also depend on whether they are working individually or group based. Usually their role is to make information about their organization which is to be accessed by their staff and public. It also aims to the accountability and their involvement in the reforms that are taking place.

Early management theories assumed bosses should be dominant, paternal, and rational in the use of communication to direct employees' work. The body of knowledge relevant to that managerial philosophy can be reduced to one directive: Give instructions clearly and firmly. From that limited beginning, research and theory progressed to explain the impact organizations have on how people communicate and why communication helps or harms organizations. Many research studies revealed that human relationship empower-ing employee's interest in their work and a positive attitude about themselves and about the organization. This leads to the use of advanced management philosophy.

Employee's involvement in the design and execution of work recognized by the managers and researchers and they emphasized bosses cannot control workers as per human resource approach. There is a cooperative balance between bosses and employees in the Revolutionizing management theory, where the human resources shifted the locus of control. A recent version of this approach reduces organizational excellence and productivity to the axiom "Work smarter, not harder." That approach to management treats employees and organizational processes as being thoughtful.

Corporate Communications is the processes a company uses to communicate all its messages to key constituencies. It encodes and promotes a strong corporate culture, a coherent corporate identity, an appropriate and professional relationship with the media, and quick, responsible ways of communicating in a crisis. It also defines how an organization communicates with its stakeholders and how that brings a company's values to life. Corporate Communications are often defined as the products of communications, memos, letters, reports, Web sites, community engagement, social and environmental initiatives or programs. These make up most importantly an aggregate of messages that a company sends to its constituencies whether internal or external.

It is important to build up an image of a company by demonstrating its integrity and to listen and speak to its stakeholders honestly. This makes corporate social responsibility as a vital component of Corporate Communications, making it as a strategic tool in which a company stand out by creating competitive advantage

Interpersonal communication in an organization, realise the fact that the interpersonal communication transpires when people inside a company interact with out side people like products sale and services to customers or clients. All means of communication occurs in large companies, employees routinely communicate interpersonally with one another, for instance by phone or writing, without ever meeting face to face. A variety of new electronic innovations offer many possibilities for interpersonal contact through mediated channels. "Interpersonal communication," Weick observed, "is the essence of organization because it creates structures that then affect what else gets said and done and by whom" Organizational performances are interactional, contextual, episodic, and improvisational.

Interpersonal communication is important for the exchange of information and coordination of activities. Employees' perception of the quality of communication in their organization depends on their interaction with their supervisors, the climate in the company, and appraisal others make of their work performance.

Employees are approaching their immediate head to get job related information which will affect their performance, satisfaction, team work and turn over. They are also seeking information from the top management to extent the scope of their efforts in the outcome especially productivity, commitment, morale, loyalty and trust. The crisis issues of the company like risk management, environment, social investment and community engagement are forcing companies to become more deliberately engaged through communicators. Communication is the key factor in the creation, implementation, monitoring and reporting on all corporate activities. Through communication, stakeholders understand company's purpose, goals and values.

Communication also aimed to influence employee's attitude toward the workplace loyalty and pride in the company in which they are working. Theoretically speaking, Corporate Communication plays a critical role in building and maintaining relationships with the stakeholders of a corporation. Communication is an unavoidable tool in the corporate sector. Media communi-cations are an essential channel through which all stakeholders receive information and develop perceptions of a company.

Specific responsibilities of a corporate communicator include:

- Supervise the status of the organization
- Develop, execute and evaluate communications strategies
- Ensuring effective two-way internal communications
- Taking the lead on media handling, proactively placing good news stories, dealing with enquiries and producing media releases
- Developing links with other departments, which enhances the smooth functioning.
- Planning proactive communications
- Leading public relations, including customer services
- Playing a key role in issue management and planning
- Ensuring that other health organizations are kept fully briefed on developments, plans and any incidents in your organization
- Producing high quality information service

- Advising senior colleagues on strategic communi-cations and related issues
- Engaging in business promotion campaigns

Typically, the following skills would be necessary for a communications role:

- Ability to work equally well both on your own and within a team
- Ability to write, speak and brief others clearly
- Ability to assess and select appropriate communi-cations routes for different messages and audiences
- Ability to remain calm under pressure
- Ability to recognize sensitive situations and act appropriately
- Negotiating and influencing skills
- Ability to work well with others at all levels both within and outside your company
- Ability to gain the trust and respect of senior colleagues
- Ability to provide creative input to projects
- Ability to think strategically

Now a days communication professional are facing lot of challenges in the areas of global corporate and brand positioning, internal relations in change situations, corporate identity shaping, and brand management. All communication is based on organizational strategy and the communication professionals are expected to fulfill the objectives of the organization.

Corporate Communication experts are the advocates for an organisations in managing the complex communications that take places between organisations and their external and internal audiences.

These specialist communicators are representing the organisation and make the organisation to aware of public views and attitudes. Other responsibilities of corporate communicators include media contacts, drafting press release,arrange and conduct programmes of internal and external communications. The process of corporate communication includes both theory and practice. It is important to identify the role of communication in corporate relationship for the effective functioning as well as to provide organisational objectives.

Apart from these to create a personal portfolio which portrait the skills across the range of professional communication areas. Other areas like skills in managing and planning projects in the areas of corporate communication is also essential. Enhance the knowledge of corporate communication to an advanced level, developing and presenting plans for corporate communication in a range of different scenarios, including crisis management and the development of corporate brands. Effective communication is closely related to the suceess of the organisation. Through which company's reputation, survival and its success is communicating to the public as well as its own employees and stakeholders. Communication is closely linked to business objectives and strategies. It is essential if organisations are to inform and influence external stakeholders including their customers, and to harness the efforts of all their members towards the successful accomplish-ment of organisational objectives. In conclusion, corporate communications represents the corporation's voice, its reputation, integrity and the images it projects of itself on a global and regional stage populated by its various audiences and stakeholders.

CORPORATE COMMUNICATION: AN ESSENTIAL TOOL IN AN ORGANIZATION

A company resident reviews a feasibility study for an environment protection project in a small community where the company's headquarters building is located. A personnel manager discusses with union leaders the forthcoming collective bargaining agreement. A marketing manager reviews videos of proposed media campaigns. A group of employees discuss the latest changes in the top management over coffee at the cafeteria.

What do each of these activities share? They all involve corporate communication. Some have this notion that corporate communication is the same as organizational communication. Others think it is a mere "rehash" of public relations. Still there are those who equate it with advertising, company publications, and management information systems.

If corporate communication is not generally well understood, it may be because corporate communication is still evolving. The concept is an offshoot of the growing recognition by top management of communication as a strategic resource in achieving corporate goals and objectives.

As the term implies, corporate communication encompas-ses all the communication activities undertaken within the corporate context, whether formal or informal, regardless of direction or flow of information (i.e. top-down, bottom-up, horizontal). What corporate communication aims to achieve is to integrate the various communication activities within the corporate organization and recognize them as key management functions. It seeks to upgrade public relations. It seeks to upgrade public relations, organizational communication, and advertising into the level of scientific discipline quite removed from the level of gut feel. As the International Management Magazine noted, corporate communication-related activities a common direction or framework. The growth of corporate communication can be attributed to the trend among progressive companies to appoint a communication man to top managerial positions (and even in the executive board). Corporate Executive Officers (CEOs) are beginning to realise that the success or failure of corporate strategies depends on how communication resources are harnessed.

COMMUNICATION: THE NERVOUS SYSTEM OF ORGANIZATIONS

A review of definitions of the term organization indicates how critical communication is the very existence of an organization. Koontz and O'Donnel define organization as a communication decision-making network. Peter Drucker states, "The organization is above all, an information decision-making system." Communication is not a secondary or derived aspect of an organization, but rather the essence of organized activity and is the basic process out of which all functions derive. It is quite clear then that communication links the various parts of an organization; it is the principal tool of managers. Through communication, the manager receives the information needed in making the right decision, and once the decision is made, manager must communicate it to others. Perhaps you often hear managers saying, "Our problem is communication."

Indeed, many managers use communi-cation as an excuse if they are not able to achieve their goal or objective. While it is true that communication as an excuse if they are not able to achieve their goal or objective. While it is true that communication is a vital skill of managers, it would be wrong to conclude that an effective communicator alone makes a good manager. An effective communication for a wrong decision will not do any good to the company. Conversely, for a manager to be an effective planner and decision-maker is not enough. A good decision (or action plan) must be translated into action.

7

Marketing Association

Marketing is the process by which companies determine what products or services may be of interest to customers, and the strategy to use in sales, communications and business development. It is an integrated process through which companies create value for customers and build strong customer relationships in order to capture value from customers in return.

Marketing is used to identify the customer, to keep the customer and to satisfy the customer. With the customer as the focus of its activities, it can be concluded that *marketing management* is one of the major components of business management. The evolution of marketing was caused due to mature markets and overcapacities in the last decades. Companies then shifted the focus from production to the customer in order to stay profitable.

The term *marketing concept* holds that achieving organizational goals depends on knowing the needs and wants of target markets and delivering the desired satisfactions. It proposes that in order to satisfy its organizational objectives, an organization should anticipate the needs and wants of consumers and satisfy these more effectively than competitors.

DEFINITIONS

Marketing is defined by the American Marketing Association [AMA] as "the activity, set of institutions, and processes for creating, communicating, delivering, and exchanging offerings that have value for customers, clients, partners, and society at large." The term developed from the original meaning which referred literally to going to a market to buy or sell goods or services. Seen from a systems point of view, sales process engineering views marketing as "a set of processes that are interconnected and interdependent with other functions, whose methods can be improved using a variety of relatively new approaches."

The Chartered Institute of Marketing defines marketing as "the management process responsible for identifying, anticipating and satisfying customer requirements profitably." A different concept is the value-based marketing which states the role of marketing to contribute to increasing shareholder value. In this context, marketing is defined as "the management process that seeks to maximise returns to shareholders by developing relationships with valued customers and creating a competitive advantage."

Marketing practice tended to be seen as a creative industry in the past, which included advertising, distribution and selling. However, because the academic study of marketing makes extensive use of social sciences, psychology, sociology, mathematics, economics, anthropology and neuroscience, the profession is now widely recognized as a science, allowing numerous universities to offer Master-of-Science (MSc) programmes. The overall process starts with marketing research and goes through market segmentation, business planning and execution, ending with pre and post-sales promotional activities. It is also related to many of the creative arts. The marketing literature is also adept at re-inventing itself and its vocabulary according to the times and the culture.

EVOLUTION OF MARKETING

An orientation, in the marketing context, relates to a perception or attitude a firm holds towards its product or service, essentially concerning consumers and end-users. Throughout history marketing has changed considerably as consumer tastes are changing faster.

Customer Orientation

A firm in the market economy survives by producing goods that persons are willing and able to buy. Consequently, ascertaining consumer demand is vital for a firm's future viability and even existence as a going concern. Many companies today have a customer focus (or market orientation). This implies that the company focuses its activities and products on consumer demands. Generally there are three ways of doing this: the customer-driven approach, the sense of identifying market changes and the product innovation approach.

In the consumer-driven approach, consumer wants are the drivers of all strategic lubna khalil marketing decisions. No strategy is pursued until it passes the test of consumer research. Every aspect of a market offering, including the nature of the product itself, is driven by the needs of potential consumers.

The starting point is always the consumer. The rationale for this approach is that there is no point spending R&D funds developing products that people will not buy. History attests to many products that were commercial failures in spite of being technological breakthroughs.

A formal approach to this customer-focused marketing is known as SIVA (Solution, Information, Value, Access). This system is basically the four Ps renamed and reworded to provide a customer focus. The SIVA Model provides a demand/customer centric version alternative to the well-known 4Ps supply side model (product, price, place, promotion) of marketing management.

Product	→	Solution
Promotion	→	Information
Price	→	Value
Placement	→	Access

Organizational Orientation

In this sense, a firm's marketing department is often seen as of prime importance within the functional level of an organization. Information from an organization's marketing department would be used to guide the actions of other departments within the firm. As an example, a marketing department could ascertain (via marketing research) that consumers desired a new type of product, or a new usage for an existing product. With this in mind, the marketing department would inform the R&D department to create a prototype of a product/service based on consumers' new desires.

The production department would then start to manufacture the product, while the marketing department would focus on the promotion, distribution, pricing, etc. of the product. Additionally, a firm's finance department would be consulted, with respect to securing appropriate funding for the development, production and promotion of the product. Inter-departmental conflicts may occur, should a firm adhere to the marketing orientation. Production may oppose the installation, support and servicing of new capital stock, which may be needed to manufacture a new product. Finance may oppose the required capital expenditure, since it could undermine a healthy cash flow for the organization.

Herd Behaviour

Herd behaviour in marketing is used to explain the dependencies of customers' mutual behaviour. *The Economist* reported a recent conference in Rome on the subject of the simulation of adaptive human behaviour. It shared mechanisms to increase impulse buying and get people "to buy more by playing on the herd instinct." The basic idea is that people will buy more of products that are seen to be popular, and several feedback mechanisms to get product popularity information to consumers are mentioned, including smart card technology and the use of Radio Frequency Identification Tag technology. A "swarm-moves" model was introduced by a Florida Institute of Technology researcher, which is appealing to supermarkets because it can "increase sales without the need to give people discounts."

Other recent studies on the "power of social influence" include an "artificial music market in which some 14,000 people downloaded previously unknown songs" (Columbia University, New York); a Japanese chain of convenience stores which orders its products based on "sales data from department stores and research companies;" a Massachusetts company exploiting knowledge of social networking to improve sales; and online retailers who are increasingly informing consumers about "which products are popular with like-minded consumers" (e.g., Amazon, eBay).

Further Orientations

- An emerging area of study and practice concerns *internal marketing*, or how employees are trained and managed to deliver the brand in a way that positively impacts the acquisition and retention of customers.
- *Diffusion of innovations* research explores how and why people adopt new products, services and ideas.
- With consumers' eroding attention span and willingness to give time to advertising messages, marketers are turning to forms of *permission marketing* such as *branded content, custom media* and *reality marketing*.

Marketing Research

Marketing research involves conducting research to support marketing activities, and the statistical interpretation of data into information. This information is then used by managers to plan marketing activities, gauge the nature of a firm's marketing environment and attain information from suppliers. Marketing researchers use statistical methods such as quantitative research, qualitative research, hypothesis tests, Chi-squared tests, linear regression, correlations, frequency distributions, poisson distributions, binomial distributions, etc. to interpret their findings and convert data into information. The marketing research process spans a number of stages including the definition of a problem, development of a research plan, collecting and interpretation of data and disseminating information formally in form of a report.

The task of marketing research is to provide management with relevant, accurate, reliable, valid, and current information. A distinction should be made between marketing research and market research. Market research pertains to research in a given market. As an example, a firm may conduct research in a target market, after selecting a suitable market segment. In contrast, marketing research relates to all research conducted within marketing. Thus, market research is a subset of marketing research.

Market Segmentation

Market segmentation pertains to the division of a market of consumers into persons with similar needs and wants. As an example, if using Kellogg's cereals in this instance, Frosties are marketed to children. Crunchy Nut Cornflakes are marketed to adults. Both goods aforementioned denote two products which are marketed to two distinct groups of persons, both with like needs, traits, and wants. The purpose for market segmentation is conducted for two main issues. First, a segmentation allows a better allocation of a firm's finite resources. A firm only possesses a certain amount of resources. Accordingly, it must make choices (and appreciate the related costs) in servicing specific groups of consumers. Furthermore the diversified tastes of the contemporary Western consumers can be served better. With more diversity in the tastes of modern consumers, firms are taking noting the benefit of servicing a multiplicity of new markets. Market segmentation can be defined in terms of the *STP* acronym, meaning *Segment, Target* and *Position*.

Types of Marketing Research

Marketing research, as a sub-set aspect of marketing activities, can be divided into the following parts:

- Primary research (also known as field research), which involves the conduction and compilation of research for the purpose it was intended.
- Secondary research (also referred to as desk research), is initially conducted for one purpose, but often used to support another purpose or end goal.

By these definitions, an example of primary research would be market research conducted into health foods, which is used *solely* to ascertain the needs/wants of the target market for health foods. Secondary research, again according to the above definition, would be research pertaining to health foods, but used by a firm wishing to develop an unrelated product.

Primary research is often expensive to prepare, collect and interpret from data to information. Nonetheless, while secondary research is relatively inexpensive, it often can become outdated and outmoded, given it is used for a purpose other than for which is was intended.

Primary research can also be broken down into quantitative research and qualitative research, which as the labels suggest, pertain to numerical and non-numerical research methods, techniques. The appropriateness of each mode of research depends on whether data can be quantified (quantitative research), or whether subjective, non-numeric or abstract concepts are required to be studied (qualitative research).

There also exists additional modes of marketing research, which are:

- Exploratory research, pertaining to research that investigates an assumption.
- Descriptive research, which as the label suggests, describes "what is".
- Predictive research, meaning research conducted to predict a future occurrence.
- Conclusive research, for the purpose of deriving a conclusion via a research process.

Marketing Planning

The area of marketing planning involves forging a plan for a firm's marketing activities. A marketing plan can also pertain to a specific product, as well as to an organization's overall marketing strategy. Generally speaking, an organisation's marketing planning process is derived from its overall business strategy. Thus, when top management are devising the firm's strategic direction or mission, the intended marketing activities are incorporated into this plan. There are several levels of marketing objectives within an organization. The senior management of a firm would formulate a general business strategy for a firm. However, this general business strategy would be interpreted and implemented in different contexts throughout the firm.

Marketing Strategy

The field of marketing strategy encompasses the strategy involved in the management of a given product. A given firm may hold numerous products in the marketplace, spanning numerous and sometimes wholly unrelated industries. Accordingly, a plan is required in order to manage effectively such products. Evidently, a company needs to weigh up and ascertain how to utilise effectively its finite resources. As an example, a start-up car manufacturing firm would face little success, should it attempt to rival immediately Toyota, Ford, Nissan or any other large global car maker. Moreover, a product may be reaching the end of its life-cycle. Thus, the issue of divest, or a ceasing of production may be made. With regard to the aforesaid questions, each scenario requires a unique marketing strategy to be employed. Below are listed some prominent marketing strategy models, which seek to propose means to answer the preceding questions.

Marketing Specializations

With the rapidly emerging force of globalization, the distinction between marketing within a firm's home country and marketing within external markets is disappearing very quickly. With this occurrence in mind, firms need to reorient their marketing strategies to meet the challenges of the global marketplace, in addition to sustaining their competitiveness within home markets.

Buying Behaviour

A marketing firm must ascertain the nature of the customers buying behaviour, if it is to market its product properly. In order to entice and persuade a consumer to buy a product, marketers try to determine the behavioural process of how a given product is purchased. Buying behaviour is usually split in two prime strands, whether selling to the consumer, known as business-to-consumer (B2C) or another business, similarly known as business-to-business (B2B).

B2C Buying Behaviour

This mode of behaviour concerns consumers, in the purchase of a given product. As an example, if one pictures a pair of sneakers, the desire for a pair of sneakers would be followed by an information search on available types/brands.

This may include perusing media outlets, but most commonly consists of information gathered from family and friends.If the information search is insufficient, the consumer may search for alternative means to satisfy the need/ want. In this case, this may be buying leather shoes, sandals, etc. The purchase decision is then made, in which the consumer actually buys the product. Following this stage, a post-purchase evaluation is often conducted, comprising an appraisal of the value/utility brought by the purchase of the sneakers. If the value/utility is high, then a repeat purchase may be bought. This could then develop into consumer loyalty, for the firm producing the pair of sneakers.

B2B Buying Behaviour

This mode of behaviour relates to organisational/industrial buying behaviour. B2C and B2B behaviour are not exact, as similarities and differences exist. Some of the key differences are listed below:

In a straight rebuy, the fourth, fifth and sixth stages are omitted. In a modified rebuy scenario, the fifth and sixth stages are precluded. In a new buy, all aforementioned stages are conducted.

USE OF TECHNOLOGIES

Marketing management can also note the importance of technology, within the scope of its marketing efforts. Computer-based information systems can be employed, aiding in a better processing and storage of data. Marketing researchers can use such systems to devise better methods of converting data into information, and for the creation of enhanced data gathering methods. Information technology can aid in improving an MKIS' software and hardware components, to improve a company's marketing decision-making process.

In recent years, the netbook personal computer has gained significant market share among laptops, largely due to its more user-friendly size and portability. Information technology typically progress at a fast rate, leading to marketing managers being cognizant of the latest technological developments. Moreover, the launch of smartphones into the cellphone market is commonly derived from a demand among consumers for more technologically advanced products. A firm can lose out to competitors, should it refrain from noting the latest technological occurrences in its industry.

Technological advancements can facilitate lesser barriers between countries and regions. Via using the World Wide Web, firms can quickly dispatch information from one country to another, without much restriction. Prior to the mass usage of the Internet, such transfers of information would have taken longer to send, especially if via snail mail, telex, etc.

SERVICES MARKETING

Services marketing, as the label suggests, relates to the marketing of services, as opposed to tangible products (in standard economic terminology, a tangible product is called a good).

A typical definition of a service (as opposed to a good) is thus:

- The use of it is inseparable from its purchase (,i.e. a service is used and consumed simultaneously)
- It does not possess material form, and thus cannot be smelt, heard, tasted, or felt.
- The use of a service is inherently subjective, in that due to the human condition, all persons experiencing a service would experience it uniquely.

As examples of the above points, a train ride can be deemed as a service. If one buys a train ticket, the use of the train is typically experienced concurrently with the purchase of the ticket. Moreover, a train ride cannot be smelt, heard, tasted or felt as such. Granted, a seat can be felt, and the train can be evidently heard, nonetheless one is not paying for the permanent ownership of the tangible components of the train.

Services (by comparison with goods) can also be viewed as a spectrum. Not all products are pure goods, nor are all pure services. The aforementioned example of a train ride can be deemed a pure service, whilst a packet of potato chips can be deemed a pure good. An intermediary example may be a restaurant (as the waiter service is intangible, and the food evidently is tangible in form).

BRAND

A brand is a name, sign, symbol, slogan or anything that is used to identify and distinguish a specific product, service, or business. A legally protected brand name is called a proprietary name.

Concepts

Brand is the image of the product in the market. Some people distinguish the psychological aspect of a brand from the experiential aspect. The experiential aspect consists of the sum of all points of contact with the brand and is known as the brand experience. The psychological aspect, sometimes referred to as the brand image, is a symbolic construct created within the minds of people and consists of all the information and expectations associated with a product or service.

People engaged in branding seek to develop or align the expectations behind the brand experience, creating the impression that a brand associated with a product or service has certain qualities or characteristics that make it special or unique. A brand is therefore one of the most valuable elements in an advertising theme, as it demonstrates what the brand owner is able to offer in the marketplace. The art of creating and maintaining a brand is called brand management. Orientation of the whole organization towards its brand is called brand orientation. Careful brand manage-ment seeks to make the product or services relevant to the target audience. Therefore cleverly crafted advertising campaigns, can be highly successful in convincing consumers to pay remarkably high prices for products which are inherently extremely cheap to make. This concept, known as creating value, essentially consists of manipulating the projected image of the product so that the consumer sees the product as being worth the amount that the advertiser wants him/her to see, rather than a more logical valuation that comprises an aggregate of the cost of raw materials, plus the cost of manufacture, plus the cost of distribution.

Modern value-creation branding-and-advertising campaigns are highly successful at inducing consumers to pay, for example, 50 dollars for a T-shirt that cost a mere 50 cents to make, or 5 dollars for a box of breakfast cereal that contains a few cents' worth of wheat. Brands should be seen as more than the difference between the actual cost of a product and its selling price - they represent the sum of all valuable qualities of a product to the consumer.

There are many intangibles involved in business, intangibles left wholly from the income statement and balance sheet which determine how a business is perceived. The learned skill of a knowledge worker, the type of metal working, the type of stitch: all may be without an 'accounting cost' but for those who truly know the product, for it is these people the company should wish to find and keep, the difference is incomparable.

Failing to recognize these assets that a business, any business, can create and maintain will set an enterprise at a serious disadvantage. A brand which is widely known in the marketplace acquires brand recognition. When brand recognition builds up to a point where a brand enjoys a critical mass of positive sentiment in the marketplace, it is said to have achieved brand franchise.

One goal in brand recognition is the identification of a brand without the name of the company present. For example, Disney has been successful at branding with their particular script font (originally created for Walt Disney's "signature" logo), which it used in the logo for go.com. Consumers may look on branding as an important value added aspect of products or services, as it often serves to denote a certain attractive quality or characteristic.

From the perspective of brand owners, branded products or services also command higher prices. Where two products resemble each other, but one of the products has no associated branding (such as a generic, store-branded product), people may often select the more expensive branded product on the basis of the quality of the brand or the reputation of the brand owner.

Brand Awareness

Brand awareness refers to customers' ability to recall and recognize the brand under different conditions and link to the brand name,logo, jingles and so on to certain associations in memory. It helps the customers to understand to which product or service category the particular brand belongs to and what products and services are sold under the brand name. It also ensures that customers know which of their needs are satisfied by the brand through its products.

BRAND SALIENCE

Brand salience measures the awareness of the brand."To what extent is the brand top-of-mind and easily recalled or recognized? What types of cues or reminders are necessary?" The tendency of a brand to be thought of in a buying situation is known as "brand salience". Brand salience is "the propensity for a brand to be noticed and/or thought of in buying situations" and the higher the brand salience the higher it's market penetration and therefore its market share. Salience refers not to what customers think about brands but to which ones they think about.

Brands which come to mind on an unaided basis are likely to be the brands in a customer's consideration set and thus have a higher probability of being purchased. Advertising weight and brand salience are cues to customers indicating which brands are popular, and customers have a tendency to buy popular brands. Also, an increase in the salience of one brand can actually inhibit recall of other brands, including brands that otherwise would be candidates for purchase. It is widely acknowledged that buyer's do not see their brand as being any different from other brands that are available. They buy a particular brand because they are more aware of it, not because it is more distinctive, or has a point of difference.

We now know that all decisions made by humans involve memory processes to a greater or lesser extent. Incoming information from the external environment travels by the sensory memory into the short-term (or working) memory (STM) but if it is not acted upon in a very short time the brain simply discards it. But salient information that is important and received on a regular basis through different channels is passed to the long-term memory (LTM) where it can be stored for many years. Memories are stored or filed via connections between new and existing memories in the different parts of the memory. They are laid down in a framework making some memories easier to access than others. Recall is the process by which an individual reconstructs the stimulus itself from memory, removed from the physicality's of that reality.

Global Brand

A global brand is one which is perceived to reflect the same set of values around the world.Global brands transcend their origins and creates strong, enduring relationships with consumers across countries and cultures.Global Brands are brands which sold to international markets. Examples of Global Brands include Coca-Cola, McDonald's, Marlboro, Levi's etc.. These brands are used to sell the same product across multiple markets, and could be considered successful to the extent that the associated products are easily recognizable by the diverse set of consumers.

Benefits of Global Branding

In addition to taking advantage of the outstanding growth opportunities, the following drives the increasing interest in taking brands global:

- Economies of scale (production and distribution)
- Lower marketing costs
- Laying the groundwork for future extensions worldwide
- Maintaining consistent brand imagery
- Quicker identification and integration of innovations (discovered worldwide)
- Preempting international competitors from entering domestic markets or locking you out of other geographic markets
- Increasing international media reach (especially with the explosion of the Internet) is an enabler
- Increases in international business • and tourism are also enablers

Global Brand Variables

The following elements may differ from country to country:

- Corporate slogan
- Products and services
- Product names
- Product features
- Positionings
- Marketing mixes (including pricing, distribution, media and advertising execution)
- These differences will depend upon:
- Language differences
- Different styles of communication
- Other cultural differences
- Differences in category and brand development
- Different consumption patterns
- Different competitive sets and marketplace conditions
- Different legal and regulatory environments
- Different national approaches to marketing.

Local Brand

A brand that is sold and marketed (distributed and promoted) in a relatively small and restricted geographical area. A local brand is a brand that can be found in only one country or region. It may be called a regional brand if the area encompasses more than one metropolitan market. It may also be a brand that is developed for a specific national market, however an interesting thing about local brand is that the local branding is mostly done by consumers then by the producers. Examples of Local Brands in Sweden are Stomatol, Mijerierna etc..

BRAND NAME

The brand name is quite often used interchangeably within "brand", although it is more correctly used to specifically denote written or spoken linguistic elements of any product. In this context a "brand name" constitutes a type of trademark, if the brand name exclusively identifies the brand owner as the commercial source of products or services. A brand owner may seek to protect proprietary rights in relation to a brand name through trademark registration. Advertising spokespersons have also become part of some brands, for example: Mr. Whipple of Charmin toilet tissue and Tony the Tiger of Kellogg's. Local Baranding is usually done by the consumers rather then the producers.

TYPES OF BRAND NAMES

Brand names come in many styles.

A few include:

- *Acronym*: A name made of initials such as UPS or IBM
- *Descriptive*: Names that describe a product benefit or function like Whole Foods or Airbus
- *Alliteration and rhyme*: Names that are fun to say and stick in the mind like Reese's Pieces or Dunkin' Donuts
- *Evocative*: Names that evoke a relevant vivid image like Amazon or Crest
- *Neologisms*: Completely made-up words like Wii or Kodak
- *Foreign word*: Adoption of a word from another language like Volvo or Samsung
- *Founders' names*: Using the names of real people like Hewlett-Packard or Disney
- *Geography*: Many brands are named for regions and landmarks like Cisco and Fuji Film
- *Personification*: Many brands take their names from myth like Nike or from the minds of ad execs like Betty Crocker

The act of associating a product or service with a brand has become part of pop culture. Most products have some kind of brand identity, from common table salt to designer jeans. A brandnomer is a brand name that has colloquially become a generic term for a product or service, such as Band-Aid or Kleenex, which are often used to describe any kind of adhesive bandage or any kind of facial tissue respectively.

BRAND IDENTITY

A product identity, or brand image are typically the attributes one associates with a brand, how the brand owner wants the consumer to perceive the brand - and by extension the branded company, organization, product or service. The brand owner will seek to bridge the gap between the brand image and the brand identity.

Effective brand names build a connection between the brand personality as it is perceived by the target audience and the actual product/service. The brand name should be conceptually on target with the product/service (what the company stands for). Furthermore, the brand name should be on target with the brand demographic. Typically, sustainable brand names are easy to remember, transcend trends and have positive connotations. Brand identity is fundamental to consumer recognition and symbolizes the brand's differentiation from competitors.

Brand identity is what the owner wants to communicate to its potential consumers. However, over time, a products brand identity may acquire (evolve), gaining new attributes from consumer perspective but not necessarily from the marketing communications an owner percolates to targeted consumers. Therefore, brand associations become handy to check the consumer's perception of the brand. Brand identity needs to focus on authentic qualities - real characteristics of the value and brand promise being provided and sustained by organisational and/or production characteristics.

VISUAL BRAND IDENTITY

The recognition and perception of a brand is highly influenced by its visual presentation. A brand's visual identity is the overall look of its communications. Effective visual brand identity is achieved by the consistent use of particular visual elements to create distinction, such as specific fonts, colors, and graphic elements. At the core of every brand identity is a brand mark, or logo. In the United States, brand identity and logo design naturally grew out of the Modernist movement in the 1950's and greatly drew on the principals of that movement – simplicity (Mies van der Rohe's principle of "Less is more") and geometric abstraction. These principles can be observed in the work of the pioneers of the practice of visual brand identity design, such as Paul Rand, Chermayeff & Geismar and Saul Bass. *Brand parity*: Brand parity is the perception of the customers that all brands are equivalent.

BRANDING APPROACHES

Company Name

Often, especially in the industrial sector, it is just the company's name which is promoted (leading to one of the most powerful statements of "branding"; the saying, before the company's downgrading, "No one ever got fired for buying IBM"). In this case a very strong brand name (or company name) is made the vehicle for a range of products (for example, Mercedes-

Benz or Black & Decker) or even a range of subsidiary brands (such as Cadbury Dairy Milk, Cadbury Flake or Cadbury Fingers in the United States).

Individual Branding

Each brand has a separate name (such as Seven-Up, Kool-Aid or Nivea Sun (Beiersdorf)), which may even compete against other brands from the same company (for example, Persil, Omo, Surf and Lynx are all owned by Unilever).

Attitude Branding and Iconic Brands

Attitude branding is the choice to represent a larger feeling, which is not necessarily connected with the product or consumption of the product at all. Marketing labeled as attitude branding include that of Nike, Starbucks, The Body Shop, Safeway, and Apple Inc.. In the 2000 book *No Logo*, Naomi Klein describes attitude branding as a "fetish strategy". "A great brand raises the bar — it adds a greater sense of purpose to the experience, whether it's the challenge to do your best in sports and fitness, or the affirmation that the cup of coffee you're drinking really matters." - Howard Schultz (president, CEO, and chairman of Starbucks) Iconic brands are defined as having aspects that contribute to consumer's self-expression and personal identity. Brands whose value to consumers comes primarily from having identity value comes are said to be "identity brands". Some of these brands have such a strong identity that they become more or less "cultural icons" which makes them iconic brands. Examples of iconic brands are: Apple Inc., Nike and Harley Davidson. Many iconic brands include almost ritual-like behaviour when buying and consuming the products.

There are four key elements to creating iconic brands:

1. *"Necessary conditions"*: The performance of the product must at least be ok preferably with a reputation of having good quality.
2. *"Myth-making"*: A meaningful story-telling fabricated by cultural "insiders". These must be seen as legitimate and respected by consumers for stories to be accepted.
3. *"Cultural contradictions"*: Some kind of mismatch between prevailing ideology and emergent undercurrents in society. In other words a difference with the way consumers are and how they some times wish they were.
4. *"The cultural brand management process"*: Actively engaging in the myth-making process making sure the brand maintains its position as an icon.

"No-brand" Branding

Recently a number of companies have successfully pursued "No-Brand" strategies by creating packaging that imitates generic brand simplicity.

Examples include the Japanese company Muji, which means "No label" in English ("Mujirushi Ryohin" – literally, "No brand quality goods"), and the Florida company No-Ad Sunscreen. Although there is a distinct Muji brand, Muji products are not branded. This no-brand strategy means that little is spent on advertisement or classical marketing and Muji's success is attributed to the word-of-mouth, a simple shopping experience and the anti-brand movement. "No brand" branding may be construed as a type of branding as the product is made conspicuous through the absence of a brand name.

Derived Brands

In this case the supplier of a key component, used by a number of suppliers of the end-product, may wish to guarantee its own position by promoting that component as a brand in its own right. The most frequently quoted example is Intel, which secures its position in the PC market with the slogan "Intel Inside".

Brand Extension

The existing strong brand name can be used as a vehicle for new or modified products; for example, many fashion and designer companies extended brands into fragrances, shoes and accessories, home textile, home decor, luggage, (sun-) glasses, furniture, hotels, etc. Mars extended its brand to ice cream, Caterpillar to shoes and watches, Michelin to a restaurant guide, Adidas and Puma to personal hygiene. Dunlop extended its brand from tires to other rubber products such as shoes, golf balls, tennis racquets and adhesives.

There is a difference between brand extension and line extension.A line extension is when a current brand name is used to enter a new market segment in the existing product class, with new varieties or flavors or sizes. When Coca-Cola launched "Diet Coke" and "Cherry Coke" they stayed within the originating product category: non-alcoholic carbonated beverages. Procter & Gamble (P&G) did likewise extending its strong lines (such as Fairy Soap) into neighboring products (Fairy Liquid and Fairy Automatic) within the same category, dish washing detergents.

MULTI-BRANDS

Alternatively, in a market that is fragmented amongst a number of brands a supplier can choose deliberately to launch totally new brands in apparent competition with its own existing strong brand (and often with identical product characteristics); simply to soak up some of the share of the market which will in any case go to minor brands.

The rationale is that having 3 out of 12 brands in such a market will give a greater overall share than having 1 out of 10 (even if much of the share of these new brands is taken from the existing one). In its most extreme manifestation, a supplier pioneering a new market which it believes will be particularly attractive may choose immediately to launch a second brand in competition with its first, in order to pre-empt others entering the market.

Individual brand names naturally allow greater flexibility by permitting a variety of different products, of differing quality, to be sold without confusing the consumer's perception of what business the company is in or diluting higher quality products.

Once again, Procter & Gamble is a leading exponent of this philosophy, running as many as ten detergent brands in the US market. This also increases the total number of "facings" it receives on supermarket shelves. Sara Lee, on the other hand, uses it to keep the very different parts of the business separate — from Sara Lee cakes through Kiwi polishes to L'Eggs pantyhose. In the hotel business, Marriott uses the name Fairfield Inns for its budget chain (and Ramada uses Rodeway for its own cheaper hotels).

Cannibalization is a particular problem of a "multibrand" approach, in which the new brand takes business away from an established one which the organization also owns. This may be acceptable (indeed to be expected) if there is a net gain overall. Alternatively, it may be the price the organization is willing to pay for shifting its position in the market; the new product being one stage in this process.

Private Labels

With the emergence of strong retailers, private label brands, also called own brands, or store brands, also emerged as a major factor in the marketplace. Where the retailer has a particularly strong identity (such as Marks & Spencer in the UK clothing sector) this "own brand" may be able to compete against even the strongest brand leaders, and may outperform those products that are not otherwise strongly branded.

Individual and Organizational Brands

There are kinds of branding that treat individuals and organizations as the "products" to be branded. Personal branding treats persons and their careers as brands. The term is thought to have been first used in a 1997 article by Tom Peters. Faith branding treats religious figures and organizations as brands. Religious media expert Phil Cooke has written that faith branding handles the question of how to express faith in a media-dominated culture. Nation branding works with the perception and reputation of countries as brands.

The word "brand" is derived from the Old Norse *brandr*, meaning "to burn." It refers to the practice of producers burning their mark (or brand) onto their products. Although connected with the history of trademarks and including earlier examples which could be deemed "protobrands" (such as the marketing puns of the "Vesuvinum" wine jars found at Pompeii), brands in the field of mass-marketing originated in the 19th century with the advent of packaged goods. Industrialization moved the production of many household items, such as soap, from local communities to centralized factories.

When shipping their items, the factories would literally brand their logo or insignia on the barrels used, extending the meaning of "brand" to that of trademark. Bass & Company, the British brewery, claims their red triangle brand was the world's first trademark. Lyle's Golden Syrup makes a similar claim, having been named as Britain's oldest brand, with its green and gold packaging having remained almost unchanged since 1885.

Cattle were branded long before this; the term "maverick", originally meaning an unbranded calf, comes from Texas rancher Samuel Augustus Maverick who, following the American Civil War, decided that since all other cattle were branded, his would be identified by having no markings at all. Even the signatures on paintings of famous artists like Leonardo Da Vinci can be viewed as an early branding tool.

Factories established during the Industrial Revolution introduced mass-produced goods and needed to sell their products to a wider market, to customers previously familiar only with locally-produced goods. It quickly became apparent that a generic package of soap had difficulty competing with familiar, local products. The packaged goods manufacturers needed to convince the market that the public could place just as much trust in the non-local product. Campbell soup, Coca-Cola, Juicy Fruit gum, Aunt Jemima, and Quaker Oats were among the first products to be 'branded', in an effort to increase the consumer's familiarity with their products.

Many brands of that era, such as Uncle Ben's rice and Kellogg's breakfast cereal furnish illustrations of the problem. Around 1900, James Walter Thompson published a house ad explaining trademark advertising. This was an early commercial explanation of what we now know as branding. Companies soon adopted slogans, mascots, and jingles that began to appear on radio and early television. By the 1940s, manufacturers began to recognize the way in which consumers were developing relationships with their brands in a social/psychological/anthropological sense. From there, manufacturers quickly learned to build their brand's identity and personality, such as youthfulness, fun or luxury. This began the practice we now know as "branding" today, where the consumers buy "the brand" instead of the product. This trend continued to the 1980s, and is now quantified in concepts such as brand value and brand equity.

Naomi Klein has described this development as "brand equity mania". In 1988, for example, Philip Morris purchased Kraft for six times what the company was worth on paper; it was felt that what they really purchased was its brand name. Marlboro Friday: April 2, 1993 - marked by some as the death of the brand - the day Philip Morris declared that they were to cut the price of Marlboro cigarettes by 20%, in order to compete with bargain cigarettes. Marlboro cigarettes were notorious at the time for their heavy advertising campaigns, and well-nuanced brand image. In response to the announcement Wall street stocks nose-dived for a large number of 'branded' companies: Heinz, Coca Cola, Quaker Oats, PepsiCo. Many thought the event signalled the beginning of a trend towards "brand blindness", questioning the power of "brand value".

Brand Building Tools

There are various tools used by the marketers to build their brands. In early days, TV advertisement was the most effective brand building tool.there were very few TV channels and people watched movies and ads with equal interest. Nowadays, most of the viewers are ignoring the ads. In fact, many more are simply not watching TV or switched to internet and other recreational activities.So the major challenge to the marketers is to use effective tools, in order to attract the attention of the consumers to their brands. Some of the important brand building tools are: 1.Public relations 2.Press releases 3.Sponsorships 4.Corporate websites 5.Exhibitions 6.Event marketing 7.Public facilities 8.Online advertisements 9.broadcast media

BRAND ARCHITECTURE

Brand architecture is the structure of brands within an organizational entity. It is the way in which the brands within a company's portfolio are related to, and differentiated from, one another. The architecture should define the different leagues of branding within the organization; how the corporate brand and sub-brands relate to and support each other; and how the sub-brands reflect or reinforce the core purpose of the corporate brand to which they belong.

According to Rajagopal Brand architecture may be defined as an integrated process of brand building through establishing brand relationships among branding options in the competitive environment. The brand architecture of an organisation at any time is, in large measure, a legacy of past management decisions as well as the competitive realities it faces in the marketplace.

TYPES OF BRAND ARCHITECTURE

There are three key levels of branding:

1. *Corporate brand, umbrella brand,* and *family brand*: Examples include Virgin Group and Heinz. These are consumer-facing brands used across all the firm's activities, and this name is how they are known to all their stakeholders – consumers, employees, shareholders, partners, suppliers and other parties. These brands may also be used in conjunction with product descriptions or sub-brands: for example Heinz Cream of Tomato Soup, or Virgin Trains.

2. *Endorsed brands,* and *sub-brands*: For example, Nestle KitKat, Cadbury Dairy Milk, Sony PlayStation or Polo by Ralph Lauren. These brands include a parent brand - which may be a corporate brand, an umbrella brand, or a family brand - as an endorsement to a sub-brand or an individual product brand. The endorsement should add credibility to the endorsed sub-brand in the eyes of consumers.
3. *Individual product brand*: For example, Procter & Gamble's Pampers or Unilever's Dove. The individual brands are presented to consumers, and the parent company name is given little or no prominence. Other stakeholders, like shareholders or partners, will know the producer by its company name.

BRAND COMMUNITY

A brand community is a community formed on the basis of attachment to a product or marque. Recent developments in marketing and in research in consumer behaviour result in stressing the connection between brand, individual identity and culture. Among the concepts developed to explain the behaviour of consumers, the concept of a brand community focuses on the connections between consumers. A brand community can be defined as an enduring self-selected group of actors sharing a system of values, standards and representations (a culture) and recognizing bonds of membership with each other and with the whole.

The term "brand community" was first presented by Albert Muniz Jr. and Thomas C. O'Guinn in a 1995 paper for the Association for Consumer Research Annual Conference in Minneapolis, MN. In a 2001 article titled " Brand Community", published in the Journal of Consumer Research (SSCI), they defined the concept as "a specialized, non-geographically bound community, based on a structured set of social relations among admirers of a brand." This 2001 paper recently has been acknowledged by Thomson Scientific & Healthcare to be one of the most cited papers in the field of economics and business. Brands which are used as examples of brand communities include Apple Inc. (Macintosh, iPod, iPhone), Ford Bronco, Holga and Lomo cameras, Jeep, Lego, Miata, Mini Cooper, Palm, PocketPC, Royal Enfield motocycles, Saab, Saturn automobiles and Subaru, and Harley Davidson. Brand communities are characterized in shared consciousness, rituals and traditions, and a sense of moral responsibility.

BRAND ENGAGEMENT

Brand Engagement is a term loosely used to describe the process of forming an attachment (emotional and rational) between a person and a brand. It comprises one aspect of brand management. What makes the topic complex is that brand engagement is partly created by institutions and organizations, but is equally created by the perceptions, attitudes, beliefs and behaviors of those with whom these institutions and organizations are communicating or engaging with. As a relatively new addition to the marketing and communication mix, brand engagement sits in the space between marketing, advertising, media communication, social media, organizational development, internal communications and human resource management. There is still lack of clarity and debate about whether this is a "soft" or hard measure, and whether it can be linked to any consumer or employee behaviour change – e.g. sales activity, trial, or recommendation.

External Brand Engagement

Brand engagement between a brand and its consumers/potential consumers is a key objective of a brand marketing effort. In general, the ways a brand connects to its consumer is via a range of "touchpoints" — that is, a sequence or list of potential ways the brand makes contact with the individual. Examples include retail environments, advertising, word of mouth, online, and the product/service itself.

Internal ("close stakeholder") Brand Engagement

There are two broad areas where brand engagement is relevant within an organization (employees and close stakeholders such as franchise staff, call centers, suppliers or intermediaries). The first area is ensuring that the employer brand promised to employees is delivered upon once employees join the firm. If the employee experience is not what is promised, this could result in increased employee turnover and/or decreased performance.

The second area is ensuring employees and close stakeholders of an organization completely understand the organization's brand, and what it stands for—and to make sure that their activities on a day to day basis are contributing to expressing that brand through the customer experience.

In general, this requires an ongoing effort on the part of the organization to ensure that its employees and close stakeholders understand what the brand is promising to its customers, and to help all employees clearly understand how their actions and behaviors, on a day to day basis, either support or undermine the effort. This often raises the issue of the value of investment in "brand engagement." It is a discretionary expense on the part of the organization. Proponents of brand engagement would argue that this is an investment—that is, the benefits to the organization outweigh the cost of the programme.

Within any organization there is competition for resources, so there is a significant need to demonstrate Return on Investment in employee engagement/internal communi-cations. While it is generally accepted that it is important for internal communications professionals to demonstrate the value this function delivers to the organization, it is difficult to place a discrete figure on this contribution.

Best practice in internal communications generally adheres to certain principles:

- Understanding the stakeholder (audiences)
- Knowing what messages and information is appropriate for each audience
- Ensuring that there is a feedback mechanism in place so communication is a dialogue
- Measuring effectiveness
- Enhancing participation and collaboration.

An aspect of internal brand engagement is Brand orientation which refers to "the degree to which the organization values brands and its practices are oriented towards building brand capabilities." Thought leaders are increasingly placing employee engagement at the forefront of the fight for greater authenticity in the workplace, increased employee satisfaction and ultimately greater retention and improved customer service.

They are passionate about the link to bottom line benefits and strongly advocate working on brands from the inside out. There are a range of experts and service providers who have created offers to bring the brand to life—all agree that the employee side of the equation is far more important than has been historically acknowledged.

The measurement Angle

Much internal communication and employee engagement practice is based on measurement of effectiveness or business contribution. The key elements in creating a model of employee engagement is the measurement of "engagement drivers" — that is, what are the factors or combinations of factors which have an impact on productivity and commitment and can be monitored and addressed through people, process or technology changes?

Many of the "engagement drivers" currently in use internally are HR focused, and in many cases do not delve deeply into the employee's role in delivering the brand/customer experience as a distinct element.

Example

Probably the most compelling example of this is the service-profit chain. The first real case study of this appeared in "The Service Profit Chain". This statistical model tracks increases in employee "engagement drivers" to correlated increases in customer satisfaction and loyalty, and then correlates this to increases in Total Shareholder Return (TSR), revenue and other financial performance measures. Since the service-profit chain emerged, it's been developed, and criticized, but the general consensus is that employee engagement can contribute roughly 20% to an organization's TSR.

Collaboration and Connectivity vs. Content Management

While some organizations are realizing the benefits of collaboration and work flow online, there appears to be significant focus on publishing and managing content, generally via Content Management Systems. There is an emerging school of thought that organizational perspectives on technology are frequently misaligned with the actual requirements and desires of the users of the technology. That is, the nature (or intention) of a technology may not always determine the nature of its use – the telephone, for example, was originally intended as a broadcast medium. Its designers were focused on delivering content, while its users sought – and still value – connectivity.

The social media phenomenon presents emerging evidence that this quest for connectivity is rapidly becoming a core focus of communication technology within organizations. This potentially creates a disconnect with more traditional content-driven models of internal communication —delivering (or making easily available) the right content at the right time to the right people using the right media. Therefore, there could be a great deal of potential within organisations, using their existing technologies, to derive cultural and performance benefits from re-thinking how they communicate, make decisions and work virtually.

BRAND EQUITY

Brand equity refers to the marketing effects or outcomes that accrue to a product with its brand name compared with those that *would* accrue if the same product did not have the brand name. And, at the root of these marketing effects is consumers' knowledge. In other words, consumers' knowledge about a brand makes manufacturers/advertisers respond differently or adopt appropriately adept measures for the marketing of the brand. The study of brand equity is increasingly popular as some marketing researchers have concluded that brands are one of the most valuable assets that a company has. Brand equity is one of the factors which can increase the financial value of a brand to the brand owner, although not the only one.

Measurement

There are many ways to measure a brand. Some measurements approaches are at the firm level, some at the product level, and still others are at the consumer level.

- *Firm level*: Firm level approaches measure the brand as a financial asset. In short, a calculation is made regarding how much the brand is worth as an intangible asset. For example, if you were to take the value of the firm, as derived by its market capitalization - and then subtract tangible assets and "measurable" intangible assets- the residual would be the brand equity. One high profile firm level approach is by the consulting firm Interbrand. To do its calculation, Interbrand estimates brand value on the basis of projected profits discounted to a present value. The discount rate is a subjective rate determined by Interbrand and Wall Street equity specialists and reflects the risk profile, market leadership, stability and global reach of the brand.

- *Product level*: The classic product level brand measurement example is to compare the price of a no-name or private label product to an "equivalent" branded product. The difference in price, assuming all things equal, is due to the brand. More recently a revenue premium approach has been advocated.
- *Consumer level*: This approach seeks to map the mind of the consumer to find out what associations with the brand that the consumer has. This approach seeks to measure the awareness (recall and recognition) and brand image (the overall associations that the brand has). Free association tests and projective techniques are commonly used to uncover the tangible and intangible attributes, attitudes, and intentions about a brand. Brands with high levels of awareness and strong, favorable and unique associations are high equity brands.

All of these calculations are, at best, approximations. A more complete understanding of the brand can occur if multiple measures are used.

Positive Brand Equity vs. Negative Brand Equity

A brand equity is the positive effect of the brand on the difference between the prices and that the consumer accepts to pay when the brand known compared to the value of the benefit received. There are two schools of thought regarding the existence of negative brand equity.

One perspective states brand equity cannot be negative, hypothesizing only positive brand equity is created by marketing activities such as advertising, PR, and promotion. A second perspective is that negative equity can exist, due to catastrophic events to the brand, such as a wide product recall or continued negative press attention (Blackwater or Haliburton, for example).

Colloquially, the term "negative brand equity" may be used to describe a product or service where an brand has a negligible effect on a product level when compared to a no-name or private label product. The brand-related negative intangible assets are called "brand liability", compared with "brand equity".

Family Branding vs. Individual Branding Strategies

The greater a company's brand equity, the greater the probability that the company will use a family branding strategy rather than an individual branding strategy. This is because family branding allows them to leverage the equity accumulated in the core brand. Aspects of brand equity includes:

brand loyalty, awareness, association, and perception of quality. In the early 2000s in North America, the Ford Motor Company made a strategic decision to brand all new or redesigned cars with names starting with "F". This aligned with the previous tradition of naming all sport utility vehicles since the Ford Explorer with the letter "E".

The Toronto Star quoted an analyst who warned that changing the name of the well known Windstar to the Freestar would cause confusion and discard brand equity built up, while a marketing manager believed that a name change would highlight the new redesign.

The aging Taurus, which became one of the most significant cars in American auto history would be abandoned in favour of three entirely new names, all starting with "F", the Five Hundred, Freestar and Fusion. By 2007, the Freestar was discontinued without a replacement. The Five Hundred name was thrown out and Taurus was brought back for the next generation of that car in a surprise move by Alan Mulally. "Five Hundred" was recognized by less than half of most people, but an overwhelming majority was familiar with the "Ford Taurus".

8

Brand Extension

Brand extension or brand stretching is a marketing strategy in which a firm marketing a product with a well-developed image uses the same brand name in a different product category. The new product is called a spin-off. Organizations use this strategy to increase and leverage brand equity (definition: the net worth and long-term sustainability just from the renowned name). An example of a brand extension is Jello-gelatin creating Jello pudding pops.

It increases awareness of the brand name and increases profitability from offerings in more than one product category. A brand's "extendibility" depends on how strong consumer's associations are to the brand's values and goals. Ralph Lauren's Polo brand successfully extended from clothing to home furnishings such as bedding and towels. Both clothing and bedding are made of linen and fulfill a similar consumer function of comfort and hominess. Arm & Hammer leveraged its brand equity from basic baking soda into the oral care and laundry care categories.

By emphasizing its key attributes, the cleaning and deodorizing properties of its core product, Arm & Hammer was able to leverage those attributes into new categories with success. Another example is Virgin Group, which was initially a record label that has extended its brand successfully many times; from transportation (aeroplanes, trains) to games stores and video stores such a Virgin Megastores.

In 1990s, 81% of new products used brand extension to introduce new brands and to create sales. Launching a new product, is not only time consuming but also needs a big budget to create awareness and to promote a product's benefits. Brand extension is one of the new product development strategies which can reduce financial risk by using the parent brand name to enhance consumers' perception due to the core brand equity.

While there can be significant benefits in brand extension strategies, there can also be significant risks, resulting in a diluted or severely damaged brand image. Poor choices for brand extension may dilute and deteriorate the core brand and damage the brand equity. Most of the literature focuses on the consumer evaluation and positive impact on parent brand. In practical cases, the failures of brand extension are at higher rate than the successes. Some studies show that negative impact may dilute brand image and equity. In spite of the positive impact of brand extension, negative association and wrong communication strategy do harm to the parent brand even brand family.

Product extensions are versions of the same parent product that serve a segment of the target market and increase the variety of an offering. An example of a product extension is Coke vs. Diet Coke in same product category of soft drinks. This tactic is undertaken due to the brand loyalty and brand awareness they enjoy consumers are more likely to buy a new product that has a tried and trusted brand name on it. This means the market is catered for as they are receiving a product from a brand they trust and Coca Cola is catered for as they can increase their product portfolio and they have a larger hold over the market in which they are performing in.

TYPES OF PRODUCT EXTENSION

Brand extension research mainly focuses on the consumer evaluation of extension and attitude of the parent brand. Following the Aaker and Keller's model, they provide a sufficient depth and breadth proposition to examine consumer behaviour and conceptual framework. They use three dimensions to measure the fit of extension. First of all, the "Complement" is that consumer takes two product (extension and parent brand product) classes as complement to satisfy their specific needs. Secondly, the "Substitute" indicates two products have same user situation and satisfy their same needs which means the products class is very similar so that can replace each other. At last, the "Transfer" is the relationship between extension product and manufacturer which "reflects the perceived ability of any firm operating in the first product class to make a product in the second class". The first two measures focus on the consumer's demand and the last one focuses on firm's ability.

From the line extension to brand extension, however, there are many different way of extension such as "brand alliance", co-branding or "brand franchise extension".Tauber suggests seven strategies to identify extension cases such as product with parent brand's benefit, same product with different price or quality, etc. In his suggestion, it can be classified into two category of extension; extension of product-related association and non-product related association. Another form of brand extension, is a licensed brand extension. Where the brand-owner partners (sometimes with a competitor) who takes on the responsibility of manufacturer and sales of the new products, paying a royalty every time a product is sold.

CATEGORISATION THEORY

Researchers tend to use "categorisation theory" as their fundamental theory to explore the links about the brand extension. When consumers face thousands of products, they not only are initially confused and disorderly in mind, but also try to categorise the brand association or image with their existing memory. When two or more products exit in front of consumers, they might reposition memories to frame a brand image and concept toward new introduction. A consumer can judge or evaluate the extension by their category memory. They categorise new information into specific brand or product class label and store it. This process is not only related to consumer's experience and knowledge, but also involvement and choice of brand. If the brand association is highly related to extension, consumer can perceive the fit among brand extension. Some studies suggest that consumer may ignore or overcome the dissonance from extension especially flagship product which means the low perceived of fit does not dilute the flagship's equity.

BRAND EXTENSION FAILURE

Literature related to negative effect of brand extension is limited and the findings are revealed as incongruent. The early works of Aaker and Keller find no significant evidence that brand name can be diluted by unsuccessful brand extensions. Conversely, Loken and Roedder-John indicate that dilution effect do occur when the extension across inconsistency of product category and brand beliefs. The failure of extension may come from difficulty of connecting with parent brand, a lack of similarity and familiarity and inconsistent IMC messages.

"Equity of an integrated oriented brand can be diluted significantly from both functional and non-functional attributes-base variables", which means dilution does occur across the brand extension to the parent brand. These failures of extension make consumers create a negative or new association relate to parent brand even brand family or to disturb and confuse the original brand identity and meaning.

In addition, Martinez and de Chernatony classify the brand image in two types: the general brand image and the product brand image. They suggest that if the brand name is strong enough as Nike or Sony, the negative impact has no specific damage on general brand image and "the dilution effect is greater on product brand image than on general brand image". In consequence, consumer may maintain their belief about the attributes and feelings from parent brand. On the other hand, their study shows that "brand extension dilutes the brand image, changing the beliefs and association in consumers' mind".

The flagship product is a money-spinner to a firm. Marketer spends budget and time to create maximum exposure and awareness for the product. Theoretically speaking, flagship product is usually had the top sales and highest awareness in its product category. In spite of Aaker and Keller's research reported that the prestige brand do no harm from failure of extension. Evidence shows that the dilution effect has great and instant damage to the flagship product and brand family. But in some findings, even overall parent belief is diluted; the flagship product would not be harmed. In addition, brand extension is also "diminish consumer's feelings and beliefs about brand name." To establish a strong brand, it is necessary to build up a "brand ladder".

Marketers may go behind the order and model created by Aaker and Keller which they are authorities on brand management. But branding does not always follow a rational line. One mistake can damage all brand equity. A classic extension failure example would be Coca Cola launching "New Coke" in 1985. Although initially accepted a backlash against "New Coke" soon emerged among consumers. Not only did Coca Cola not succeed in developing a new brand but sales of the original flavour also decreased. Coca Cola were had to make considerable efforts to regain customers who had turned to Pepsi cola.

Although there are few works about the failure of extensions, literature still provides sufficient in depth research around this issue. Studies also suggest that brand extension is a risky strategy to increase sales or brand equity. It should consider the damage of parent brand no matter what types of extension are used. Example. BIC Pens tried to produce BIC pantyhose.

BRAND EQUITY

Brand equity is defined as the main concern in brand management and IMC campaign. Every marketer should pursue the long term equity and pay attention to every strategy in detail. Because a small message dissonance would cause great failure of brand extension. On the other hand, consumer has his psychology process in mind.

The moderating variable is a useful indication to evaluate consumer evaluation of brand extension. Throughout the categorisation theory and associative network theory, consumer does have the ability to process information into useful knowledge for them. They would measure and compares the difference between core brand and extension product through quality of core brand, fit in category, former experience and knowledge, and difficulty of making.

Consequently, in this article may conclude some points about consumer evaluation of brand extension:

- Quality of core brand creates a strong position for brand and low the impact of fit in consumer evaluation.
- Similarity between core brand and extension is the main concern of consumer perception of fit. The higher the similarity is the higher perception of fit.
- Consumer's knowledge and experience affect the evaluation before extension product trail.
- The more innovation of extension product is, the greater positive fit can perceive.

A successful brand message strategy relies on a congruent communication and a clear brand image. The negative impact of brand extension would cause a great damage to parent brand and brand family. From a manager and marketer's perspective, an operation of branding should maintain brand messages and associations within a consistency and continuum in the long way. Because the effects of negative impact from brand extension are tremendous and permanently. Every messages or brand extension can dilute the brand in nature.

BRAND IMPLEMENTATION

Brand implementation refers to the physical application of brand identity across visual identity carriers. This can include signage, uniforms, liveries and branded merchandise. Brand implementation encompasses facets of architecture, product design, industrial design, quantity surveying, engineering, procurement, project management and retail design.

Brand implementation emerged as a discipline in the 1990s when brand owners recognized the need for consistency across branded estates. Traditionally, brand implementation was handled by various parties, including shop-fitters, interior designers and sign companies. Lack of centralized project management led to inconsistencies, while information dissymmetry meant suppliers had too much control over brand issues. Brand implementation was thus coined as an umbrella term for all aspects of the application and maintenance of physical brand assets.

Today

Brand implementation is now a critical discipline focused on binding the relationship between the target audience and the brand. This allows brand implementation firms to identify the best possible manufacturing solution for each project.

Magic and Logic

Brand implementation does not involve the design or creation of brand identity. Instead, brand implementation agencies work closely with branding agencies to ensure that the latter's work is applied accurately and consistently. This relationship is referred to as Magic and Logic (RTM of Marketing Supply Chain International). Branding agencies look after the Magic (creative) and brand implementation agencies look after the Logic (implementation).

BRAND LOYALTY

Brand loyalty, in marketing, consists of a consumer's commitment to repurchase or otherwise continue using the brand and can be demonstrated by repeated buying of a product or service or other positive behaviors such as word of mouth advocacy.

Brand loyalty is more than simple repurchasing, however. Customers may repurchase a brand due to situational constraints (such as vendor lock-in), a lack of viable alternatives, or out of convenience. Such loyalty is referred to as "spurious loyalty". True brand loyalty exists when customers have a high relative attitude toward the brand which is then exhibited through repurchase behaviour. This type of loyalty can be a great asset to the firm: customers are willing to pay higher prices, they may cost less to serve, and can bring new customers to the firm. For example, if Joe has brand loyalty to Company A he will purchase Company A's products even if Company B's are cheaper and/ or of a higher quality.

An example of a major brand loyalty programme that extended for several years and spread worldwide is Pepsi Stuff. Perhaps the most significant contemporary example of brand loyalty is the dedication that many Mac users show to the Apple company and its products. From the point of view of many marketers, loyalty to the brand — in terms of consumer usage — is a key factor.

Usage Rate

Most important of all, in this context, is usually the 'rate' of usage, to which the Pareto 80-20 Rule applies. Kotler's 'heavy users' are likely to be disproportionately important to the brand (typically, 20 per cent of users accounting for 80 per cent of usage — and of suppliers' profit).

As a result, suppliers often segment their customers into 'heavy', 'medium' and 'light' users; as far as they can, they target 'heavy users'.

Loyalty

A second dimension, however, is whether the customer is committed to the brand.

Philip Kotler, again, defines four patterns of behaviour:

- *Hardcore loyals*: Who buy the brand all the time.
- *Softcore loyals*: Loyal to two or three brands.
- *Shifting loyalty*: Moving from one brand to another.
- Switchers: With no loyalty (possibly 'deal-prone', constantly looking for bargains or 'vanity prone', looking for something different).

Factors Influencing Brand Loyalty

It has been suggested that loyalty includes some degree of pre-dispositional commitment toward a brand. Brand loyalty is viewed as multidimensional construct. It is determined by several distinct psychological processes and it entails multivariate measurements. Customers' perceived value, brand trust, customers' satisfaction, repeat purchase behaviour, and commitment are found to be the key influencing factors of brand loyalty. Commitment and repeated purchase behaviour are considered as necessary conditions for brand loyalty followed by perceived value, satisfaction, and brand trust. Fred Reichheld, one of the most influential writers on brand loyalty, claimed that enhancing customer loyalty could have dramatic effects on profitability. Among the benefits from brand loyalty — specifically, longer tenure or staying as a customer for longer — was said to be lower sensitivity to price. This claim had not been empirically tested until recently. Recent research found evidence that longer-term customers were indeed less sensitive to price increases.

Industrial Markets

In industrial markets, organizations regard the 'heavy users' as 'major accounts' to be handled by senior sales personnel and even managers; whereas the 'light users' may be handled by the general salesforce or by a dealer.

Portfolios of Brands

Andrew Ehrenberg, then of the London Business School said that consumers buy 'portfolios of brands'. They switch regularly between brands, often because they simply want a change.

Thus, 'brand penetration' or 'brand share' reflects only a statistical chance that the majority of customers will buy that brand next time as part of a portfolio of brands they favour. It does not guarantee that they will stay loyal.

Influencing the statistical probabilities facing a consumer choosing from a portfolio of preferred brands, which is required in this context, is a very different role for a brand manager; compared with the — much simpler — one traditionally described of recruiting and holding dedicated customers. The concept also emphasises the need for managing continuity.

Market Inertia

One of the most prominent features of many markets is their overall stability — or inertia. Thus, in their essential characteristics they change very slowly, often over decades — sometimes centuries — rather than over months. This stability has two very important implications. The first is that those who are clear brand leaders are especially well placed in relation to their competitors and should want to further the inertia which lies behind that stable position.

This, however, still demands a continuing pattern of minor changes to keep up with the marginal changes in consumer taste (which may be minor to the theorist but will still be crucial in terms of those consumers' purchasing patterns as markets do not favour the over-complacent). These minor investments are a small price to pay for the long term profits which brand leaders usually enjoy.

The second, and more important, is that someone who wishes to overturn this stability and change the market (or significantly change one's position in it), massive investments must be expected to be made in order to succeed. Even though stability is the natural state of markets, sudden changes can still occur, and the environment must be constantly scanned for signs of these.

EXAMPLES OF BRAND LOYALTY PROMOTIONS

My Coke Rewards

My Coke Rewards is a customer loyalty marketing campaign for the Coca-Cola soft drink. Customers enter codes found on specially marked packages of Coca-Cola products on a website. Codes can also be entered "on the go" by texting them from a cell phone.

These codes are converted into virtual "points" which can in turn be redeemed by members for various prizes or sweepstakes entries. The programme was first launched in 2006. By November of that year, more than one million prizes had been redeemed. The programme has since been extended every year for the past four years with the current extension announced on November 6th, 2009 until 2010.

Limitations

The programme has always featured limits on the number of codes and points that could be redeemed at one time. Prior to February 17, 2009, members were limited to entering 10 codes per day, regardless of the number of points that this represented. Members who entered 10 codes from 24-can packages could, under this system, earn a total of 200 points per day, or 1400 per week. This represented that maximum rate at which points could be accrued without the use of bonus points and similar promotions.

On February 17, 2009, this system was changed. Members are now limited to entering 120 points per week, regardless of the number of codes redeemed per week. Bonus points and promotional offers such as "Double Points Days" are still not subject to this weekly limit. My Coke Rewards now has a meter that tells the member how many points they earned during the current week, and whether they have reached the 120 point-per-week limit. Attempts to enter codes that exceed the limit (for example, entering 10-point code once you have accumulated 119 points) do not cause overflow; the participant is told to "hold on to that code".

In addition, MyCokeRewards features an expiration date of codes that are entered. Currently, points expire after 90 days of user account inactivity, meaning a customer must either add points to their account or claim a prize within 90 days to ensure their points do not expire.

Code Reuse

There are two types of codes: single-use and multi-use codes. Single-use codes like those found on Coke products contain a mix of letters and numbers.

These codes can only be used once; if they have been entered in any account they will not work again. By contrast, multi-use codes are identified by being all numeric and may be entered by multiple users. Thus far the multi-use codes have all started with the digits 10008. They have been distributed through email, including during the 2006 Christmas holiday season, as well as through direct mail and print advertising campaigns in various magazines and other publications. Both Blockbuster and Disney (with Pirates of the Caribbean) have participated in such special promotions.

Controversy

The programme is one of several marketing campaigns that have come under fire from the Centre for Digital Democracy, an advocacy group interested in regulating how food products are marketed to children.

Coca-Cola's online marketing techniques are included in a 98-page report issued in May 2007 by the centre and the American University called "Interactive Food & Beverage Marketing: Targeting Children and Youth" which criticizes the programme for collecting personal information from children and for promoting obesity.

Childhood obesity was also a concern for weight-loss instructor Julia Griggs Havey who sued Coca-Cola over the programme in 2006, but dropped her lawsuit a few weeks later. The lawsuit was dropped for the specific reason of it being frivolous, since there was a misinterpretation as to what was required of a user in order to accumulate Coke points and obtain the currently available reward prizes.

The first assumption—that those who have Coke codes must purchase the product in order to redeem them—was shown to be untrue, as Coke stated they took into consideration that users may obtain codes from others. Second, it was pointed out that the CocaCola Company has other products besides Coca-Cola, including Powerade and Dasani water that are available for those who do not wish to consume high amounts of high fructose corn syrup or caffeine.

Some customers have further accused Coca-Cola of utilizing "bait-and-switch" tactics in the programme. They claim that the prizes for which they had been saving are either constantly out of stock or are no longer available. Some items have experienced steep unexpected price increases, as well; for example the coupons for a free 20 ounce bottle of Coke increased 25% (from 24 points to 30), a $75 Blockbuster gift card which used to cost 722 points went up to 1020 points (a 41% increase), and the price of a GPX docking station went up from 975 points to 1820 (an 87% increase).

These increases, it should be noted, took place at the same time as Coca-Cola was taking drastic measures to decrease the number of points awarded (through its February 2009 rule changes which reduced the maximum number of points from 1400 per week to 120 per week).

For its part, Coca Cola has maintained that all prizes in the My Point Rewards programme are available "while supplies last," and that there is no guarantee expressed or intended that a given prize will either continue to be offered or continue to be offered at the same price. Some prizes are advertised as "free." For example, you may redeem points for a "free 20 oz. sparkling product." What you receive is a manufacturers coupon. These coupons are not accepted at all retailers who sell Coca-Cola products, which can be frustrating to customers. Also, when you find a retailer who does accept the coupons, you are responsible for sales tax on the retail price of the product plus any state container deposits.

In California, for example, redeeming a "free" coupon for a 20 oz. beverage will cost the consumer $.20. Ounce-for-ounce, that is only slightly less than paying full retail for bulk packaging of the same product.

Pepsi Stuff

Pepsi Stuff refers to a promotion launched by PepsiCo, first in North America and then around the world, in the 1990s and continuing into the 2000s featuring merchandise that could be purchased with Pepsi Points. Customers can acquire points from specially marked Pepsi packages and fountain cups. Additional points have been sold both by Pepsi and by consumers, the latter mainly enabled by eBay.

1990s Campaigns

Points were distributed on billions of packages and cups and millions of consumers participated. According to some sources, the first Pepsi Stuff campaign significantly outperformed The Coca-Cola Company's much-anticipated Atlanta Olympics Summer with growth 3 times larger than Coca-Cola's and 2 points of share gained by Pepsi.

Pepsi Stuff continued to run throughout North America due to consumer and bottler demand, and was eventually expanded to include Mountain Dew and other drinks, and into many international markets. In response to the campaign, The Coca-Cola Company accelerated and extended its discount pricing programs.

Pepsi Stuff was one of the first major consumer promotions to feature a dedicated interactive Web site. Celebrities like Andre Agassi, David Beckham, Beyoncé, Cindy Crawford, Jimmy Fallon, Jeff Gordon, Derek Jeter, John Lee Hooker, Shaquille O'Neal, Deion Sanders, Shakira, Britney Spears, and the Spice Girls appeared in TV, print, and Internet advertising promoting Pepsi Stuff. PepsiCo produced over 200 million catalogs each year, billions of Pepsi points, and an extensive line of free merchandise.

2000s Campaigns

In the years after the initial Pepsi Stuff promotion, both Pepsi and Coca-Cola have introduced other promotions in a similar vein to the original campaign. Some promotions involved a variety of merchandise, while others involved specific products, such as Cash or MP3s. Permanent merchandise campaigns began in 2005 when The Coca-Cola Company launched iCoke, a very similar programme in which consumers collect points printed on packages, in Canada, with its introduction in the United States in 2006 as "My Coke Rewards."

Also in 2006, Pepsi introduced Pepsi Access in Canada to compete with iCoke, although that campaign ended in 2007. In 2008, Pepsi relaunched the programme, this time in partnership with Amazon MP3 and with a dedicated website that provides a "shopping" experience modeled on the Amazon website. Amazon's partnership follows to Amazon's actual website, where the option to pay for certain designated items with Pepsi Points instead of traditional payment methods, is available. Pepsi is once again relying on celebrities to advertise the promotion, including a Super Bowl spot starring Justin Timberlake and featuring Andy Samberg from Saturday Night Live.

Different product have codes worth different point values; single bottles generally have one point while can 12-packs have two and 24-packs have four. Codes from Pepsi NFL Kickoff 12-packs are worth four points. Items available for redemption through the promotion range in value from 5 points (MP3 song download) to 175 points (Vintage Pepsi logo hoodie sweatshirt). Customers can also redeem points for entry in various sweepstakes.

BRAND ORIENTATION

Brand orientation is a deliberate approach to working with brands, both internally and externally. The most important driving force behind this increased interest in strong brands is the accelerating pace of globalization. This has resulted in an ever-tougher competitive situation on many markets. A product's superiority is in itself no longer sufficient to guarantee its success. The fast pace of technological development and the increased speed with which imitations turn up on the market have dramatically shortened product lifecycles. The consequence is that product-related competitive advantages soon risk being transformed into competitive prerequisites. For this reason, increasing numbers of companies are looking for other, more enduring, competitive tools – such as brands. Brand orientation refers to "the degree to which the organization values brands and its practices are oriented towards building brand capabilities".

BRAND MANAGEMENT

Brand management is the application of marketing techniques to a specific product, product line, or brand. It seeks to increase the product's perceived value to the customer and thereby increase brand franchise and brand equity. Marketers see a brand as an implied promise that the level of quality people have come to expect from a brand will continue with future purchases of the same product. This may increase sales by making a comparison with competing products more favorable. It may also enable the manufacturer to charge more for the product. The value of the brand is determined by the amount of profit it generates for the manufacturer. This can result from a combination of increased sales and increased price, and/or reduced COGS (cost of goods sold), and/or reduced or more efficient marketing investment.

All of these enhancements may improve the profitability of a brand, and thus, "Brand Managers" often carry *line-management* accountability for a brand's P&L (Profit and Loss) profitability, in contrast to marketing *staff* manager roles, which are allocated budgets from above, to manage and execute. In this regard, Brand Management is often viewed in organizations as a broader and more strategic role than Marketing alone.

The annual list of the world's most valuable brands, published by Interbrand and *Business Week*, indicates that the market value of companies often consists largely of brand equity. Research by McKinsey & Company, a global consulting firm, in 2000 suggested that strong, well-leveraged brands produce higher returns to shareholders than weaker, narrower brands. Taken together, this means that brands seriously impact shareholder value, which ultimately makes branding a CEO responsibility. The discipline of brand management was started at Procter & Gamble PLC as a result of a famous memo by Neil H. McElroy.

Principles

A good brand name should:

- Be protected (or at least protectable) under trademark law.
- Be easy to pronounce.
- Be easy to remember.
- Be easy to recognize.
- Be easy to translate into all languages in the markets where the brand will be used.
- Attract attention.
- Suggest product benefits (e.g.: Easy-Off) or suggest usage (note the tradeoff with strong trademark protection.)
- Suggest the company or product image.
- Distinguish the product's positioning relative to the competition.
- Be attractive.
- Stand out among a group of other brands.

Types of Brands

A number of different types of brands are recognized. A "premium brand" typically costs more than other products in the same category. These are sometimes referred to as 'top-shelf' products. An "economy brand" is a brand targeted to a high price elasticity market segment. They generally position themselves as offering all the same benefits as a premium product, for an 'economic' price. A "fighting brand" is a brand created specifically to counter a competitive threat. When a company's name is used as a product brand name, this is referred to as corporate branding. When one brand name is used for several related products, this is referred to as family branding. When all a company's products are given different brand names, this is referred to as individual branding.

When a company uses the brand equity associated with an existing brand name to introduce a new product or product line, this is referred to as "brand extension." When large retailers buy products in bulk from manufacturers and put their own brand name on them, this is called private branding, store brand, white labelling, private label or own brand (UK). Private brands can be differentiated from "manufacturers' brands" (also referred to as "national brands"). When different brands work together to market their products, this is referred to as "co-branding". When a company sells the rights to use a brand name to another company for use on a non-competing product or in another geographical area, this is referred to as "brand licensing."

An "employment brand" is created when a company wants to build awareness with potential candidates. Earlier it was not existing but now we see commodities being branded, this is called commodity branding.

Brand awareness

Functions of Brand

For Consumers Identification of source of product, Assignment of responsibility to product maker, Risk reducer, Search cost reducer, Symbolic device, Signal of quality. For Manufacture Means of identification to simplify handling or tracing, Means of legally protecting unique features, Signal of quality level to satisfied customers, Means of endowing products with unique associations, Source of competitive advantage, Source of financial returns.

Brand Architecture

The different brands owned by a company are related to each other via brand architecture. In "product brand architecture", the company supports many different product brands with each having its own name and style of expression while the company itself remains invisible to consumers. Procter & Gamble, considered by many to have created product branding, is a choice example with its many unrelated consumer brands such as Tide, Pampers, Abunda, Ivory and Pantene.

With "endorsed brand architecture", a mother brand is tied to product brands, such as The Courtyard Hotels (product brand name) by Marriott (mother brand name). Endorsed brands benefit from the standing of their mother brand and thus save a company some marketing expense by virtue promoting all the linked brands whenever the mother brand is advertised. The third model of brand architecture is most commonly referred to as "corporate branding". The mother brand is used and all products carry this name and all advertising speaks with the same voice. A good example of this brand architecture is the UK-based conglomerate Virgin. Virgin brands all its businesses with its name

Techniques

Companies sometimes want to reduce the number of brands that they market. This process is known as "Brand rationalization." Some companies tend to create more brands and product variations within a brand than economies of scale would indicate. Sometimes, they will create a specific service or product brand for each market that they target.

In the case of product branding, this may be to gain retail shelf space (and reduce the amount of shelf space allocated to competing brands). A company may decide to rationalize their portfolio of brands from time to time to gain production and marketing efficiency, or to rationalize a brand portfolio as part of corporate restructuring. A recurring challenge for brand managers is to build a consistent brand while keeping its message fresh and relevant. An older brand identity may be misaligned to a redefined target market, a restated corporate vision statement, revisited mission statement or values of a company. Brand identities may also lose resonance with their target market through demographic evolution. Repositioning a brand (sometimes called rebranding), may cost some brand equity, and can confuse the target market, but ideally, a brand can be repositioned while retaining existing brand equity for leverage. Brand orientation is a deliberate approach to working with brands, both internally and externally.

The most important driving force behind this increased interest in strong brands is the accelerating pace of globalization. This has resulted in an ever-tougher competitive situation on many markets. A product's superiority is in itself no longer sufficient to guarantee its success. The fast pace of technological development and the increased speed with which imitations turn up on the market have dramatically shortened product lifecycles. The consequence is that product-related competitive advantages soon risk being transformed into competitive prerequisites. For this reason, increasing numbers of companies are looking for other, more enduring, competitive tools – such as brands. Brand Orientation refers to "the degree to which the organization values brands and its practices are oriented towards building brand capabilities".

Challenges

There are several challenges associated with setting objectives for a brand or product category.

- Brand managers sometimes limit themselves to setting financial and market performance objectives. They may not question strategic objectives if they feel this is the responsibility of senior management.

- Most product level or brand managers limit themselves to setting short-term objectives because their compensation packages are designed to reward short-term behaviour. Short-term objectives should be seen as milestones towards long-term objectives.
- Often product level managers are not given enough information to construct strategic objectives.
- It is sometimes difficult to translate corporate level objectives into brand- or product-level objectives. Changes in shareholders' equity are easy for a company to calculate. It is not so easy to calculate the change in shareholders' equity that can be attributed to a product or category. More complex metrics like changes in the net present value of shareholders' equity are even more difficult for the product manager to assess.
- In a diversified company, the objectives of some brands may conflict with those of other brands. Or worse, corporate objectives may conflict with the specific needs of your brand. This is particularly true in regard to the trade-off between stability and riskiness. Corporate objectives must be broad enough that brands with high-risk products are not constrained by objectives set with cash cows in mind. The brand manager also needs to know senior management's harvesting strategy. If corporate management intends to invest in brand equity and take a long-term position in the market (i.e. penetration and growth strategy), it would be a mistake for the product manager to use short-term cash flow objectives (ie. price skimming strategy). Only when these conflicts and tradeoffs are made explicit, is it possible for all levels of objectives to fit together in a coherent and mutually supportive manner.
- Brand managers sometimes set objectives that optimize the performance of their unit rather than optimize overall corporate performance. This is particularly true where compensation is based primarily on unit performance. Managers tend to ignore potential synergies and inter-unit joint processes.
- Overall organisation alignment behind the brand to achieve Integrated Marketing is complex.
- Brands are sometimes criticized within social media web sites and this must be monitored and managed (if possible)

Online Brand Management

Companies are embracing brand reputation management as a strategic imperative and are increasingly turning to online monitoring in their efforts to prevent their public image from becoming tarnished. Online brand reputation protection can mean monitoring for the misappropriation of a brand trademark by fraudsters intent on confusing consumers for monetary gain. It can also mean monitoring for less malicious, although perhaps equally damaging, infractions, such as the unauthorized use of a brand logo or even for negative brand information (and misinformation) from online consumers that appears in online communities and other social media platforms. The red flag can be something as benign as a blog rant about a bad hotel experience or an electronic gadget that functions below expectations.

DIGITAL BRAND ENGAGEMENT

Due to the way the Internet is fast evolving, especially through the social web and social media, there is now a plethora of digital channels which can be used to hold a dialogue between a Brand and a Consumer, or groups of consumers. Digital brand engagement is brand engagement with a key focus on communication via the web. The Cluetrain Manifesto written by four visionaries in 1999 (which is now a very long time ago) predicted the Internet would evolve to a point where the consumer holds the "power" and no longer could the corporate world continue to communicate to their markets (the people they wish to interact with) in a push marketing or broadcast manner. How right they were. The Internet has evolved and people/consumers can now be very selective about which brands they choose to interact with; and have the ability to communicate their thoughts and feelings globally.

Such mediums on the social web including blogs, micro-blogs, forums, social networks, groups within social networks, bookmarking sites, imagery and video sites can all be utilised by consumers; and they are doing just this in their thousands. Brands can take notice of what is being said about them, their product or service by monitoring conversations taking place outside of their own website, through "buzz monitoring" tools and there are a number of tools to chose from. The value of the information provided is proportional to the time and expertise dedicated to configuring and analysing the data provided. This value can be increased further when the buzz monitoring data is correlated with onsite web analytics data. It's important to listen and observe the buzz, and analyse its impact prior to engaging. The key elements to consider when listening and observing, before formulating a digital engagement strategy, are:

People/Consumer:

- Who are they?
- What are their values?
- What motivates them?
- How do they behave?

Location:

- Where are they?
- Are they just an Observer?

- Are they a Participant?
- Or are they Active Contributor?

Influence:

- Reach of conversation?
- Authority of dialogue and site?
- Volume and amount of buzz?
- Sentiment - (positive, negative, neutral)?
- Brand Association
- Are they inquisitive and looking for info?
- Are they about to commit to the Brand?
- Are they loyal brand advocates?
- Are they brand opponents?

Once you have an overview of what the current brand/consumer situation is online, you are far better informed to create an engagement strategy. The information above will provide a "Factual" position as it is based upon what people are actually doing and saying. There is another level of research that can be carried out which adds a "Predictive" element. i.e. undertake some consumer testing prior to implementing and engagement approach.

Typically, and traditionally this is carried out in a conscious level manner of research, such as focus groups, surveys and interviews. However, it is becoming recognised that conscious level research on its own can be flawed, as it is based upon the assumption that people are prepared to and are able to articulate what they are think on all levels. Therefore a combination of research at the conscious and unconscious level is recommended. Having obtained meaningful and valuable information from all the research and analysis, the time should now be right to start formulating the digital engagement strategy. In order to put some structure and process around this, the following approach is recommended, although there may be other methods which can be used.

People/Consumer:

- Create virtual representative consumer groups
- Understand why they need your brand
- Outline what aspects of the brand appeal to them
- Create content that has a value to each group

Location:

- Be present and available in the relevant online areas
- Be visible and offer free information
- Provide a platform/mechanism for interaction
- Engage with them observing the right etiquette

Influence:

- Prioritise the key influences
- Stimulate inter consumer dialogue
- Provide status and recognition for influencers
- Address negative comments by helping

Brand Association :

- Maximise your advocacy into creating interest
- Encourage inter consumer dialogue to minimise risk of commitment
- Reward your advocates and people loyal to your brand
- Reduce brand opponency where possible

The other key area to consider is full integration with "offline" brand engagement/marketing strategy. To maximise the returns, these need to be full synchronised and complemen-tary. Typically, offline marketing can be used to drive online interaction. Encouraging people to communicate with the brand.

9

Directors, Powers, Managerial Remuneration

INTRODUCTION

When a company is incorporated under the Companies Act, 1956, it becomes a legal entity capable of exercising all its functions. This impersonal creation of law can only act through some agency, and it must be a human agency. It being impracticable for all the members of a company to conduct its affairs they elect their representatives for this purpose. These elected representatives are usually known as directors. Under Section 2, a director "includes any person occupying the position of director by whatever name called" Directors of a company collectively are referred to as:'the Board of Directors[1]' or the "Board". Any person, in accordance with whose directions or instructions the Board of Directors of a company is accustomed to act. is also deemed to be a director of the comDanv.

LEGAL POSITION OF DIRECTORS

- *As trustees*: Although a director is described as a trustee, yet he is not a trustee in the true sense of the term; he is so only in a limited sense, *viz.*, he stands in a fiduciary relationship with his company. It has been said that directors are trustees. If this means no more than those directors in the performance of their duties stand in a fiduciary relationship to the company, the statement is true enough. But if this statement is meant to be an indication by way of analogy of what those duties are, it appears to me to be wholly misleading. I can see but little resemblance between the duties of a director and the duties of a trustee of a will or of a marriage settlement ". Since he is in a fiduciary relationship with the company, he is, to that extent, also a trustee of the company's assets which are under the director's control or which have come into their hands. He is a trustee in the sense that he must act in the interest of the company and not in his own interest. Because of his fiduciary relationship he must exercise the powers just as to the best of his judgement for good of the company and its shareholders. It is his duty to abide by the provisions of the articles and to exercise his power after due deliberation and careful consideration of what he is intending to do. His transactions must be fair and proper. Though the directors are trustees, even in the limited sense, for the company and the shareholders, they are not trustees for the creditors or for individual shareholders or for outsiders.

- *As agents*: Although directors are not agents in the legal sense, the law of agency governs the relationship between the company and its directors. Whenever an agent acting on behalf of his principal will be liable, the directors would also be liable in the like circumstances; where the liability would attach to the principal and the principal only. The liability is the liability of the company. Thus when directors act properly on behalf of the company, they do not incur personal liability; if they exceed their powers but the acts are *intra vires* the company, it can ratify the acts. They are not in the position of agents to shareholders. In certain respects, their powers are more extensive than those of agents because the shareholders who appoint them do not have much opportunity to control their acts.
- *As managing partners*: The directors who look after a company does so for themselves as well as for the shareholders. Their position is similar to that of managing partners, for they are appointed to their offices by an arrangement between them and other members. But they do not have all the powers or liabilities of managing partners. Even amongst the directors themselves there is no mutual agency as in the case of partners.

  "Directors" are described as trustees, agents of managing partners, not as exhausting their powers or responsibilities but as indicating useful points of view. It does not matter much what you call them, so long as you understand what their true position is, "they are commercial men managing a trading concern for the benefit of themselves and all other shareholders in it". The best way to describe their position is to say that they stand in a fiduciary position towards the company in regard to powers conferred on them by the articles.
- *Number of Directors*: The articles generally specify the maximum number of directors that a company may have. Every public company must have at least three directors. Every other company must have at least two directors.

APPOINTMENT OF DIRECTORS

You will appreciate that the competence and integrity of directors of a company go a long way in bringing about its success. The company, therefore, must be pretty choosy in selecting the proper persons to vest them with its management. Only an individual can be a director of a company.

Consequently a body corporate, firm or other association of persons cannot be appointed as director. Usually the articles of a company name the first directors but their appointment will be valid only if the conditions prescribed by Section 266(1) of the Act have been complied with namely

- That the director has given his consent in writing and the same has been filed with the Registrar; and
- That he has subscribed to the memorandum undertaking to purchase the qualification shares or has acquired the number of shares prescribed as the qualification for a director or has an affidavit with the Registrar to the effect that he shall take or pay for his qualification shares or that shares of the value not less than qualification shares, are registered in his name.
- Section 257 provides that a person who is not a retiring director and is other wise not disqualified must either himself or some other member intending to propose him must give a written notice of at least 14 days before the meeting along with a deposit of ₹500 which shall be refunded to such person or, as the case may be, to such member, if the person succeeds in getting elected as a director. The Amendment Act, 1988 has added this requirement of deposit of ₹500 to discourage frivolous notice to contest for election as director of a company. These restrictions, however, do not apply to the case of a private company.

Section 254 provides that "in default of and subject to any provisions in the articles" subscribers to the memorandum who are individuals shall be deemed to be the directors of the company till the company under Section 255 appoints directors. Generally, however, the articles name the first directors. Sometimes articles may also provide that both the number and the names of the first directors have to be determined in writing by subscribers to the memorandum or a majority of them. In such a case it has been held that a majority or subscribers should be present before the first directors could be validly appointed.

The Section 255, unless the articles provide for the retirement of all directors in every general meeting, at least 2/3rds of the total number of directors of the public limited company in question must, in the first place, be appointed, save as otherwise expressly provided in the Act by the company in general meeting; secondly, they must be persons whose period of office is liable to be determined by rotation. The remaining directors of such company must also be appointed in the same way unless some other provision for such appointments is made in the articles of the company concerned as where, for instance, the articles authorise a financial institution, which may have advanced large loans to the company to induct a director on the Board of the Company. Now, the general meeting italicised above may be either an annual general meeting or an extraordinary general meeting. But in practice, appointments of directors pursuant to Section 255 are made, at the first annual general meeting after the in corporation of the company. Persons who are named, as directors in the articles of the public company have to retire from office at such meeting unless any of them had been appointed under an authority conferred upon some person by the articles as aforesaid. The provisions as regards the retirement of directors by rotation are designed, in the words of Justice Sarkar "to eradicate the mischief caused by self-perpetuating managements" *Oriental Metal pressing works vs. Bhaskar A.I.R 1961.* In Section 256, out of the 2/3rds rotational directors only 1/3rds must retire by rotation at one general meeting. If the number is not three or multiple of three, then the number nearest to 1/3 must retire from office.

First those directors who are the longest in office must retire. If two directors have been appointed on the same day, their retirement will be determined either mutually or by lot. The vacancies caused by such retirement may be filled in the same annual general meeting by appointing either the retiring directors or some other person. But the meeting may also decide that the vacancies shall not be filled. Where, however, the meeting has not done either of two, and then the meeting is deemed to have been adjourned for a week. If at the adjourned meeting held after the said week, fresh appointment is not made and if no resolution against appointment is passed, then the retiring directors shall be deemed to have been appointed except in the following cases:

- Where at the meeting or at the previous meeting the resolution for the reappointment of a particular director was put to vote but lost;
- Where the retiring director has expressed his unwillingness to be reappointed by a written notice addressed to the company or its Board of Directors;
- Where he is unqualified or has been disqualified for appointment; and
- Where any special or ordinary resolution is required for his appointment or reappointment.

You should also remember that a director who is to retire by rotation at an annual general meeting cannot continue in office after the last day on which the meeting ought to have been called as required by Section 166. It should further be noted that a company, which does not carry on business for profit, or a company, which by its articles prohibits the payment of dividend to its members, would not be affected by the provisions of Sections 177, 255, 256 and 263. Section 177 provides that at any general meeting a resolution put to vote at the meeting shall unless a poll is demanded be decided on a show of hands.

Section 255 provides that at least 2/3rds of the directors shall retire by rotation Section 256 provides that 1/3rds of the retiring directors shall retire every year. Section 263 provides each director should be elected separately.

Such a company, which does not carry on business for profit or prohibits the payment of dividend to its members may provide by its articles for election of directors by ballot. The Companies that will come under this section would be mostly the Chambers of Committee, Clubs and other associations licensed under Section 25 of the Act where, in most cases, there exists a practice of electing office bearers by ballot. In some companies where the articles provide election of directors by ballot, if the context permits the word 'ballot' would probably mean 'poll'.

- *Right of person other than retiring Director to stand for Directorship*: In terms of Section 257 as amended by the Amendment Act of 1988, a person other than a retiring director proposing himself as a director, or any member proposing him for directorship has to not less than fourteen days before the meeting give notice signifying his candidature along with depositing with the company concerned a sum of ₹500 which shall be refunded to such person or member in the event the person concerned succeeds in getting elected as a director of the company. Conversely as clarified by circular nos. of 1989 dt. 15.9.89, in case such a person is not elected as director, he or the member, as the case may be, will not be entitled to the refund of ₹500 and the amount deposited shall stand forfeited by the company.

This provision, it may be noted, does not apply to the appointment of directors otherwise than by the company in the general meeting. Nor does it apply to a private company, which is not subsidiary of a public company. The company shall inform its members of the candidature of a person for the office of director or the intention of a member to propose such person as a candidate for that office, by serving individual notices on the members not less than seven days before the meeting.

But the company may avoid serving individual notices as aforesaid if the company advertises such candidature or intention not less than seven days before the meeting in at least two newspapers circulating in the place where the registered office of the company is located, of which one is published in the English language and the other in the regional language of that place. Sub-section (1A) will have to be complied with by all companies, public and private.

- Appointment by proportional representation: But the articles of a public company or a private company which is subsidiary of a public company may adopt the principal of proportional representation for appointing not less than $2/3^{rd}$ if the total number of the directors, whether by a single transferable vote or by a system of cumulative voting or otherwise. In such a case, appointments will be so made once in every three years and interim casual vacancies will be filled in conformity with the provisions of Sections 262 and 265.

Cumulative voting denotes that if there are five candidates or distributes his five votes. He can cast all the five votes in favour of one candidate or distribute his five votes among different candidates. This system of voting ensures that the Board will have fair representation of the minority interest.

- *Increase in the number of Directors*: A public company may by an ordinary resolution, increase or reduce the number of its directors within the limits fixed by the articles buy any increase in the number of its directors beyond the maximum permissible under the articles must be by a special resolution and have the approval of the Central Government. Where, however, such permissible maximum is 12 or less, no approval of the Central Government shall be required if the increase does not make the total number of directors more than 12. In other words, the approval of the Government would not be required for increase in the number of director's upto 12 irrespective of the provision in the articles of association.
- If the articles fix no maximum or minimum, the provision as to minimum required by Section 252 will govern. Any resolution in any manner increasing the number above twelve as fixed by the proviso will have to require Central Government approval.
- Appointment of Small Shareholders as Director: The Companies (Amendment) Act, 2000 has provided that a Public Company,
  - With a Paid-up Capital of ₹5 crores or more
  - 1000 or more small shareholders may have a director elected by such small shareholders as may be prescribed. In exercise of the powers conferred by Section 642 read with Section 252 of the Companies Act, 1956, the Central Government has framed the following rules, called the Companies Rules, 2001.

They shall come into force on the date of their publication in the Official Gazette Notification No. GSR 168(E), dated 9.3.2001. In this rules, unless the context otherwise requires "small Shareholder" means shareholder holding shares of nominal value of twenty thousand rupees or less in public company to which Section 252 of the Act applies.

These rules shall apply to public companies having:

1. Paid-up capital of five crores rupees or more;
2. One thousand or more small shareholders.

Manner of election of small shareholders' director:

- A company may act *suo moto* to elect a small shareholders' director from amongst small shareholders or upon the notice of small shareholders, who are not less than $1/10^{th}$ of total small shareholders and have proposed name of person who shall also be a small shareholder of the company.
- Small shareholders intending to propose a person shall leave a notice

of their intention with the company at least 14 days before the meeting under the signature of at least 100 small shareholders specifying name, address, shares held and folio number and particulars of share with differential rights as to divided and voting, if any, of the person whose name is being proposed for the post of director and of other small shareholders proposing such person as a candidate for the post of director or small shareholders.

- A person whose name has been proposed for the post of small shareholders' director shall sign, and file with the company, his consent in writing to act as a director.
- The listed public company shall elect small shareholders nominee subject to sub-rules (1), (2) and (3) above through the postal ballot.
- The unlisted company may appoint such small shareholders' nominee subject to conditions if majority of small shareholders recommend his candidates for the post of director in their meeting.
- Tenure of such small shareholders' director shall be for a maximum period of 3 years subject to meeting the requirement of provisions of Companies Act except that he need not have to retire by rotation.
- On expiry of his tenure, the same person if so desired by small shareholders, may be elected for another period of 3 years.
- Such director shall be treated as director for all other purposes except for appointment as whole time director or managing director.

Disqualification: A person shall not be capable of being appointed as small shareholders' director of a company, if:

- He has been found to be of unsound mind by a court of competence jurisdiction and the finding is in force;
- He is an un-discharged insolvent;
- He has applied to be adjudicated as an insolvent and his application is pending;
- He has been convicted by a court of any offence involving moral turpitude and from the date of expiry of the sentence;
- He has not paid any call in respect of shares of the company held by him, whether along or jointly with others, and six months from the last day fixed for the payment of call; or
- An order disqualifying him for appointment as director has been passed by a Court in pursuance of Section 203 and is in force, unless the leave of the court has been obtained for his appointment in pursuance of that section.

Vacation of office: A person appointed as small shareholders' director shall have to vacate the office if,

- Such person so elected, as director of small shareholders ceases to be a small shareholders' director on and from such date on which he ceased to be a small shareholder;

- He has been rendered disqualified by virtue of sub-rule (1) of rule 5;
- He fails to pay any call in respect of shares of the company held by him, whether alone or jointly with others, within six months from the last date fixed for the payment of the call;
- He absents himself from three consecutive meetings of the Board of directors, or from all meetings of the Board for a continuous period of three months, which ever is longer, without obtaining leave of absence from the Board;
- He is a partner of any private company of which he is a director, accepts, a loan, or any guarantee or security for a loan, from the company in contravention of Section 295;
- He acts in contravention of Section 299;
- He becomes disqualified by an order of court under Section 203;
- He is removed in pursuance of Section 284.

Restriction on number of directorship: No person shall hold office at the same time as small shareholders director in more than two companies.

- *Additional Directors*: When empowered by the articles, the Board of Director can appoint
- *Additional directors*: But such additional directors shall hold office only up to the date of
- *The next annual general meeting*: Also the total number of additional directors and other
- Directors together must not exceed the maximum strength fixed for the Board by the
- *Articles (Section* 260): This Section applies to all companies, public and private,
- *Additional Directors must acquire the qualification shares within two months*: The power under Section 260 can be exercised by a board even enough the strength of the board has fallen below the minimum. However, such appointment of additional Directors must be in the interest of the general body of shareholders.
- Can an additional Director Continue to be in office where the annual general
- Meeting is not held as per Section 166? In Krishna Prasad Pilani vs. Colaba Land Mills latest on the date on which the annual general meeting could have been held under Section 166. He cannot continue in office on the ground that the meeting was not held or could not be called within the time prescribed.
- Can an additional Director be appointed in general meeting? Where the articles have conferred the power of appointing additional directors on the Board of Directors the company in a general meeting is precluded from appointing additional directors. However, though

in ordinary circumstances the company in general meeting is precluded from appointing such directors yet if owing to a deadlock or otherwise there is no board capable of making the necessary appointment the company in a general meeting may do so.

- Casual Vacancy: Where the office of a director appointed by the public company in general meeting is vacated before his term of office expires in the normal course, resulting in a casual vacancy may, in default of and subject to any regulations in the articles, be filled by the Board of Directors at a meeting of the Board. (Section 262) Since Section 262 requires the filling of casual vacancy at a Board meeting, appointment can be made only by a validly convened and constituted Board meeting. This cannot be done by a resolution by circulation.
- Regarding the tenure of a director appointed against casual vacancy, sub-section (2) of Section 262 provides that the person appointed in the casual vacancy shall hold office only upto the date to which the director in whose place he is appointed would have held office.
- Appointment of directors by Central Government: Section 408 empowers the Central Government to appoint such number of persons as the Central Government may, by order in writing, specify as being necessary to effectively safeguard the interest of the company or its shareholders or the public interest for a maximum period of 3 years at a stretch, with a view to preventing the oppression of the members or mismanagement of the affairs of the company provided the conditions prescribed by the section are fulfilled.
- Appointment of alternate directors: The Board of Directors of a Company may, if authorised by its articles or by a resolution passed by the company in general meeting, appoint an alternate director to act for a director during his absence (for a period of not less than 3 months from the State in which meetings of the Board are ordinarily held). Such a director only officiates for the permanent incumbent and cannot hold office for a period longer than that permissible for the original director and as such vacates the office on the return of the original director. Also, if the term of office of the original director is determined before he returns, any provision for the automatic reappointment of retiring director in default of another appointment shall apply to the original director and not to the alternate director (Section 313).
- Assignment of office by director: Any assignment of office made after the commencement of the Act by any director is void [Section 312].
- It was held in *Oriental Metal Pressing Works Private Ltd. vs. B.K.*

Thakoor 1960 Bom. 167 that the appointment of person as Managing Director by the will executed by the existing Managing Director was void in view of the provisions contained in Section 312, since, just as to the High Court, the words 'any assignment' were comprehensive enough to include every assignment to transfer of a director or of the appointment by a director of a person to the office of a director in his place, whether by a deed *inter vivos* or by will. But this ruling has been reversed by the Supreme Court. The Court considers that the word 'assignment' in Section 312 does not mean or include appointment. From its every nature transfer inevitably imports the passing of a thing from one person to another. A transfer without the passage of the thing, even when that is an office is inconceivable. On the other hand, an 'appointment' has nothing to do with passing from one person to another; it connotes the putting in of someone in a vacancy. So transfer and appointment are dissimilar. It would be an unusual statute, which by using a single word intended to prohibit at the same time, two wholly different acts. A construction leading to such a result cannot be permitted.

- Who cannot be appointed as directors? The Companies Act prohibits undischarged insolvents and fraudulent persons from discharging any of the functions of a director. Under Section 202 if an undischarged insolvent discharges any of the functions of a director he is punishable with imprisonment (extending to 2 years) or fine (extending to ` 5000) or with both. 'Company in this context includes an unregistered company as well as a foreign company having an established place of business in India). Similarly, Section 203 provides that:
  - Where a person is convicted of an offence in connection with the promotion, formation or management of a company;
  - Where in the course of winding up of a company, it appears that
  - A person has been guilty of an offence under Section 542 (whether convicted or not),
  - Has been otherwise guilty while an "officer" of the company of any fraud, misfeasance or breach of duty in relation to the company, the Court may order that such person shall not, without the leave of the Court, be a director of a company for a period not exceeding 5 years. (The court as regards (a) includes the convicting court and as regards (b) the court having jurisdiction to wind up the company).

Furthermore, under Section 274 a person cannot be appointed as director of a company in any of the following cases, namely:

- Where he has been found to be of unsound mind by a court of competent jurisdiction and the finding is in force;

- Where he is an undischarged insolvent;
- Where he has applied to be adjudged as an insolvent and his application is pending;
- Where he has been convicted by a court of an offence involving moral turpitude and sentenced to an imprisonment for not less than six months and a period of five years has not elapsed from the date of expiry of the sentence;
- Where he has failed to pay any call in respect of shares held by him, whether singly or jointly with others and six moths have elapsed since the last day fixed for the payment of the call;
- Where he has been convicted of an offence in relation to promotion, formation or management of the company, or where has been found, during the course of winding up to be guilty of fraudulent conduct of business or misfeasance in relation to the company and as a consequence the Court has disqualified him from being appointed as director for a period not exceeding 5years.

A private company, which is not, a subsidiary of a public company can provide for additional grounds for disquali-fication. But a public company or its private subsidiary cannot provide for additional grounds for disqualification.

CLARIFICATIONS FROM THE DEPARTMENT OF COMPANY AFFAIRS ON DISQUALIFICATION OF DIRECTORS UNDER SECTION 274(1) (G) OF THE COMPANIES ACT, 1956

General Circular No. 8/2002 Dated 22-03.2001

- Issued by the Ministry of Law, Justice and Company Affairs, Department of Company Affairs vide No. 2/5/2-1-CLV; As you are aware, the provisions of Section 274 of the Companies Act, 1956 were amended through Companies (Amendment) Act, 2000 and a new clause (g) was inserted to sub-section (1) of this Section. Through this clause a director of a public company, which has made defaults in filing of annual accounts and annual returns and in repaying deposits/interests thereon on due date or redeeming its debentures on due date or in paying dividend for period specified in that section, is disqualified to be appointed as director of other public companies for a period of five years from the date on which such public company (ies) so defaulted.
- A high proportion of the companies had been defaulting in filing the annual accounts and annual returns and a large number of companies were defaulting in repayment of deposits/ interest thereon and in redemption of debentures which put investor to lots of hardships and the remedial action including a deterrent punishment

to the errant directors was essential. But ironically, the errant directors were not only continuing in the defaulting companies but becoming directors in other companies too. It was in this context that in the Companies Act, 1956 the new sub-section 274(1)(g) was inserted and the RBI also took some remedial measures.

- The intention and propose of the amendment was to disqualify the errant directors, protect the investors from mismanagement, ensure compliance in filing of annual accounts and annual returns which are means of a disclosure to all the stakeholders, increase the compliance rate of filing of the statutory documents and infuse good corporate governance in the regulation of corporate affairs in the country.
- The Department, however, has received representations from public financial institutions, Government owned financial companies and other financial Institutions and Companies in respect of these provisions. The Banking Division in the Finance Ministry has also supported the apprehension of the Financial Institution. The representation have been considered carefully keeping in view on the one hand, the need for strict compliance with the provisions of the clause (g) of sub-section (1) of Section 274 of the Companies Act, 1956 and on the other hand the non-obstante clause in statutes of some of the public Financial Institutions and the special situation of the nominee directors of public Financial Institutions/banks and the nominees of Central and State Government companies.
- *The Government has decided to*:
  - Clarify the legal position in respect of the Public Financial Institutions/banks having non-obstante clause in their statute;
  - To give some relief to the nominees of the Public Financial Institutions/Banks/Central and State Government;
  - To exempt Government Companies from the applicability of the provisions of Section 274(l)(g) of the Companies Act, 1956.
- While considering the applicability of the provisions of Section 274(1)(g) of the Companies Act, 1956, the Government has taken into account the following points:
- In addition to protecting the interest of the Public Financial Institutions/banks, which they represent, the Nominee Directors are also expected to serve the best interest of sound public policy and bring about higher levels of corporate governance.
- In view of implicit disqualification in Section 274(1)(g), qualified and experienced professionals, both official and non-official, suitable for being appointed on the Boards of assisted concerns may not agree/ available, thus adversely affecting the interests of the Banks/Financial Institutions.

- Presence of the Nominee Directors on the Boards of assisted concerns and close monitoring through them of all the affairs of the assisted concerns is for more desirable when the company is in default to the Banks/Financial Institutions.
- However, the Government hereby further clarifies that the Nominee Directors of public Financial Institutions/Banks/Government should in order to avail the relief granted are expected to comply with the following:
- The Nominee Directors are expected to work assiduously towards observance of good corporate governance practices in the company with due regard to the legitimate interest of the various shareholders. The various provisions relating to good corporate governance has been introduced in the Companies Act Rules/Regulations and clauses 49 of the Listing Agreement introduced by the SEBI. The Nominee Directors are expected to study these provisions of corporate governance and have them implemented.
- Ensure that the operations of the company are conducted in consonance with public policy.
- Ensure strict compliance in letter and spirit of all the statutory provisions in particular the provisions of the Companies Act and the regulations, clarifications etc. issued there under. It is the duty of the nominee directors to fully acquaint themselves in the relevant provisions of the Company Law and ensure that measures are instituted to monitor and certify that these statutory provisions are being observed.
- The Nominee Directors should see that important committees of the Board of Directors are constituted and are functioning effectively such as Audit Committee, Nominations Committee, Remuneration Committee etc. The Nominee Directors are expected to seek membership of these important committees and through their active participation in such committees ensure that the objectives of setting up these committees are being achieved. Public The Nominee Directors are expected to regularly attended and actively participate in the proceedings of the Boards and in committee on which they are included. Their frequent absence for sufficient reasons from the meetings of the Board of Directors/Committees would negate the purpose for which the Institutions have nominated the Nominee Directors and they would not be able to perform the various responsibilities listed out in this paragraph. Duly safeguard the interest of the Government/Banks/Financial Institutions, which they represent. Ensure proper utilisation of financial assistance by the assisted company and prevent any misuse/diversion of funds by the promoters/management of the companies.

- Provide adequate feedback to the nominating Institutions/banks/ Companies on the affairs and operations of the assisted concerns.
- The Financial Institutions are expected to closely monitor the participation by the Nominee Directors in the Boards/Committees as above and to ensure that they are discharging their responsibilities. In case any Nominee Director is failing to discharge his/her responsibilities the Institutions are expected to take steps to replace him/her. The Institutions are also expected to send a six monthly report to the Department of Company Affairs (DOCA) bringing out the steps taken by them to ensure that their Nominee Directors are discharging their responsibilities. The Financial Institutions should also in a separate section of their annual Report clearly bring out the measures instituted by them to ensure that the system of Nominee Directors is functioning effectively.

It is clarified that:

- Nominee Directors appointed by the Public Financial Institutions and Companies established under the Acts of Parliament having non-obstante provisions over the Companies Act, 1956, like IDBI, LIC, UTI, IIBI etc, in their respective statutes shall not be liable to be disqualified for appointment as directors by virtue of Section 274(1)(g) of the Companies Act, 1956.
- Nominee Directors appointed on the Boards of assisted concerns or other public companies by - (a) public financial institutions within the meaning of Section 4A of the Companies Act, 1956; (b) Central or State Government; and (c) banking companies are also exempt from the provisions of Section 274(1)(g) of the Companies Act, 1956.

Further in continuation of the Department's Circular No. 8/2002_dated 22nd March, 2002, it has been further clarified that default of privately placed bonds/ debentures/debt instruments by public financial institutions will not be considered as default to disqualify directors u/s 274(1)(g) of the Companies Act of 1956.

In exercise of the powers conferred by clause (b) of sub-section (1) of section 642 of the Companies Act, 1956 (1 of 1956), the Central Government hereby makes the following rules to carry out the purpose of clause (g) of sub-section (1) of section 274 of the said Act, namely.

Short title, commencement and extent:

- These rules may be called the Companies (Disqualification of Directors under section 274(1)(g) of the Companies Act, 1956) Rules, 2003.
- These rules shall come into force from the date of their notification in the Official Gazette.
- These rules shall apply to all public limited companies registered under the Companies Act, 1956.

Definitions

In these rules, unless the context otherwise requires,:

- "Disqualifying company" is the company in which the default has occurred on account of which a director stands disqualified;
- "Appointing company" is the company in which an individual is seeking appointment as a director, including re-appointment as director.

Disqualifications under clause (g) of sub-section (1) of section 274 of the Companies Act, 1956:

- Whenever a company fails to file the annual accounts and annual returns, as described in sub-clause (A) of clause (g) of sub-section (1) of section 274, persons who are directors on the last due date for filing the annual accounts and the annual returns for any continuous three financial years commencing on and after the first day of April, 1999, shall be disqualified.
- If a company has failed to repay any deposit, irrespective of the enactment, rules or regulations under which the deposits have been accepted by the companies, or interest thereon, or redeem its debentures, or pay any dividend declared on the respective due dates, and if such failure continues for one year, as described in sub-clause (B) of clause (g) of sub-section (1) of section 274, then the directors of that company shall stand disqualified immediately on expiry of that one year from the respective due dates:
- Provided that all the directors who have been directors in the relevant year, from the due date to the expiry of one year after the due date, will be disqualified:
- Provided further that disqualification on account of the reasons cited under this Rule shall also apply to the reappointment as a director.

Explanation- For the purpose of this rule, it is clarified that non-payment of dividend referred to in sub-clause (B) of clause (g) of sub-section (1) of section 274 due to the reason of dividend not being claimed or kept in separate bank account as required under section 205A of Companies Act, 1956 or paid into Investors Education and Protection Fund as required under section 205C of that Act shall not be deemed to be a failure to make payment of dividend.

DUTY OF STATUTORY AUDITOR TO REPORT ON DISQUALIFICATION

- It shall be the duty of statutory auditor of the appointing company as well as disqualifying company, as required under section 227(3)(f) to report to the members of the company whether any director is disqualified from being appointed as director under clause (g) of sub-section (1) of section 274 and to furnish a certificate each year as to whether on the basis of his examination of the books and records of the company, any director of the company is disqualified for appointment as a director or not.

- It shall be the duty of the statutory auditors of the "disqualifying company" as required in section 227(3)(f) to report to the members of the company whether any director in the company has been disqualified during the year from being re-appointed as director, or being appointed as director in another company under clause (g), of sub-section (1) of section 274.

DUTY OF COMPANY TO INTIMATE DISQUALIFICATION

- Whenever a company fails to file the annual accounts and returns, or fails to repay any deposit, interest, dividend, or fails to redeem its debentures, as described in clauses (A) and (B) of clause (g) of sub-section (1) of section 274, the company shall immediately file a return in duplicate in Form 'DD-B', prescribed under these rules for this purpose, to the Registrar of Companies, furnishing therein the names and addresses of all the Directors of the company during the relevant financial years:
- Provided that names of such directors who have been exempted from application of Section 274(1)(g) by the Central Government, from time to time, shall be excluded.
- Provided further that no unusual abbreviations or short forms shall be used in filling up the Form 'DD-B', which shall give such details as may be necessary to distinguish and identify each director without any ambiguity.

FAILURE TO INTIMATE DISQUALIFICATION SHALL RENDER DIRECTOR AS OFFICER IN DEFAULT

- When a company fails to file the Form 'DD-B' within 30 days of the failure that would attract disqualification under Section 274(1)(g), officers of the company listed in section 5 of the Companies Act, 1956 shall be officers in default.
- Upon receipt of the Form 'DD-B' in duplicate under Rule 5, the Registrar of Companies
- Shall immediately register the document and place one copy of it in the document file for public
- inspection.
- The Registrar of Companies shall forward the other copy to the Central Government.

NAMES OF THE DISQUALIFIED DIRECTORS ON THE WEB-SITE ETC

- The Central Government shall place on the web site of the

Department of Company Affairs the names and addresses and such other details including names and details of the companies concerned, as may be necessary, in respect of all the disqualified directors.

- The Central Government may also publicize the names of disqualified directors in such manner, as it may consider appropriate.
- The Central Government shall take such steps as may be required to update its web-sit to ensure that name of the person, in whose respect disqualification period has expire after 5 years, is deleted from the web-site.

DUTY OF EVERY DIRECTOR

- Every director in a public company registered under the Companies Act, 1956 shall file Forr 'DD-A', prescribed under these Rules, before he is appointed or re-appointed.
- If any question arises as to whether these rules are or are not applicable to a partials company, such question shall be decided by the Central Government.

PUNISHMENT FOR CONTRAVENTION OF THE RULES

If a company or any other person contravenes any provision of these rules for which n punishment is provided in the Companies Act, 1956, the company and every officer of the company who is in default or such other person shall be punishable with fine which ma extend to five thousand rupees and where the contravention is a continuing one, with a further fine which may extend to five hundred rupees for every day after the first, during which the contravention continues. On the commencement of these rules, all rules, orders or directions in force in relation t any matter for which provision is made in these Rules shall stand repealed, except as respect things done or omitted to be done before such repeal.

In exercise of the powers conferred by clause (a) of sub-section (1) of section 620 of the Companies Act, 1956 (1 of 1956), the Central Government hereby directs that clause (g) of sub-section (1) of section 274 of the said Act shall not apply to a Government company, a copy of this notification having been laid in draft before both Houses of Parliament as required by sub-section (2) of section 620 of the said Act.

- Can a Minor be appointed as a Director? In case of a minor there is no provision in the Act expressly disqualifying him. However, since a minor is not competent to contract. He cannot file with the Company or with the Registrar any valid consent to act as Director, as required under Section 264. But, as Section 264 applies only to public companies and private companies, which are their subsidiaries, there is nothing to prevent a minor becoming a Director of independent private companies. Restrictions on number of directorships: A person cannot hold office at the same time as director in more than *fifteen* companies excluding a private company which is not subsidiary or holding company of a public company, and unlimited company, an association not for profit and a company in which such person is only an alternate director (Sections 275 and 278). In this context let us now consider an illustration. A is director in 14 public limited companies. He is offered the directorship of,

- BC Private Limited;
- XYZ Ltd.;
- Indian Automobile Association, a company registered under Section 25 of the Companies Act. Can A accept these directorships? In the first case, A can accept the directorship of BC private Ltd. In view of the provisions of Section 278(l)(a), because private company, which is neither a subsidiary nor a holding company of a public company, is not to be counted in calculating the number of directorships as prescribed by Section 275. In the second case too; A can accept the directorship of XYZ Ltd. Because with this he becomes a director of 15 companies which is the prescribed maximum limit. In the third case as well, A can accept the directorship of the Indian Automobile Association because the directorship is also to be excluded from the computations of 15 directorships under Section 278(l)(c).

- Choice by person becoming director of more than 15 companies: Section 277 provides that where a person already holding the office of director in 15 companies is appointed as a director of any other company, the appointment:
  - Shall not take effect unless such person has within 15 days thereof, effectively vacated his office as director in any of the companies in which he was already a director; and
  - Shall become void immediately on the expiry of the 15 days if he has not before such expiry, effectively vacated his office as director in any of the other companies aforesaid.
- Where a person already holding office of director in 14 companies or less is appointed as a director of other companies, making the total number of his directorships more than 15, he shall choose the directorships which he wishes to continue to hold or to accept, so however that the total number or the directorships, old and new, held by him shall not exceed fifteen. Please note that none of the new appointments of Directors shall take effect until the aforesaid choice is made; and all the new appointments shall become void if the choice is not made within 15 days from the day on which the

last of them was made. According to Section 279 any person who holds office or act as a director of more than 15 companies in contravention of the aforesaid provisions shall be punishable with fine, which may extend to ₹.50,000 in respect of each of those companies exceeding fifteen.

- Consent of candidate for directorships: A person who is proposed as a candidate for the office of director, is required to sign and file with the company his consent to act as director (if appointed). However, a director retiring by rotation or otherwise or a person who has left at the office of the company a notice under Section 257 signifying his candidature for the office of a director, is not required to do so [Section 264(1)]. A person shall not act as a director unless he has signed and filed with the Registrar his consent in writing to act as director within 30 days of his appointment [Section 264(2)]. The aforesaid provision does not apply to:
  - Director reappointed after retirement by rotation or immediately on the expiry of term of his office;
  - An additional or alternate director, or a person filling a casual vacancy under Section 262 appointed as director or reappointed as an additional or alternate director immediately on the expiry of his term office,
  - A person named as director under the articles as first registered.
- Appointed of directors must be voted individually: Each director shall be appointed by a separate resolution in the case of a public company unless the meeting first agreed by resolution that the appointment shall be made by single resolution and no vote has been cast against it. A resolution moved in contravention of this provision shall be void, whether or not objection thereto was raised at the time it was so moved. Thus, two or more directors of a company cannot be elected as directors by a single resolution unless it is done in conformity with the provisions of Section 263. When such a resolution is passed, provision for automatic re-appointment of directors retiring by rotation shall not apply. Section 263 does not apply to a company whose articles provide for election of directors by ballot and which does not carry on business or prohibits the payment of a dividend to the members (Section 263A).
- *Principle of proportional representation for appointment of directors*: Under Section 265, a company can adopt the principle of proportional representation for the appointment of its directors, buy only if its articles so provide. In such a case, not less than 2/3rds of the total number of directors shall be appointed just as to the aforesaid principle, whether by the single transferable vote by a system of cumulative voting or otherwise. Such appointments are to be made

once in every three years and interim casual vacancies can be filled in accordance with the provision, *mutatis mutandis,* of Section 263.

SHARE QUALIFICATION FOR DIRECTORS

It is that number of shares which a shareholder must hold in order to be eligible for election as a director. The Companies Act, 1956 does not prescribe for any share qualification for a director. The articles of a company usually prescribe for such qualifications so that a director has a personal interest in the company. In the event of such a provision by the articles, it becomes incumbent on the part of every director to hold qualification shares and if does not hold them at the time of his appointment as director, he must acquire them within two months after his appointment as director. Any provision, made in the articles of the company requiring a person proposed for directorship to hold qualification shares either before appointment or within a third shorter than two months after his appointment will be void.

The nominal value of qualification shares must not exceed ₹5,000 and if the nominal value of each share is ₹5,000 or more than the number of shares prescribed, as qualification will be only one. It is, of course, not necessary for any company to insist upon the holding of shares for the purpose of qualification for directors. For the purpose of share qualification, the bearer of a share warrant is not deemed to be the holder of the shares mentioned in the warrant (Section 270). A Director acting without qualification shares is punishable with fine, which may extend to ₹500/- for every day during which he continues as director (Section 272). The provisions relating to the share qualification of a director do not apply to a private company, unless it is subsidiary of a public company (Section 273): nor do they apply to directors appointed by the Central Government under Section 408.

- *Vacation of office by director*: The office of a director shall become vacant if
  - He fails to obtain with in the prescribed time (two months) or ceases to hold thereafter the qualification shares when he is so required by the articles;
  - He is found to be of unsound mind by the Court;
  - He applies to be adjudged an insolvent;
  - He is adjudged as an insolvent;
  - He is convicted by a court of an offence involving moral turpitude and is sentenced to imprisonment for not less than six months;
  - He does not pay the call in respect of shares held by him within six months from the last date fixed for the payment. The Central Government can, by notification in Official Gazette, remove this disqualification;
  - Without obtaining leave of absence from the Board, he absents

himself from three consecutive meetings of the Board or from all meetings thereof for a continuous period of 3 months, whichever is longer;
- He, whether by himself or by any person for his benefit or on his account or any firm in which he is a partner or any private company of which he is a director, accepts a loan or any guarantee or security for a loan from the company without previous approval of the Government as required by Section 295;
- Having been appointed a director by virtue of his holding any office or other employment in the company, he ceases to hold such office or other employment in the company
- He fails to disclose his interest in contract or a proposed contract by the company as required by Section 299
- He is disqualified by an order of Court under Section 203 from acting as director of the company
- He is removed by the company in annual general meeting in pursuance of Section 284;
- He holds any office or place of profit in the company or its subsidiary without the consent of the company accorded by a special resolution.

• *Note*:
  - An alternate director vacates office when the original director returns [Section 313(2)].
  - A person vacates the office of director automatically in such other company after the expiry of 15 days if he, while holding directorship in 20 companies, is appointed director in other companies unless he gives notice of choice [Section 277(l)(b)].
• *Resignation of director*: A director can resign from his office. For this purpose, he must service a notice of his resignation upon the company. Palmer, however is of the view that if the articles permit a director to resign at any time, the resignation will be effective from the time of the service of the notice. There is no need for its acceptance by the Board or the company in general meeting. If, however, the articles contain no such provision then the resignation of the director will be effective only when he serves notice on the company or the Board and resignation is accepted by them.
• A verbal resignation is enough, though articles usually provide for a written notice. But a managing or governing or whole-term director cannot resign merely by giving a notice. In his case, a formal acceptance of resignation by the company is essential so as to make it complete and effective. This is because he occupies two positions or possesses two capacities, *viz.*,

- One that of a director,
- The other that of manager or officer of the company in the sense of a whole-time employee. An employee cannot give up office at his pleasure, simply by giving notice. The notice or the letter of resignation is required to be approved or accepted by the company and officer concerned has to be relieved of his duties and responsibilities attaching to the office which he has resigned from. However, in the case of an ordinary director, formal acceptance of resignation is not needed. A director cannot withdraw his resignation, without the consent of the company, even if such withdrawal is sought before the Board considered the resignation. Where the articles of a company provide that a person shall be a director for life or until he resigns, a director so appointed will not be entitled to damages against the company tor wrongful termination of contract on the company going into liquidation; the reason is that the articles operate so long as company exists and it must be deemed to have been contemplated by articles that office shall come to an end on the company going into liquidation.

REMOVAL OF DIRECTORS [SECTION 284]

A director may be removed from the office by an ordinary resolution before the period of office expires. But he cannot be removed in this way if he is the director of a company holding office for life on 1-4-1953. It is further provided that the directors appointed on the principle of proportional representation under Section 265 cannot be removed by an ordinary resolution as aforesaid.

Special notice shall be required for a resolution to remove a director under Section 284. On receiving the notice of this resolution the company must forthwith send a copy thereof to the director concerned, and the director shall be entitled to be heard on the resolution at the meeting. The director can make a representation in writing, a copy of which shall have to be sent to every member to whom the notice of the meeting is sent. If the copy of the representation is not sent either due to its having been received too late or due to the company's default, the director may get the representation read out at the meeting. However, the copy of the representation need not be sent out at the meeting if on the application of either the company or any person claiming to be aggrieved, the Court is satisfied that these rights are being abused to secure needless publicity for defamatory matter.

The right under the section is a statutory right given to the company to remove by an ordinary resolution, any director in whatsoever manner or on whatsoever terms appointed. Where the directors attempt to avoid their removal by omitting to call a meeting or by not attending with a view to creating a situation of no quorum, the Court/the Central Government will convene the necessary meeting under Section 186. Thus, where one of the only two director shareholders who was holding 51% shares wanted to remove his fellow director who did not attend the meeting to frustrate him because the articles required quorum of two, the Court (here it would have to be CLB) ordered a meeting to be called with the presence of one as sufficient quorum. What is important in this decision is the judicial recognition of the importance of a statutory right. The right of the majority shareholder to remove a director whom he fell out cannot be permitted to be vetoed by the quorum requirements.

The vacancy resulting from the aforesaid removal may be filled in by the appointment of another director at the same meeting at which the director is removed, provided special notice of the proposed appointment has been given. A director so replaced holds office for the remaining period for which the director who has been removed would have held office had he not been removed. If the members of the company do not fill the vacancy, the Board of Directors may fill it as casual vacancy. But the director who was so removed from office shall not be reappointed to the Board when the casual vacancy is filled.

The provisions do not deprive any director, so removed of his rights to compensation or damages payable to him in respect of the premature termination of the directorship, or of any appointment terminating with that as a director (Section 284).

REMOVAL OF MANAGERIAL PERSONNEL

In the principal Act, in part VI, (VIA) and Sections 388B, 388C, 388D and 388E dealing with the powers of the Central Government to remove managerial personnel from office on recommendation of the Company Law Board have been added by the Companies (Amendment) Act, 1963 the object of introduction of these Sections, as explained by the Finance Minister, being that the existing provisions in Sections 397 and 398 of the Companies Act and other that follow provide for the removal from office in a company of persons found to have been guilty of mismanagement in regard to the affairs of that company only. Section 274 disqualifies a person from being appointed as a director of a company if he is convicted by a court for any offence involving moral turpitude and sentenced to imprisonment for a period of not less than 6 months. But under these Sections, a conviction by a court is a prerequisite. This process, being very difficult and lengthy process, the Central Government has tried to find an alternative procedure for effecting removal of such persons from position of authority when the Central Government comes into possession of certain facts which indicate that any person concerned with the management of the affairs of a company has been guilty of negligence or default etc. in carrying out of his obligations and functions.

These Sections apply to companies both public and private, but do not apply to such body corporate as foreign companies, which are incorporated outside India, as they are not companies within the definition given in Section 3 of the Companies Act, 1956. Further, these Sections deal only with the person who is or has been in management and not with one whose concern with the management has ceased. These Sections will apply to a whole body of individuals constituting the Board of Directors. Though the explanation "managerial personnel" as enumerated in Section 197A does not include the Board of Directors or individual director, they will also come within the scope of Section 388B because they supervise, control and direct the manager. It may be construed from the construction of these Sections that directors come within the scope of the provisions of these Sections.

Reference to Company Law Board of cases against managerial personnel: There can be circumstances relating to the affairs of a company, which might suggest:

- That any person, concerned in the conduct and management of the affairs of a company is or has been guilty of fraud, misfeasance persistent negligence or default in carrying out his obligation and functions under the law or breach of trust in connection therewith;
- That the business of a company is not or has not been conducted and managed by such; person in accordance with sound business principles or prudent commercial practices;
- That the company is or has been conducted and managed by such person in a manner which is likely to cause or has in fact caused serious injury or damage to the interest of the trade, industry or business to which such company pertains;
- That the business is or has been conducted and managed by such person with an intent to defraud its creditors, members or any other persons or otherwise for a fraudulent or unlawful purpose or in a manner prejudicial to public interest.

If the Central Government is convinced that any one of the aforementioned circumstances exist, it may state a case against the person aforesaid and refer it to the Company Law Board with a request that the Board may enquire into the case and record its findings as to whether or not such a person is fit and proper to hold the office of director or any other office concerned with the conduct and management of any company. The statement of the case should be in the form of an application presented to the Company Law Board or such officer thereof as it may appoint in this behalf, and the person against whom such a case is stated and referred, should be joined as a respondent to the application.

The application should contain concise statement of such circumstances and materials, as the Central Government may consider necessary for purpose of enquiry to be made by the Company Law Board. The application must be signed and verified in the manner laid down in the Code of the Civil Procedure, 1908 for the signature and verification of a plaint in a suit by the Central Government. At any stage of the proceedings, the Company Law Board may allow the Central Government to alter or amend the application in such manner and on such terms as may be just and all such alterations or amendments shall be made may be necessary for the purpose of determining the real questions in the enquiry (Section 388B)

Interim order by Company Law Board:

- During the pendency of case before the Company Law board, certain situations might come to the knowledge of the Board which might necessitate the passing of an interim order restraining, in the interest of the members or creditors of the company, the delinquent person against whom the case is pending. In such situations, the Board may either on the application of the Central Government or on its own motion, by order, direct that the respondent (delinquent person) shall not discharge any of the duties of his office until further order and appoint in his stead another suitable person to discharge the duties connected with the office of the respondent subject to such terms and conditions as the Board may specify in the order. There person, who is temporarily called upon to discharge the duties in lieu of the respondent, will be regarded as a public servant within the meaning of Section 21 of the Indian Penal Code [Section 388C].

Findings of the Company Law Board:

- At the end of hearing of the case, the Company Law Board shall record its findings. In the findings it must specifically state as to whether or not the respondent is a fit and proper person to hold the office of director, or any office and to be concerned with the conduct and management of the company [Section 388D].

Power of the Central Government to remove managerial personnel:

- Either on the basis of the aforesaid finding of the Company Law Board or upon a decision of the Board, the Central Government may, notwithstanding any other provisions contained in this Act, by order remove the delinquent respondent from his office. An order of removal having been passed under Section 388E the person concerned will be debarred from holding the office for a period of five years from the date of the order of removal. This time-limit may, however, be relaxed by the Central Government with the previous concurrence of the Company Law Board, and the Central Government may accordingly permit such person to hold the office of a director or any other office connected with the conduct and management of the affairs of the company, even before the expiry of the period of five years. But, for the loss or termination of his office, he will not be entitled to or be paid any compensation in any event, even if there is anything contained in any other provisions of the Act, or any other law or contract, memorandum or articles. On the removal of the person the company may, with the previous approval of the Central Government, appoint another person to that office in accordance with the provisions of this Act. [Sections 388E(3), (4) and (5)].

DIRECTORS TO ACT AS A BOARD

Directors must act together as a body and generally, at meeting properly convened, unless special powers are delegated to an individual director. Every company must hold a meeting of the Board of Directors. Once in every three months and at least four such meetings shall be held in every year. (The Central Government can by notification direct that the provision of Section 285 shall not apply to any class of companies or shall apply in a modified form.) These provisions shall not be deemed to have been contravened merely by reason of the fact that the meeting of the Board, which had been properly called, could not be held for want of a quorum [Section 288(2)]. Notice of the Board's meeting must be given in writing to every director for the time being in India, and at his usual address in India (Section 286).

The quorum for a meeting of the Board of Directors must be one-third of its total strength (any fraction contained in that one-third being rounded off as one), or two directors whichever is higher. However, where at any time, the number of interested directors exceeds or is equal to two thirds of the total strength the number of directors who are not interested and who are present at the meeting not being less than two shall be the quorum. There must be at least 2 non-interested directors (Section 287). If the meeting could not be held for want of quorum, then unless the adicles otherwise provide, the meeting shall automatically stand adjourned till the same day in the next week at the same time and place, or if that day is a public holiday, till the next succeeding day which is not a public holiday at the same time and place (Section 288(1)].

Section 289 contains conditions, which must be complied with for the passing of a resolution by circulation. The resolution must be circulated in draft along with necessary papers to all the directors, or to all the members of the Committee not being less than the quorum fixed for the Board meeting then in India and to other directors and members at their usual addresses in India. Also the resolution must have been approved by such of the directors as are there in India, or by a majority of such of them as are entitled to vote on the resolution.

- *Passing of resolution by circulation*: Powers of the directors which are not expressly required to be exercised at the Board's meeting can also be exercised by means of resolutions passed by circulation. Moreover, a resolution in writing, signed by all the members of the Board or of a committee thereof, for the time being entitled to receive notice of a meeting of Board or Committee, shall be as valid and effectual as if it had been passed at a meeting of the Board or Committee, duly convened and held. Section 289 lays down the procedure for the passing of resolution by circulation. A resolution is deemed to have been duly passed by the Board or by Committee thereof by circulation only if:

- The resolution has been circulated in draft along with the necessary papers to all the directors or to all the members of the committee then in India (not being less in number than the quorum fixed for a meeting of the Board or Committee) and to all other directors or members at their usual address in India; and
- The resolution has been approved by such of the directors as are then in India, or by a majority or them as are entitled to vote on the resolution.

POWERS OF DIRECTORS AND RESTRICTIONS THEREON

The board of directors in entitled to exercise all such powers of the company and to do all such acts and things as the company is authorised to exercise and do. But the Board shall not exercise any power or do any act or thing which is, by the Act or any other statute or by the memorandum or articles of the company or otherwise required to be exercised by the company in general meeting. In exercising such powers the Board shall be subject to regulation made by the company in that general meeting (Section 291). But this 'subject to regulation' does not mean that the company in general meeting can override the Board's powers of carrying on the business, by prescribing a regulation, or passing a resolution, taking away the powers which have been conferred upon the Board by the articles. In generality the statement in the question is quite correct. The powers cover all the day-to-day activities for the company and the actions of the Board of Directors cannot be called into question. However in no case, can the directors usurp the powers vested by the articles in the body of shareholders, nor can the shareholders usurp the power vested likewise in the Board of Directors. The directors, being agents, are naturally subject to the will of their principal, *viz.*, the shareholders. Also because of the need to protect the interest of the shareholders, of the company and in the public interest the law has imposed certain restrictions on the powers of the Directors the most important of these are contained in Section 293 of the Companies Act.

The general powers of the Directors are subject to the following limitations:

- The Board of Directors must necessarily act just as to the Memorandum and the Articles of Association. The implication of this is that the Board or the shareholders cannot exercise certain powers, which are ultra vires the company. The acts which are *intra vires* the company *i.e.*, those powers which the company is entitled to exercise and the activities that the company engage itself in, fall within the purview of the Board of Directors generally, unless the Articles specifically reserve them for shareholders. For example, it is common that declaration of the dividend is reserved for the shareholders, to be decided upon at the Annual General Meeting. In case, power is reserved for the shareholders by the articles and the Directors happen to exercise that power, it is possible for the shareholders to ratify the action of the Board: in the final analysis, the power is exercised by the shareholders and not by the Directors.

- Certain power can be exercised only by the shareholders under law. In these, the Directors clearly have no authority. Some of the prominent examples are given below:
- Issue of shares at a discount [Section 79(2)(i)]
- Undertaking lines of business other than those mentioned in Memorandum as the main objects including auxiliary to those [Section 149(2A)].
- Selling or otherwise disposing of company's undertaking or substantial part of the undertaking (Section 293)].
- Investing, otherwise than in trust securities, the amount of compensation received by the company in respect of compulsory acquisition of the company's undertaking or of any premises or property used for in such undertaking (Section 293).
- Borrowing in excess of the aggregate of paid up capital plus free reserves (Section 293).
- Contributing in any financial year, to charitable and other funds not relating to the company's business, amounts exceeding ₹.50,000 or 5% of its average net profits during the three preceding financial years whichever is greater (Section 293 as amended by the Companies) (Amendment) Act, 1977).
- Issuing bonus shares or debentures.
- Reorganisation of capital and amendment of Articles or Memorandum of Association (Sections 94, 31 and 16 respectively).
- Winding up unless ordered by the Court (Section 484).
- Appointment of sole selling agents except that the Board can make the appointment subject to approval of the company in a general meeting within 6 months of the appointment (Section 294).

It follows that except in certain special matters, the Board of Directors can exercise all the powers and carry on all the activities that are necessary to achieve the object of the company.

A distinction, however, is necessary between the following three categories of powers and activities:

1. Those powers and activities in respect of which the Directors have complete discretion.
2. Those activities where approval of the shareholders is required but the third parties would be protected if the Board acts without the consent of the company.

3. Power, which only the shareholders can exercise, sometimes, subject to the approval of the Central Government.

Certain powers exercisable with the consent of the general body meeting: Under Section 293 the Board of Directors of a public company cannot, except with the consent of the company in general meeting:

- Sell, lease or otherwise dispose of the whole, or substantially the whole, of the company's undertaking or where the company owns more than one undertaking, of the whole or substantially the whole of any such undertaking. Any resolution permitting the aforementioned transaction may attach such conditions to the permission as may be specified in the resolution. Such conditions may include those regarding the use, disposal or investment of the sale proceeds, which may result from the transaction;
- Remit, or give time for the repayment of, any debt due by a director;
- Invest otherwise than in trust securities, the amount of compensation received by the company in respect of the compulsory acquisition of any such undertaking as is referred to in clause (i) or of any premises or properties used for any such undertaking and without which it cannot be carried on or can be carried on only after a considerable time;
- Borrow moneys where the moneys to be borrowed together with moneys already borrowed by the company will exceed the aggregate of the paid up capital of the company and its free reserves, (*i.e.*, reserves not set apart for any specific purpose). Temporary loans (*i.e.*, loans repayable on demand or within 6 months from the date of the loans, such as, short-term cash credit arrangements, the discounting of bills and the issue of other short-terms loans of a seasonal character but does not include loans raised for the purpose of financing expenditure of a capital nature) obtained from the company's bankers in the ordinary course of business are not covered by this provision.
- However, if a bank, in the ordinary course of its business, accepts deposits of money from the public repayable on demand or otherwise, and withdrawable by cheque, draft, order or otherwise, such acceptance must not be deemed to be a borrowing by the bank within the meaning of clause (iv) above. A debt incurred by the company in excess of the ceiling placed by clause (iv) above, shall not be valid or effectual, unless the lender proves that he advanced the loan in good faith and without knowledge that the aforesaid limit had been exceeded; and
- Contribute to charitable and other funds not directly related to the business of the company or the welfare of its employees, any amounts the aggregate of which will in any financial year, exceed

₹.50,000 or 5% of its average net profits during the immediately preceding three financial years, whichever is greater. The resolution in the general meeting must specify the total amount upto which moneys may be borrowed or total amount which may be contributed to charitable and other funds in any financial year.

- Appoint a sole selling agent for any area; the appointment may be made in the first instance without the approval of the general meeting but it will be subject to the subsequent approval by the company in the first general meeting held after the date on which the appointment is made [Section 294 (2)].
- Appoint a director to hold any office or place of profit (excepting that of managing director, manager, legal or technical advisers, banker or trustees for the holders of debentures of the company) special resolution being needed therefore; the consent of the company or its subsidiary in general meeting is necessary (Section 314).
- Make loan to or give guarantee, or provide security in connection with a loan made by any person to or to any person by, another company except where the aggregate of loans made to companies not under the same management as the lending company does not exceed the prescribed percentage of the aggregate of the subscribed capital and free reserve of the lending company (not applicable to banking, insurance and purely privates companies and companies established for financing industrial enterprises)
- To commence any new business; there is the necessity of a special resolution being passed by the company in its general meeting [Section 149(2A)].
- *Tutorial Note*: The list of the powers is not exhaustive but illustrative. It should be borne in mind that there are instance of other powers needing general body meeting's consent.

Powers to be exercised by Board only at its meeting: In Section 292, the following powers can be exercised by the Board only by means of resolution passed at its meetings:

- To make calls; (aa) to authorise the buy back of shares
- To issue debentures;
- To borrow money otherwise than on debentures;
- To invest the funds of the company;
- To make loans.

The Board may, however, by resolution passed at meeting, delegate the last three powers to the extent specified hereunder.

Such a delegation can be made to any committee of directors, the managing director, the manager or any other principal officer of the company or in the case of a branch office of the company, a principal officer thereof.

Every resolution delegating the power referred to in (c), (d) and (e) above shall specify:

- The total amount outstanding at any time up to which money may be borrowed by the delegate;
- The total amount up to which the funds may be invested as well as the nature of investment;
- The total amount of loans and the purpose thereof up to which and for which loans may be raised respectively. It is to these extents that the delegate may exercise the aforesaid three powers.

In connection with the power mentioned in (c) above a question may arise whether borrowing on a promissory note is within the powers of the directors. It has been held in that where such a borrowing permissible under the company's articles and moneys were borrowed on promissory notes, such transaction would come within the powers of the director, It has also been held in the same case that where a person was appointed as the managing director of the company by the Board's resolution vested with full powers of the management of the affairs of the company and authorised to sign all the papers of the company, he would have full powers to borrow money on a promissory note even without a resolution of the Board as contemplated by Section 292(c) of the Act.

In addition to Section 292, some other Sections also require the Board to exercise its powers in its meeting which are:

- Receive notice of disclosure of shareholdings of directors under Sections 307 [Section 308(2)].
- Fill in casual vacancies in the Board (Section 262);
- Sanction or give consent to contracts of or with any directors [Section 294(4); and
- Receive notice of disclosure of interest (Section 299)

The following powers may be exercised by a resolution passed at the meeting only with the consent of all the directors present at the meeting.

- To appoint a managing director or manager a person who is already a managing director or manager of another company [Sections 316(2) & 386(2)]
- To the sanction investment in companies in the same group [Section 372(5)].

Validity of acts of directors:

- All the acts of a director or a committee of the Board shall be valid not withstanding that his appointment was afterwards discovered to be invalid by reason of any defect or disqualification or by reason of the appointment being terminated by virtue of any provision contained in the Act or in the articles of the company. But this provision of law shall not have the effect of validating the acts of a director after his appointment has been shown to the company to be invalid or to have been terminated (Section 290). But where there was no appointment at all, the acts of such *de facto* directors are not protected. This protection applies only to defects in appointment discovered after the appointment. Thus, if a director, whose term of office has expired, acts as director, such acts cannot be regarded as valid; that is not a defect.

- It has been held in *Morris vs. Kaneseen 19451 All E.R. 586* that this rule is intended to be machinery to avoid calling into question the validity of transactions when there has been a slip or irregularity in the appointment of directors and to override substantive provisions of law relating to such appointments. The presumption as to the validity of acts of directors would not cover the case where there has not been any appointment at all.

Consideration of a few complicated problems based on power of directors:

- Having read the directorial powers in detail it would be worthwhile to consider a few problems on these powers.
- The Directors of X & Co. Ltd. desire to authorise the Managing Director to enter into the following transactions namely,
  - Invest from time to time surplus funds in the purchase of shares of other companies:
  - Borrow from banks money required for the purpose:
  - Give loans to persons, including firms in which directors or their relatives are partners;
  - Give donations to charitable trusts in which any of the directors may be interested as trustees.

Let us now examine the measures to be taken for the proper implementation of the proposals:

- Although Section 292 empowers the Board of Directors of a company to delegate to the Managing Directors the power to invest, in general terms, the funds of the company nevertheless because of the overriding provisions of Section 372(5) the transaction in the instant case would be invalid. Section 372(5) provides that no investment in shares of a company can be made by the Board of Directors of an investing company in pursuance of sub-section (2), unless it is sanctioned by a resolution passed at a meeting of the Board with the consent of all the directors present at the meeting except those not entitled to vote thereat, and unless further notice of the resolution to be moved at the meeting has been given to every director in the manner specified in Section 286. Since Section 372 does not provide for delegation of the power, the proposed delegation to the Managing Director in question, notwithstanding the general provision of Section 292, cannot be made.
- In terms of Section 292 the Board of Directors may also delegate to

the Managing Director the power to borrow money otherwise than debentures, which it can exercise only by means of resolutions passed at Board meetings. As per Explanation to Section 292(1), it is the arrangement for an overdraft or cash credit that constitutes the exercise of the borrowing power and not the actual utilisation of the arrangement. In other words, an arrangement for an overdraft or cash credit to the tune of say ₹.5 lakhs constitutes the exercise of the borrowing power and not the actual drawing of this amount on the basis of the overdraft or cash credit. Consequently, the transaction in the instant case shall be valid. But before implementation of the proposal, the Board must pass a resolution at its meeting authorising the Managing Directors to borrow from banks money required for the purpose of the company's business. Also the resolution delegating this power shall specify the total amount outstanding at any one time up to which the delegate may borrow money.

If however, the moneys to be borrowed together with the money already borrowed by the company (apart from temporary loans obtained from the Company's bankers in the ordinary course of business) will exceed the aggregate of the paid up capital of the company and its free reserves, [that is to say, reserves not set apart for any specific purpose] the Board of Directors of the company in question must obtain the consent of the company in its general meeting. Consequently, care should be taken to ensure that while delegating the power to the managing director the aforesaid provision has not been violated; also it should be ensured that the memorandum of association permits borrowing. Since just as to Section 295(1), (which we shall discuss later) without obtaining prior approval of the Central Government in that behalf, a company can not directly or indirectly lend money to persons including firms, in which directors or their relatives are partners, the company in question must in the first instance seek the Central Government's approval.

Secondly since the power to make loans may be delegated under Section 292(1)(e), the Board of Directors of the company in question must pass a resolution therefore and every resolution delegating this power to the Managing Director shall specify the total amount up to which loans may be made by the delegate, the purpose for which loans may be made and the maximum amount of loans which may be made for each such purpose in individual cases. Thirdly, by virtue of Section 291(1), the Board must see with reference to the memorandum and articles whether the company is authorised to exercise the power.

Under Section 293(1) (e), the Board of Directors of a public company can contribute or donate to charitable and other funds not directly related to the business of the company or the welfare of its employees any amount the aggregate of which will not, in any financial year exceed ₹.50,000 or 5% of its average net profits during the three financial years preceding whichever is greater. If this power of the company is not *ultra vires* the memorandum of the company, then only the Board can act in pursuance of the resolution of the company and in so acting, it can authorise the Managing Director to exercise the power on behalf of the Board. *It may be noted that the power of the Board to donate to general charities is not conditional to the existence of any profits. In such* case, *they may contribute up to the limit given in Section 293(1)(e), even though the company may be working at a loss.*

DUTIES OF DIRECTORS

The duties of directors may now be summarised as follows:

- Since the directors are in fiduciary position, their duties are onerous. As you know, they are trustees of the money of the company in the bank as well as of the property of the company. They are also agents in the transactions entered into by them on behalf of the company. Therefore they must act in utmost good faith and take as much care as a man of ordinary prudence would take in respect of his own affairs. In other words, they will have to exercise all the powers they are vested with only in this fiduciary capacity. You must remember that a director is a trustee only of the company and not of the shareholder thereof. Therefore, though he may possess inside information which may augment the value of shares, yet he is not obliged to disclose the information to a shareholder who offers to sell his shares to the director. However, in exceptional circumstances, the director may owe a fiduciary duty to shareholders as well *e.g.* where directors are negotiating terms of sale of issued shares of the company. That is where the directors approach the shareholders and not *vice versa* for sale of shares.
- He is required to evince as much skill as is expected from a person of his knowledge and experience-thus far and no further.
- Every director must act honestly. A director shall be liable to the company for any of his underhand dealings irrespective of whether or not the company suffers on account of such underhand dealings. Causing shares to be allotted to a minor, sale by director to company without the disclosure of his interest, fraudulent misrepresentation to co-directors enticing them into advancing money to him on insufficient security, taking of bribes, etc... are some of the instances of dishonest acts. Where a director derives any secret benefits or accept any bribes or any other illegal gratifications, he must account for them and make them over to the company *Eden vs. Ridsdale Co. 23 A.B.D. 336.* A company may repudiate a contract if it has been induced by bribes.
- It is normally not the duty of the director to detect the frauds of the

manager and the chairman of the company. He can therefore, rely on co-directors and officers. If the duty of detection of fraud is cast on a director, anything like an intelligent devolution of labour will be impossible. But if there is anything that gives rise to the slightest suspicion, then he will be put on an enquiry. If he fails to make the requisite enquiry to allay his suspicion then he will be guilty of dereliction of duty and be liable for damage emerging from such dereliction.

- It is the duty of a director to see that company's moneys are kept properly invested, unless the articles warrant the delegation of this duty to others.
- It is incumbent upon directors to insist on some independent valuation of investment and fixed assets at appropriate intervals. Revaluation of immovable property may not be necessary for a considerable time, but revaluation of shares must be made once a year. In this regard, a director should not put any reliance on the assurances of the chairman or on the expression of the auditor's belief. Likewise auditor too must not rely on the directors' assurance.
- Directors are required to ensure the accurate compilation of the stock sheets and the physical checking of certain of these items being done by the auditors.
- Palmer a list of cheques that the Board authorises is to be placed before each meeting of the Board.
- It is the duty of the directors not to act in a manner prejudicial to public interest or oppressive to any members. If they so act, proceedings will be against them under Section 397.
- Duties of directors regarding take-over under Section 395.

DIRECTORS NOT TO HOLD OFFICE OR PLACE OF PROFIT

Any office or place shall be deemed to mean office or place of profit under the company [within the meaning of the Section 314(3)]:

- In case the office or place is held by a director, if the director holding it obtains from the company anything by way of remuneration over and above the remuneration to which he is entitled as such director, whether as salary, fees, commission, perquisites, the right to occupy free of rent any premises as a place of residence or otherwise.
- In case the office or place is held by an individual other than a director or by any firm, private company or other body corporate, if the individual, firm, private company of body corporate holding it obtains from the company anything by way of remuneration whether as salary, fees commission, perquisites, the right to occupy free of rent any premises as a place of residence, or otherwise.

Except with consent of the company accorded by a special resolution:

- No director of a company shall hold any office or place of profit,
- No partner or relative of his, no firm in which he or his relative is a partner, no private company of which he is a director or member and no director or manager of such a private company shall hold any office or place of profit carrying a total monthly remuneration of such sum as may be prescribed.

However, any of the aforesaid persons may be appointed as a managing director or manager, banker or trustee for the debentureholders under any subsidiary of the company, unless the remuneration received from such subsidiary in respect of such office or place of profit is paid over the company or its holding company. The special resolution may be passed before or at the general meeting of the company held for the first time after the holding of such an office or place of profit. Further, where a relative of a director, or a firm in which such a relative is a partner is appointed to an office or place of profit in the company or a subsidiary thereof without the knowledge of the director, the consent of the company may be obtained either in the general meeting held for the first time after the holding of such an office within 3 months from the date of the appointment whichever is later [Section 314(1) and the provision thereof]. But the provisions of sub-section (1) shall not be applicable in a case where the relative of a director or firm in which such relative is a partner holds any office or place of profit under the company or its subsidiary, if the said relative's or firm's appointment had taken place before the director in question became the director of the company [Section 314(1A)].

A partner or a relative of a director or manager, a firm in which such director or manager or relative of either is a partner, or a private company of which such a director or manager or relative of either is director or member cannot hold any office or place of profit which carries a total monthly remuneration of such sum as may be prescribed [The Govt, vide its notification of 5th February, 2003 has fixed this amount as ₹.50,000 or more], except with the *prior consent* of the company by *special* resolution and the approval of the Central Government. When an office is held in contravention of the provision in sub-section (I), the director, partner, relative, firm etc., concerned shall be deemed to have vacated office from the date next following the date of the general meeting of the company referred to above or at the expiry of the period of the three months, as the case may be, and shall be liable to refund the company any remuneration received or the monetary equivalent of any perquisite or advantage enjoyed by him for the period immediately preceding the date aforesaid in respect of such an office or place of profit [Section 314(2)(a)]. The company shall not waive recovery of any sum refundable to it under Section 314(2)(a), unless permitted to do so by Central Government [Section 314(2)(b)].

Every individual, firm, private company or other body corporate proposed to be appointed to any office or place of profit shall, before shall, before or at the time of such appointment declare in writing whether he or it is not connected with a director of the company in any of the ways referred to in sub-section (I) [Section 314(2A]. If may happen that after the commencement of 1947 Amendment Act, an office or place of profit is held without the prior consent of the company by a special resolution and the approval of the Central Government. In such a case, the partner, relative, firm or private company appointed to it shall be liable to refund to the company any remuneration received or the monetary equivalent of any perquisite or advantage enjoyed by him on and from the date on which the office was so held by him [Section 314(28)].

The company shall not waive the recovery of any sum refundable to it under sub-section (2B) or (2c) as the case may be, unless permitted to do so by the Central Government [Section 314(2D)]. It may be noted that nothing in Section 314 shall apply to a person who, being the holder of any office or place of profit in the company, is appointed by the Central Government under Section 408 as director of the company [Section 314(4)]. The aforementioned provisions are calculated to prevent directors from obtaining unfair advantage from the company by providing sinecures to their business associates and relations without the knowledge of the shareholders.

Let us examine the following problems:

- Mr. Smart is a director of ABC Ltd., accepts the offer of employment as "Chief Executive-Technical Operations" of the same company on a monthly remuneration of ₹.15,000. Can he be an employee at the same time being the director of the company? In case his son is appointed to the same post$_f$ does it attract any provisions of the Companies Act?
- *Answer*: Ordinarily, the shareholders in general meeting elect a director, and once so elected, he enjoys well-defined rights and powers under the Act. An employee is appointed by the company under a contract of service is a servant of the company and the company can always direct his actions and interfere with his work. *I*t was observed that directors are elected representatives of the shareholders engaged in directing the affairs of the company on its behalf. However, there is nothing in law to prevent a director from accepting employment under the company under a special contract, which he may enter into with the company. Section 314 provide for a director holding an office or place of profit under a company.

Except with the consent of the company accorded by a special resolution no director shall hold any office or place of profit and no partner or relative of his, no firm in which he or his relative is a partner, no private company of which he is a director or member and no director or manager of such a private company shall hold any office or place of profit carrying a monthly remuneration of ₹10,000 or more. The special resolution may be passed before or a general meeting of the company held for the first time after the holding of such an office or profit. If it is done without the knowledge of the director, the consent of the company may be obtained either in the general meeting held for the first time after the holding of such an office or within 3 months from the date of appointment whichever is later. If a partner or a relative of a director or manager, a firm in which such director or manager or relative of either is a partner or a private company of which such a director or manager or relative of either is director or member can not hold any office or place of profit which carries a total monthly remuneration of ₹20,000 or more except with the prior consent of the company by special resolution and the approval of the Central Government.Thus, in the instance case, Mr. Smart can accept the offer of employment as Chief Executive-Technical Operations.

If his son is appointed to the said post, it requires the consent of the company:

- Mr. True is a director of a company and also a chartered accountant by profession and one of the partners in M/s True and Fair Co. The company appointed the said firm as chartered accountant of the company on a regular basis. Does Mr. True holds any office or place of profit in the company. Would your answer be different if his appointment is on a case-to-case basis?
- *Answer*: Chartered Accountants appointed by a company on a regular basis are hit by a restrictive provisions of sub-sections I and 1(b) of Section 314 if he is a director receiving remuneration over and above to which he is entitled. In case the office or place of profit is held by an individual other than a director or by any firm, private company or other body corporate, if it obtains from the company anything by way of remuneration whether as salary, fees, commission perquisite or otherwise, approval of the company is not required where the monthly remuneration is less than ₹10,000/-. If a director is holding the place of chartered accountants for the company he would be covered by Section 314(3) irrespective of the fact that office or place of profit carries a total monthly remuneration less than ₹10,000/-.

LIABILITIES OF DIRECTORS

The liability of a director should be considered from the following stand points:

- Directors may become liable to shareholders in multifarious ways,
- They may also become liable to third parties in certain cases: the liability may be civil and/or criminal.

LIABILITY TO SHAREHOLDERS

Negligence: A director may become liable to shareholders for negligence.

Where the directors acting within their powers, fail to exercise as much reasonable skill and diligence as may be expected from persons with their knowledge and experience in the management of the affairs of the company, they can be held liable for negligence. They are, however, not liable for errors of judgement as a result of which a loss might have been caused to the company provided they acted bonafide for the benefit of the company and with such a care as may be reasonably expected of them. The burden of proving bad faith in such a case lies on the person who challenges the act of the directors.

- *Misfeasance and breach of trust:* "Misfeasance" and "breach of trust" are allied heads of liability. The former is defined as any breach of duty in the conduct of the company's affairs, which causes loss to the company: the latter is confined to any misapplication of the funds of the company. Thus, the payment of dividend out of capital is a breach of trust. On the other hand, allotment of shares to an infant or giving a fraudulent preference to a creditor, or to commit any breach of articles would be misfeasance.
- *Ultra vires acts:* Where directors do any act which is in excess of their powers, *e.g.* borrow money or create a mortgage which is beyond their *authority* as defined by the articles such an act is called *ultra vires* the directors. If, however, it is not beyond the powers of the company as laid down by the memorandum, the shareholders may, by subsequent ratification, make the act, which is ultra vires the directors but *intra vires* the company, valid and binding on the company.
- *Act of co-directors:* A director is not responsible for the acts and defaults of co-director, unless he has expressly or impliedly authorised the same *[Cargil vs. Bower 10 Ch.D.502]*. The directors are jointly and severally liable for a breach of trust.

LIABILITY TO THIRD PARTIES

- Insofar as contracts entered into by directors on the company's behalf are concerned, the directors cannot be generally held personally liable for the some, for they act as agents of the company. But they may be personally liable if they act, without the authority of the company, on the ground of a breach of warranty of authority. This personal liability may attach to them when they have expressly or impliedly undertaken to be personally responsible for their act.
- If the directors commit or authorise a tortious act, they are personally liable therefore even if they have been acting as agents of the company. Likewise they would be personally liable for commitment or authorisation of fraud, *e.g.*, issue of a fraudulent prospectus. But a director would not be liable for the fraud of his co-director, unless it has been authorised by him, or he has participated therein.

- Certain liabilities have also been imposed by the Act as regards director *qua* third parties, *e.g.*, for misstatement in prospectus under Section 62 to prospective subscribers; for irregular allotment under Section 71: for failure to return application moneys where minimum subscription has not been raised within the prescribed period, under Section 69; for similar failure mentioned under Section 73 etc.

Directors' rights and liabilities for their ultra vires acts: The acts of directors which may be regarded as *ultra vires* are two-fold in nature, namely,

- The acts which are beyond their authority but within the company's powers (*i.e. intra vires* the company)
- The acts which are beyond the director's authority as well as the company's.

The rights and duties which emanate from ultra vires acts, we shall discuss here under:

- Under the Act, the funds of a company can be applied in carrying out its permitted objects. Therefore, if the directors of the company make an ultra vires payment, *e.g.*, payment of the interest out of capital they may be compelled to repay the money to the company even after it goes into liquidation. But the directors so compelled to refund the money to the company could claim to be indemnified by the payees who received the money from the directors with the knowledge that the payment to them was *ultra vires.* The reason for this rule of indemnification is that in such a case, the payees would be constructive trustees of that money.
- The directors are the agents of the company. That's why they cannot do anything, which the company itself cannot do under its memorandum. But if they make a contract within the powers of the company (*i.e. intra vires* the memorandum) but *ultra vires* the powers which the company by its articles has conferred upon them, then the company may ratify the contract in general meeting and be bound by it. If, however the company does not ratify such contract then the company will not be bound by the contract. Consequently, the directors will remain liable to the other party to the contract for the breach of an implied warranty of their authority.

Directors with unlimited liability:

- In a company with limited liability, the liability of the directors, like that of any other members, is limited to the amount remaining unpaid on their shares. However, a limited company may, if the memorandum permits, have directors with an unlimited liability. If a limited company has the powers under its articles it may also alter its memorandum by a special resolution so as to make the liability of its directors unlimited (Sections 322 and 323).

Director's reports:

- Section 217, the directors are under an obligation to make out and attach to every balance sheet laid before a company; in general meeting a report with regard to the state of affairs of the company-, the amount (if any) which they recommend as dividends, the amount if any, which they propose to carry any reserves in such balance sheet and the material changes and commitments (if any) affecting the financial position of the company which have occurred between the end of financial year to which the balance sheet relates and the date of the report.

The report shall deal with any changes, which have occurred during the financial year:

- To the nature of the company's business,
- In the company's subsidiaries or in the nature of the business carried on by them
- Generally in the class of business in which the company has an interest.

However, such matters are to be disclosed so far as these are material for the application of the state of the company's affairs by its members and will not, in the board's opinion be harmful to the business of the company or any of its subsidiaries. The Board must also give the fullest information and explanation in its report or in case falling under the proviso to Section 222, in an addendum to the report, on every reservation, qualification or adverse remark contained in the auditor's report.

The report and any addendum thereto must be signed by the chairman of the Board if he is authorised by the Board; otherwise, it is to be signed by such number of directors as are required to sign the balance sheet and profit and loss account of the company by virtue of Section 215. In default of compliance with these provisions, each of the directors and chairman signing the report without the Board's authority shall be punishable with imprisonment for a term extending up to six months or with fine up to ₹.20,000 or with both. But no person is to be sentenced to imprisonment for such offence unless it was committed willfully.

DIRECTOR'S RESPONSIBILITY STATEMENT [SECTION 217]

This section deals with the Report of Board of Directors to be placed before the general meeting. A new sub-section (2AA) has now been inserted [by the Companies (Amendment) Act, 2000] to provide that the Report of Board of Directors shall also include a Directors' Responsibility Statement as under:

- That the applicable accounting standards have been followed in preparing the annual accounts. If there is material departure, explanation for the same should be given.
- That the directors have selected such accounting policies and applied

them consistently and made judgements and estimates that are reasonable and prudent so as to give a true and fair view of the state of affairs of the company while preparing the annual accounts.

- That the Directors have taken proper and sufficient care,
  - For maintenance of adequate accounting records as required by the Act,
  - For safeguarding the assets of the company
  - For preventing and detecting fraud and other irregularities.
- That the Directors have prepared the annual accounts on a going concern basis.

LOANS TO DIRECTORS [SECTION 295]

As suggested, presently see from our discussion hereunder that a company's power of lending money to its directors is strictly regulated by the Act. A company without obtaining prior approval of the Central Government in that behalf, cannot directly or indirectly lend moneys or guarantee or secure the loans advanced by the other person to:

- A director of the lending company or that of its holding company or partner or relative of any such director
- Any firm in which any such director or relative is a partner;
- Any private company of which any director is a director or member;
- Any body corporate 25% or more of whose total voting power may be exercised or controlled by any such or by two or more such directors together
- Any body corporate the Board of Directors, managing director or manager whereof is accustomed to act in accordance with the directions or instructions of the board or of any director or directors of the lending company [Section 295(1)].

The impact of the aforesaid provision is that it prohibits the company not only from directly lending money to its directors but also from giving any guarantee for a loan taken by a director from any other person and providing any security for such loan. The Section too prohibits the providing of any guarantee or security for a loan advanced by a director to any person. The provisions do not apply to loans, etc. advanced by a private company (unless it is a subsidiary of a public company) or by a holding company to its subsidiary. Similarly, any guarantee or security provided by the holding company in respect of any loans made to its subsidiary does not attract the provisions.

It is thus clear from the foregoing discussion that under Section 295, a company cannot give loan or advance to its directors without obtaining the prior sanctions of the Central Government in that behalf. Now suppose that the directors of a public company have to travel often for company's business. The company makes some advances to them for this purpose, which sometimes exceeds the actual requirements. In such a case can the company be deemed to have, contravened the provision of Section 295? It seems that advances pertaining to travelling expenses are outside the ambit of Section 295, because such advances are not in the nature of loans, and are meant to meet expenses on behalf of the company. Therefore, the provisions of Section 295(1) are not contravened, but the directors are bound to keep the advances in excess in trust for the company.

In case a director of a public company has take a loan from the company without the approval of the Central Government,

- Is it possible to avoid prosecution by applying to the central Government for approval or by refunding the loan? And
- *Whether the offence is compoundabie before or after institution of prosecution and the authority can compound the offence?*
  - Section 295 of the Companies Act, no public company shall make any loan to any of its directors either directly or indirectly without obtaining the previous approval of the Central Government. As the Act envisages prior approval, Central Government will not entertain any application from the company seeking approval for a loan already given to its director. The company has, therefore, contravened the provisions of Section 295(1) and for this offence every person who is knowingly a party to this contravention including the person to whom the loan is made shall be punishable either with fine which may extend to `50,000 or with simple imprisonment for a term which may extend to six months [Section 255(4)]. Where any such loan has been repaid in full, no punishment by way of imprisonment shall be imposed and where the loan has been repaid in part, the maximum punishment, which may be imposed by way of imprisonment, shall be proportionately reduced. So, by refunding the loan in full, it is possible to avoid punishment in the form of imprisonment, but it is not possible to a avoid prosecution and punishment in the form of fine.
  - All offences other than an offence which is punishable under the Companies Act with imprisonment only or with imprisonment and also with fine are compoundable under Section 621A. As the offence under Section 295 is punishable with fine or imprisonment is compoundable but with the permission of the Court [Section 621A(2)]. The offence m be compounded either before or after the institution of prosecution. If the offence compounded before the institution of any prosecution, no prosecution shall be instituted relation to such offence, either by the Registrar or by any shareholder or by any pers-authorised by the Central Government. Where the

composition of any offence is ma> after the institution of any prosecution, such composition shall be brought to the notice the court by the Registrar in writing and on such notice of the composition of the offen being given, the company or its officer in relation to whom the offence is so compound' shall be discharged [Section 621A(4)].

The offence may be compounded by the Regional Director where the maximum amount fine, which may impose for such offence, does not exceed ₹50,000 and in other cases the company Law Board.

In this case, Regional Director may compound the offence, as t maximum fine is only ₹50,000. On receipt of applications from the persons liable for pena under Section 295(4) along with the comments of the Registrar, the Regional Director m specify the amount no exceeding the maximum fine which shall be paid to the Cent Government for compounding of the offence.

IRECTORIAL REGISTERS

REGISTER OF CONTRACTS, COMPANIES AND FIRMS IN WHICH DIRECTORS ARE INTERESTED

Every company shall keep one or more registers in which particulars of all contracts, or arrangements to which Section 297 or Section 299 applies shall be entered.

These particulars should include the following to the extent they are applicable in each case:

- Date of the contract or arrangement;
- Names of the parties thereto;
- The principal terms and conditions thereof;
- In the case of contract to which Section 297 applies or in the case of a contract or arrangement to which Section 299(2) applies, the date on which it was placed before the Board;
- The names of the directors voting for or against the contract or arrangement and the name of those remaining neutral.

The particulars of every such contract or arrangement to which either of the Sections applies must be entered in the register within 7 days of the receipt at the registered office of the particulars of contract other than the one requiring the Board's approval or within 30 days of date of that contract whichever is later; in the case of contract requiring the Board approval within 7 days (exclusive of public holidays) of the meeting of the Board at which the contract is approved. On these entries being made, the register is required to be placed before the next meeting of the Board, whereupon it shall be signed by all the directors present at the meeting. The register must also specify, in relation to each director of the company, the names of the firms or bodies corporate of which he has given notice under Section 299(3). However, the particular as regards contracts the value of which does not exceed ₹1,000 in the aggregate in any year or as regards contracts entered into by a banking company for collection of bills or as regards any transactions referred to in Section 297(2)(c) are not required to be entered in the register. Violation of the aforementioned provision would render the company and every officer thereof (in respect of each default) punishable with fine up to ₹5000 (Section 301).

REGISTER OF DIRECTORS, MANAGING DIRECTOR, MANAGER AND SECRETARY (SECTION 303)

Every company must keep at its registered office a register of directors, managing director, manager and secretary, and send to the Registrar in the prescribed form within 30 days of the appointment of the first directors, a return in duplicate containing particulars specified in the register and must notify the Registrar of any subsequent changes within 30 days of the happening thereof. This notification also must be submitted in duplicate in the prescribed form.

The register must contain the following particulars:

i. In the case of an individual, his present (and former) name and surname in full; his father's name and surname in full or where the individual is a married woman the husband's name and surname in full; his usual residential address, nationality, business, occupation, if any particulars of office (if any *e.g.*, that of director, managing director, manager or secretary in any other body corporate), the date of birth;
ii. In the case of a body, corporate its corporate name and registered or principal office, etc.
iii. In the case of a firm, the name of the firm etc.;
iv. If any director or directors have been nominated by a body corporate, its corporate name and all the particulars mentioned (i) and (ii);
v. If any directors have been nominated by a firm, the firm name and all the particulars mentioned in (i) and (ii) above.

For the purpose of the aforesaid provision any person in accordance with whose directions, or instructions the Board of Directors of a company is accustomed to act shall be deemed to be a director of the company. [Explanation to Section 303].

- Inspection of the Register (Section 304): The register mentioned in Section 303 must be open to inspection by any member of the company free of charge. But a person other than the member can inspect it on payment of one rupee for each inspection. If the inspection is refused, the company and every officer thereof who are in default are punishable with fine extending upto ₹.50. Also the Company Law Board may, by order, compel an immediate inspection of the register.

- Register to be kept by Registrar (Section 306): The Registrar shall maintain a separate register wherein he shall enter the particulars received by him under Section 303(2) in respect of companies, so however that all entries in respect of each such company shall be together. This register shall be open to inspection by any member of the public at any time during office hours, on payment of the prescribed fee. The register should be in Form No. 34 of the Companies General Rules and Forms 1956. A decision of the Punjab High Court, where returns under Section 303(2) have been made by rival claimants, the registrar should wait for the decision of the Court on the conflicting claims before making entries in his separate register of the particulars furnished by either party.
- Register or directors' shareholding etc. (Section 307): A company must maintain a register showing, as regards each director, the number, description and the amount of shares in or debentures of the company or any other body corporate, being the company's subsidiary or holding company, or a subsidiary of the company's holding company, which are held by him, or in trust for him, or of which he has any right to become the holder whether on payment or not. Apart from these entries, there must be an indication in the register of the nature and extent of any interest or right in or any shares or debentures recorded in relation to a director. The register must also show the date of each transfer of shares or debentures and the price or other consideration therefore if the transaction has been entered into after the commencement of the Act (*i.e.,* April 1, 1956). The register shall be kept at the registered office of the company. During the period beginning 14 days before the date of company's annual meeting, and ending 3 days after the date of its conclusion, any member or holder of the debentures may inspect it; but during this period or any other period, any person acting on behalf of the Central Government or the Registrar may inspect it. Further the Central Government or the Registrar may at any time, require a copy of the register or any part thereof. Furthermore, it must be produced at the commencement of every annual general meeting and kept open and accessible during the continuance of the meeting the any person having the right to attend the meeting.

Any default in the matter or the entries referred to in Sections 307(1) and (2) is punishable with the extending to ₹ 50,000 and also with a further fine extending to ₹.200 for every day during which default continues. Similar punishment is leviable in case a copy required under this Section is not sent within a reasonable time. In the case of refusal, the Company Law Board may compel an immediate inspection of the register. The provisions of Sections 307 and 308 shall apply to managers as they apply to directors.

POLITICAL CONTRIBUTIONS

Prior to the amendment of Section 293A, by the Companies (Amendment) Act, 1985, there was a blanket ban on political contributions by companies. The amended Section seeks to continue the existing blanket ban against political contributions in the case of government companies and companies which have been in existence for less than three financial years. The new Section seeks to permit any other company to make political contributions not exceeding five per cent of the average net profits if a resolution authorising such contributions is passed at a meeting of the Board of Directors. The New Section also seeks to impose an obligation on every company to disclose in its profit and loss account any amount or amounts contributed by it to any political party or for any political purpose. Under the new Section, if a company makes any political contribution in contravention of the provisions thereof, the company would be liable to fine which may extend to three times the amount so contributed. Further every officer of the company in default, would be liable to imprisonment for a term, which may extend to three years and also to fine.

The detailed provision of Section 293A, as amended, are reproduced below:

- Notwithstanding anything contained in any other provision of this act:
- No Government company; and
- No other company which has been in existence for less than three financial years, shall contribute any amount or amounts directly or indirectly:
- To any political party; or
- For any political purpose to any person.
- A company, not being a company referred to in clause (a) or clause (b) of sub-section (1), may contribute any amount or amounts, directly or indirectly:
- To any political party, or
- For any political purpose to any person.

Provided that the amount or, as the case may be, the aggregate of the amount which may be so contributed by a company in any financial year shall not exceed five per cent of its average net profits determined in accordance with the provisions of Sections 349 and 350 during the three immediately preceding financial years.

Explanation: Where a portion of a financial year of the company falls before the commencement, of the Companies Act (Amendment) Act, 1985 and a portion falls after the amendment, the latter portion shall be deemed to be a financial year within the meaning, and for the purposes, of this sub-section. Provided further that no such contribution shall be made by a company unless a resolution authorising the making of such contribution is passed at a meeting of the Board of Directors and such resolution shall, subject to the other provision of this Section, be deemed to be justification in law for the making and the acceptance of the contribution authorised by it.

- Without prejudice to the generality of the provisions of sub-sections (1) and (2):
- A donation or subscription or payment caused to be given by a company on its behalf or on its account to a person who, to its knowledge, is carrying on any activity which, at the time at which such donation or subscription or payment was given or made, can reasonably be regarded as likely to affect public support for a political party shall also be deemed to be contribution of the amount of such donation, subscription or payment to such person for a political purpose:
- The amount of expenditure incurred, directly or indirectly, by a company on advertisement in any publication being a publication in the nature of a souvenir, brochure, tract, pamphlet or the like, by or on behalf of a political party or for its advantage shall be deemed:
- Where such publication is by or on behalf of a political party, to a contribution of such amount to such political party, and
- Where such publication is not by or on behalf of but for the advantage of a political party to be a contribution for a political purpose to the person publishing it.
- Every company shall disclose in its profit and loss account any amount or amounts contributed by it to any political party or for any political purpose to any person during the financial year to which that account relates, giving particulars of the total amount contributed and the name of the party or person to which or to whom such amount has been contributed.
- If a company makes any contribution in contravention of the provisions of this Section:
- The company shall be punishable with fine which may extend to three time the amount so contributed, and
- Every officer of the company who is in default shall be punishable with imprisonment for a term, which may extend to three year and shall also be liable to fine.

MANAGERIAL REMUNERATION

A director is not a servant of the company but he is the incharge of its management and controls its affairs. He has no implied rights to remuneration for his services as a director. However, there may be a specific provision for providing remuneration to him in the articles or the shareholders may resolve for the same in the General Meeting. The articles, however, generally provide for director's remuneration, which is in the nature of honorarium. Sections 198, 309, 310, 311, 387, 200 and Schedule XIII of the Companies Act, 1956 provide the relevant provision relating to managerial remuneration, which may be summarised as under;

3.46 *Corporate and Allied Laws*:

- For the purpose of the Sections, the term 'remuneration' includes:
- Any expenditure incurred by the company in providing any rent free accommodation or any other benefit or amenity in respect of accommodation free of charge;
- Any expenditure incurred by the company in providing any other benefit or amenity free of charge or at a concessional rate;
- Any expenditure incurred by the company in respect of any such obligation or service which but for such expenditure by the company would have been paid by the person himself; and
- Any expenditure incurred by the company to effect any insurance of the life of, or to provide any pension, annuity or gratuity for the person or his spouse or child. (Section 198) The term 'remuneration' however, does not include:
- Any sitting or attendance fees payable to directors for attending each meeting of the Board or a Committee there of [Section 198(2)]. However, in case of a managing director and whole time director, the payment of sitting fee forms a part of managerial remuneration and if the amounts is payable in accordance with Schedule XIII, no such sitting fee is payable to them.
- Remuneration payable for acting as technical expert. [Section 309(1)]
- If the articles do not provide for the payment of travelling expenses to the directors, travelling expenses incurred in attending meeting of the Board or Committee thereof or General Meeting.
- The remuneration of the directors must be fixed:
- By the articles or
- By a resolution or if the articles so require by a special resolution of the company [Section 309(1)]
- The director may be paid remuneration in one of the following modes:
- A director may receive remuneration by way of fee for each meeting of the Board or a Committee thereof attended by him.
- A director who is either in the whole time employment of the company or a managing director may be paid remuneration either by way of a monthly payment or as a specific percentage of the net profits of the company or partly by one way and partly by the other.
- A director who is neither in the whole time employment of the company nor a managing director may be paid remuneration either by way of a monthly, quarterly or annual payment with the approval of the Central Government or by way of commission if the company by a special resolution authorised such payment.

- Section 198, total managerial remuneration payable to directors, managing director(s) or manager or whole time director(s) in respect of any financial year should not exceed 11% of the net profits of that company for that financial year. The approval of the Central Government is required to pay the remuneration to a whole time director/managing director of a company if such remuneration exceeds 5% of the net profits for one such director, and 10% of net profits for all of them together. (Section 309). In case of a director who is neither in the whole time employment of the company nor a managing director, the approval of the Central Government for their remuneration is required if it exceeds 1% of the net profits of the company, if a company has a managing or a whole time director or a manager, and 3% of the net profits of the company in any other case. (Section 309) In case of a manager the need for approval of the Central Government arises when the remuneration exceeds 5% of the net profits (Section 387)
- Under sub-section (4) of Section 198 in case of loss or inadequacy of profits, the approval of the Central Government is required for payment of minimum remuneration to managerial personnel. Section 269 has dispensed with the requirement of prior approval of Central Government for appointment of managerial personnel so long as the appointment and remuneration are in accordance with Schedule XIII. Section II Part II of the Schedule specifies minimum remuneration (varying from ₹75,000 per month to ₹.2,00,000 per month and ₹1,50,000 to ₹4,00,000 as the case may be depending on the effective capital of the company). It may be inferred that no separate approval of the Central Government would be required under Sections 198(4) and 309(3) provided the remuneration paid to a managerial person in the event of absence or inadequacy of net profits in any financial year is in accordance with the provisions of Section II of Part II of Schedule XIII.
- *Note*: Earlier provision for 10 per cent reduction in salary of a managerial person has been deleted from the revised Schedule XII! effective from 14th July, 1993. In fact the remuneration specified in Part il of the Schedule as amended on 1st February, 1994 is itself the 'minimum remuneration'. Hence, where a managerial person had been appointed (with or without Central Government approval) on a specified salary with a provision for 10% reduction in salary in the event of loss or inadequacy of net profits in any financial year, the company may, if it so wishes, delete the said condition, without obtaining central Government's approval in accordance with the provisions of Section 3ffl
- Remuneration payable by a company having adequate net profits

to its managerial; personnel is governed by Section 1 of Part II of Schedule XIII, there would be no restriction on the nature or quantum of remuneration paid by a company to its managerial personnel as long as the remuneration paid during any financial year is within 5 per cent or 10 per cent of the net profits, as the case may be, of that financial year. It may be further noted that where a profit making company fixes remuneration for all its managerial personnel in accordance with the provisions of Section 1 of Part II of the Schedule but in incurred losses or earns inadequate profits in any subsequent financial year, it would be required to confirm to the provisions of Section II of Part II of the Schedule during such subsequent financial year unless it obtains the approval of the Central Government for payment of remuneration to its managerial personnel in excess of the limits specified in Section II of Part II of the Schedule.

- Section 310 prohibits any increase in the remuneration of any director, except with the approval of the Central Government. However, increase in remuneration effected by an increase in the sitting fee for each meeting of the Board or Committee thereof it such fee after the increase, does not exceed the limits prescribed by the Central Government [presently the amount of remuneration by way of fee for each meeting of the Board of Directors or a committee thereof is [(a) For companies with a paid up share capital and free reserves of ₹10 crore and above or turnover of ₹50 crore and above not to exceed ₹20,000/- and (b) For other companies not to exceed ₹10,000/-] do not require the Central Government's approval. The Amendment Act, 1998, provided that so long the increase in remuneration is in accordance with Schedule XIII, approval of the Central Government will not be required.
- In the case of an appointment or reappointment of a managing or whole-time director at a remuneration higher than the remuneration which that office previously carried with it, the approval of Central Government is required except the cases where such increase is in accordance with the conditions specified in the Schedule XIII (Section 311). Schedule XIII provides that in regard to such managerial personnel who are already in position on the date of the amendment in the Schedule, companies may themselves raise their remuneration, from a date not earlier than 1st February 1994, *i.e.*, the date of the notification of the revised Schedule, without the approval of the Central Government. This may be done even where the earlier appointment/remuneration had been approved by the Central Government in accordance with the provisions of Schedule XIII save and except in those cases where the Central Government had given

conditional approval to the appointment/remuneration. For example, in some cases the Central Government approves appointment of a person subject to the condition that the company would not increase or vary his remuneration without obtaining approval of the Central Government or that the remuneration of a managerial person shall not exceed a specified ceiling if he has been permitted to work as managerial person in more than one company and draw remuneration from both the companies. Where such specific or special conditions have been imposed by the Central Government while approving appointment/remuneration, these conditions would still have to be complied with unless varied by the Central Government. Any increase in the remuneration of managerial personnel in accordance with the revised Schedule shall be subject to the approval of the shareholders in a general meeting, when held, in specific terms so as to comply with Part III of the Schedule.

- Under Section 200, a company cannot pay its officer or employee any tax-free remuneration. Since, under Section 2(30), the term 'officer' includes a director, the payment of tax-free remuneration to a director is also forbidden. It may, however be noted that despite Section 200 of the Companies Act, Section 10(6)(vii)(a)(ii) of the Income-Tax Act, 1961, provides that in the case of a foreign technician of the class specified therein and employed by a company, the tax on his income chargeable under the head 'salaries' may be paid by the company for a period of twenty-four months following the expiry of a tax-free period of thirty-six months from the date of his arrival in India.
- The Companies (Amendment) Act, 1974 introduced a new Section 637-AA empowering the Central Government while just as approval to the appointment or remuneration of a managing or whole-time director or manager to fix the remuneration, within the statutory ceilings, at such amount or percentage of profits of the company, as it may deem fit and while fixing the remuneration, the Central Government shall have regard to:
- The financial of the position of the company;
- The remuneration or commission drawn by the individual concerned in any other capacity, including his capacity as a sole selling agent;
- The remuneration or commission drawn by him from any other company;
- Professional qualifications and experience of the individual concerned;
- Public policy relating to the removal of disparities in income.

Compensation for loss of office:

- Sections 318 to 321 lay-down elaborate provisions for regulating payment of compensation to directors for loss of office or in consideration of retirement from office or in connection with such losses or retirement. These provisions apply to all companies, *i.e.* public companies, private subsidiary of public companies and to private companies.

Under Section 318 such compensation can be paid only to managing director, director holding the office of the manager and to a whole time employee director and to no others. The compensation payable shall be on the basis of average remuneration actually earned by such persons for three years (or such shorter period as may be the case) immediately proceeding the ceasing of holding of such office, and shall be for the unexpired portion of his term or for three years (whichever is shorter). No such payment however can be m< at all if winding up of the company is commenced before or commences within 12 mor after he ceases to hold office if the assets or winding up (after deducting expenses winding up) are not sufficient to repay the shareholders the capital contributed.

No payment of such compensation can also be made in the following cases:

- Where the director resigns office due to reconstruction or amalgamation of the compi with another body or body corporate and such director is appointed manager or manac director or other office in the resulting new body.
- Where a director resigns otherwise that as on reconstruction or amalgamation.
- Where the director vacates office under Section 203 (acting-fraudently as director manager) or Section 283(1) Clauses (a) to (1) (vacation-of office by director).
- Where winding up (compulsory, voluntary or under supervision) has been due to negligence or default of the director in question.
- Where the winding up is not due to negligency or default of the director, he can be compensation for loss of office, even in the winding up. Termination of his services will be wrongful if the winding up was due to his default.
- Where the director has been guilty of any fraud or breach of trust in relation to or gross negligency or gross mismanagement of the affairs of the company or any subsidiary or holding company thereof. This also includes a breach of fiduciary obligations because that constitutes a breach of trust.

In *Bell vs. Lever Brothers, (1932)*, Lever Brothers removed their managing director of a subsidiary by paying him compensation. It was afterwards discovered that during his tenure of office he had been guilty of so many breaches of duty and corrupt practices that he could have been removed without compensation. An action was then commenced to recover back the compensation money. It was held that Bell was not bound to refund the compensation money and to disclose any breach of his fiduciary obligation so as to give the company an opportunity to dismiss him.

MANAGING DIRECTOR

A managing director is a person entrusted with any powers of management, which would not otherwise be exercisable, by him (Section 226). He exercises some or all of the director's powers and functions of managing which are delegated to him upon some terms and conditions and subject to such restrictions as are set-out in the agreement, resolution or other document appointing him.

He may be appointed by:

- An agreement with the company, or
- The resolution of the Board of Directors, or
- A resolution passed by the company in Annual General Meeting, or
- By the memorandum, or
- By the articles.

Normally, the articles empowers the Board of Directors to appoint one of their body to the office of the managing director, by a resolution passed at the Board Meeting in separate service contract stating his powers and his duties and terms of employment.

As such a managing director is a service director and he is to act under the control and supervision of the Board. As a managing director must necessarily be a director, his appointment is automatically terminated if he ceases to act as a director either because of any disqualification, *e.g.*, not purchasing qualification shares within two months of his appointment as director or because of his retirement by rotation.

Before the Amendment Act of 1988, it was not obligatory for a public company (including a deemed public company) or a private company, which is subsidiary of a public company to appoint managerial personnel, that is, a managing or whole time director or a manager. As per the amended section, it is obligatory for every public company or a subsidiary of a public limited company having a paid-up share-capital of such sum as may be prescribed (₹5 crores or more w.e.f. August 18, 1990) to appoint either a managing or whole time director or a manager.

There can be more than one managing director in a company on functional basis. But usually there is only one managing director in a company of moderate size in which he is the chief executive official of the company.

Appointment of managing or whole time director or manager to require Government approval in certain cases only:

- In the case of a public company (including a deemed public company), or a private company which is subsidiary of a public company, the Companies Act imposes certain restrictions on managing or whole time director's appointment.

If the condition specified in Schedule XIII are fulfilled, a managing or whole time director or manager in public company (including a deemed public company) or a private company which has a subsidiary thereof can be appointed, reappointed without the approval of the Central Government. A return in the prescribed form no. 25-C is, however, required to be filed within 90 days of appointment [Section 269(2)].

If the conditions specified Schedule XIII is not complied with, an application seeking approval of the appointment must be made to the Central Government within 90 days from the date of such appointment/re-appointment [Sections 269(2) and (3)].

The Central Government shall not accord its approval unless it is satisfied that:

- The proposed managing or whole time director of the company is a fit and proper person and the appointment of the such an individual as managing or whole time director is not against public interest;
- The terms and conditions of the appointment of the proposed managing or whole time director of the company are fair and reasonable [Section 269(4)].

The Central Government is also empowered to accord approval to the appointment for a period less than the period for which the person is proposed to be appointed by the company [Section 269(5)].

If the appointment re-appointment is not approved by the Central Government the appointee shall vacate office immediately on communication of the decision by the Central Government, otherwise he shall be punishable with fine up to ₹5,000/- for every day during which he fails to vacate such office [Section 269(6)].

When the Central Government is, prima-facie, of the opinion that any appointment made without its approval has been made in contravention of the requirement of Schedule XIII, the Central Government may render the letter to the Company Law Board for decision. The Company Law Board after giving reasonable opportunity of hearing to the company and the appointee may make an order declaring whether contravention of the requirements of Schedule XIII has or has not taken place. If the Company Law Board comes to he conclusion that such contravention has occurred, the appointment shall be deemed to have come to an end on the date of such declaration and the person so appointed shall, in addition to being liable to pay a fine of ₹1,00,000 refund to the company the entire amount of salaries and perquisites etc., received by him. However, all the acts of the managerial personnel, whose appointment is invalidated, will be deemed to be valid [Sections 269(7), (8), (9), (10), (12)].

- Restrictions on Appointment: An individual cannot be managing director or manager of more than two companies, public or private, where out of two companies at least one is a public company or private company, which is a subsidiary of a public company. An individual may hold the office of managing director or manager in any number of private companies, which are not subsidiaries of public company. But if the office is hold in a public company or a private company which is subsidiary of a public company, the same individual can not, in addition thereto, hold the office of managing director in more than one another company whether such every company is a public company or private company which is subsidiary of public company or any private company. (Section 316)

- *Terms of Office*: The term of office of a managing director must not exceed 5 years at a time. The term, however, may be extended for further period not exceeding 5 years at a time. (Section 317)
- It is important to note that the person ceases to be managing director with a ceasure of directorship on account of his retirement by rotation at the Annual General Meeting. But if such a person is re-elected as director at the AGM and thereby he continues as the director of the company, he shall continue as a managing director also for the period for which he is so elected by the AGM and for the unexpired period of present term of appointment as managing director.
- *Isqualifications for appointment*: A managing director has necessary to be a director and therefore, all the disqualifications rendering impossibilities for the appointment of a person as director (Section 274) will apply in the case of appointment of a managing director. Section 267 specifically provide that company must appoint or continue the appointment of a person as managing or whole time director who is:
- An undischarged insolvent or has at any time been adjudged insolvent;
- Suspends or has at any time suspended payment to his creditor or has made a composition with them or
- Has at any time been convicted of an offence involving moral turpitude.

The term moral turpitude needs a little elaboration. It comprises anything contrary to justice, honesty, and principle of good morals, an act of baseness, vileness or depravity in the private and social duties, which a man owes to his fellowmen or society in general. The term also comprises anything contrary to the accepted and customary rule of right and duty between man and man.

INTER-CORPORATE LOANS AND INVESTMENTS (SECTION 372A)

- Overall ceiling limits: No company shall directly or indirectly make
- Make any loan to any other body corporate;
- Give any guarantee or provide security in connection with a loan

made by any other person to, or to any other person by, any body corporate; and

- Acquire by way of subscription, purchase or otherwise the securities of any other body corporate, exceeding 60% of its paid-up share capital and free reserves or 100% of its free-reserves whichever is more, [sub-section (1)] Explanation:
- "Loan" includes debentures, or any deposit of money made by one company with another company, not being a banking company.
- "Free Reserves" means those reserves which, as per latest audited balance sheet of the company, are free for distribution as dividend and shall include balance to the credit of the securities premium account but shall not include share application money.
- Loans, Investments and guarantees in excess of prescribed limits: Where the
- Aggregate of the loans and investments so far made, the amounts for which guarantee or
- Security so far provided to or in all other bodies corporate, along with the investment, loan,
- Guarantee or security proposed to be made or given by the Board, exceeds the aforesaid
- Limits, no investment or loan shall be made or guarantee shall be given or security shall be
- Provided unless previously authorised by a special resolution passed in a general
- Meeting.

However, the Board may give guarantee, without being previously authorised by a special resolution if:

- A resolution is passed in the meeting of the board authorising to give guarantee in accordance with the provisions of this section;
- There exists exceptional circumstances which prevent the company from obtaining previous authorisation by a special resolution passed in a general meeting for giving a guarantee;
- The resolution of the Board under (1) as above is confirmed within twelve months, in a general meeting of the company or the annual general meeting held immediately after passing of the Board resolution, whichever is earlier.
- Matter to be specified in special resolution: The notice of special resolution shall
- Indicate clearly the specific limits, the particulars of the body corporate in which the
- Investment is proposed to be made or loan or security or guarantee to be given, the

- Purpose of the investment, loan or security or guarantee, specific sources of funding and
- Such other details.
- Other Steps: No loan or investment shall be made or guarantee or security given by the
- Company in pursuance of sub-section (1) of Section 372A unless the resolution
- Sanctioning it is passed at a meeting of the Board with the consent of all the directors
- Present at the meeting and the prior approval of the public financial institution referred to
- In Section 4A where any term loan is subsisting, is obtained.
- The prior approval of a public financial institution shall not be required where the aggregate of the loans and investments so far made, the amounts for which guarantee or security so far provided to or in all other bodies corporate, along with the investments, loans guarantee or security proposed to be made or given does not exceed the limit of sixty per cent specified in sub-section (1), if there is no default in repayment of loan instalment or payment of interest thereon as per the terms and conditions of such loan to the public financial institution, [sub-section (2)].
- Rate of interest: No loan to any body corporate shall be made at a rate of interest lower
- Than the prevailing bank rate, being the standard rate made public under Section 49 of the
- Reserve Bank of India Act, 1934. [sub-section (3)].
- Default under Section 58A: No company which has defaulted in complying with the provision of Section 58A, shall directly or indirectly make any loan to any body corporate; give any guarantee, or provide security, in connection with a loan made by any other person to, or to any other person by, any body corporate and acquire, by subscription, purchase or otherwise the securities of any other body corporate till such default is subsisting, [sub-section (4)]
- *Register of Investments and Loans*: (i) Every company shall keep a register showing the following particulars in respect of every investment or loan made, guarantee given or security provided by it in relation to any body corporate under sub-section (1), namely:
- The name of the body corporate;
- The amount, terms and purpose of the investment or loan or security or guarantee;
- The date on which the investment or loan has been made; and
- The date on which the guarantee has been given or security has been provided in connection with a loan.

- The particulars of investment, loan, guarantee referred to in sub-section (1) shall be entered chronologically in the register aforesaid within seven days of the making of such investment or loan, or the giving of such guarantee or the provision of such security, [sub-section (5)]
- The register referred to in sub-section (5) shall be kept at the registered office of the
- Company concerned and shall be open to inspection at such office and the extracts may be taken therefrom and copies thereof may be required, by any member of the company to the same extent, in the same manner, and on payment of the same fees as in the case of the register of members of the company; and the provisions of Section 163 shall apply accordingly, [sub-section (6)]
- *Guidelines*: The Central Government may prescribe guidelines for the purposes of Section 372A. [sub-section (7)]. Exemptions: Nothing contained in Section 372A shall apply,
- To any loan made, guarantee given or any security provided or any investment made by,
  - A banking company or an insurance company, or a housing finance company in the ordinary course of its business, or a company established with the object of financing industrial enterprise or of providing infrastructural facilities;
  - A company whose principal business is the acquisition of shares, stock, debentures or other securities;
  - A private company, unless it is a subsidiary of a public company;
- To investment made in shares allotted in pursuance of clause (a) of sub-section (1) of Section 81;
- To any loan made by a holding company to its wholly owned subsidiary;
- to any guarantee given or any security provided by a holding company in respect of loan made to its wholly owned subsidiary;
- To acquisition by a holding company by way of subscription, purchases or otherwise, the securities of its wholly owned subsidiary [sub-section (8)]
- Penalty for default: If default is made in complying with the provisions of this section, other than sub-section (5), the company and every officer of the company who is in default shall be punishable with imprisonment which may extend to two years or with fine which may extend to fifty thousand rupees. However where any such loan or any loan in connection with which any such guarantee or security has been given, or provided by the company, has been repaid in full, no punishment by way of imprisonment shall be imposed under this sub-section and where such loan has

been repaid in part, the maximum punishment which may be imposed under this sub-section by way of imprisonment shall appropriately be reduced. Further that all persons who are knowingly parties to any such contravention shall be liable, jointly and severally, to the company for the repayment of the loan or for making good the same which the company may have been called upon to pay by virtue of the guarantee given or the securities provided by such company, [sub-section (9)]. If default is made in complying with the provisions of sub-section (5), the company and every officer of the company who is in default shall be punishable with fine which may extend to five thousand rupees and also with a further fine which may extend to five hundred rupees for every day after the first day during which the default continues, [sub-section (10)].

10

Amalgamation of Companies

The beginning to amalgamation may be made through common agreements between the transferor and the transferee but mere agreement does not provide a legal cover to the transaction unless it carries the sanction of company court for which the procedure laid down under section 391 of the Companies Act should be followed for giving effect to amalgamation through the statutory instrument of the court's sanction. Although chapter V of the Companies Act, 1956 comprising sections 389 to 396-A deals with the issue and related aspects covering arbitration, compromises, arrangements and reconstructions but at different times and under different circumstances in each case of merger and amalgamation application of other provisions of the Companies Act, 1956 and ruled made there-under may necessarily be attracted. So, the procedure does not remain simple or literally confined to chapter V. The procedure is complex, involving not only the compromises or arrangements between the company and its creditors or any class of them or between the company and its members or any class of them but it involves, safeguard of public interest and adherence to public policy. These aspects are looked after by the Central Government through official liquidator on Company Law Board, Department of Company Affairs and the court has to be satisfied of the same.

TOP MANAGEMENT'S COMMITMENTS TOWARDS MERGER AND AMALGAMATION

Top management defines the organisation's goal and outlines the policy framework to achieve these objectives. The organisation's goal for business expansion could be accomplished, inter alia through business combinations assimilating a target corporate which can remove the present deficiencies in the organization and can contribute in the required direction to accomplish the goal of business expansion through enhanced commercial activity *i.e.* supply of inputs and market for output product diversification, adding up new products and improved technological process, providing new distribution channels and market segments, making available technical personnel and experienced skilled manpower, research and development establishments etc.

Depending upon the specific need and cost advantage with reference to creating a new set up or acquiring a well-established set-up firm.

SEARCH FOR A MERGER PARTNER

The top management may use their own contacts with competitors in the same line of economic activity or in the other diversified field which could be identified as better merger partners or may use the contacts of merchant bankers, financial consultants and other agencies in locating suitable merger partners. A number of corporate candidates may be shortlisted and identified. Such identification should be based on the detailed information of the merger partners collected from published and private sources.

Such information should reveal the following aspects viz:

- Organisational history of business and promoters and capital structure
- Organisational goals
- Product, market and competitors
- Organisational setup and management pattern
- Assets profile: Movable and immovable assets, land and building
- Manpower–skilled, unskilled, technical personnels and detailed particulars of management employees.

NEGOTIATIONS

Top management can negotiate at a time with several identified shortisted companies suited to be merger partner for settling terms of merger and pick up one of them which offers most favourable terms. Negotiations can be had with target companies before making any acquisitional attempt. Samedrill of negotiations could be followed in the cases of merger and amalgamation. There are other aspects, too, in the activity schedule covering, quantification action plan, purpose, shape, and date of merger, profitability and valuation, taxation aspects legal aspects and development plan of the company after merger.

STEPS FOR MERGER AND AMALGAMATION

SCHEME OF AMALGAMATION

The scheme of amalgamation should be prepared by the companies, which have arrived at a consensus to merge. There is no specific form prescribed for scheme of amalgamation but scheme should generally contain the following information:

- Particulars about transferee and transferor companies
- Appointed date
- Main terms of transfer of assets from transferor to transferee with power to execute on behalf or for transferee the deed or documents being given to transferee.

- Main terms of transfer liabilities from transferor to transferee covering any conditions attached to loans/debentures/ bonds/other liabilities from bank/financial institution/ trustees and listing conditions attached thereto.
- Effective date when the scheme will come into effect
- Conditions as to carrying on the business activities by transferor between 'appointed date' and 'effective date'.
- Description of happenings and consequences of the scheme coming into effect on effective date.
- Share capital of transferor company specifying authorized capital, issued capital and subscribed and paid up capital
- Share capital of transferee company covering above heads.
- Description of proposed share exchange ratio, any conditions attached thereto, any fractional share certificates to be issued, transferee company's responsibility to obtain consent of concerned authorities for issue and allotment of shares and listing.
- Surrender of shares by shareholder of transferor company for exchange into new share certificates.
- Conditions about payment of dividend, ranking of equity shares, pro rata dividend declaration and distribution.
- Status of employees of the transferor companies from effective date and the status of the provident fund, gratuity fund, super annuity fund or any special scheme or funds created or existing for the benefit of the employees.
- Treatment on effective date of any debit balance of transferor company balance sheet.
- Miscellaneous provisions covering income-tax dues, contingencies and other accounting entries deserving attention or treatment.
- Commitment of transferor and transferee companies towards making applications/petitions under section 391 and 394 and other applicable provisions of the con Companies Act, 1956 to their respective High Courts.
- Enhancement of borrowing limits of the transferee company upon the scheme coming into effect.
- Transferor and transferee companies give assent to change in the scheme by the court or other authorities under the law and exercising the powers on behalf of the companies by their respective Boards.
- Description of powers of delegatee of transferee to give effect to the scheme.
- Qualification attached to the scheme, which require approval of different agencies, etc.
- Description of revocation/cancellation of the scheme in the absence of approvals qualified in clause 20 above not granted by concerned authorities.

- Statement to bear costs etc. in connection with the scheme by the transferee company.

APPROVAL OF BOARD OF DIRECTORS FOR THE SCHEME

Respective Board of Directors for transferor and transferee companies are required to approve the scheme of amalgamation.

APPROVAL OF THE SCHEME BY SPECIALISED FINANCIAL INSTITUTIONS/ BANKS/TRUSTEES FOR DEBENTURE HOLDERS

The Board of Directors should in fact approve the scheme only after it has been cleared by the financial institutions/banks, which have granted loans to these companies or the debenture trustees to avoid any major change in the meeting of creditors to be convened at the instance of the Company Court's under section 391 of the Companies Act, 1956. Approval of Reserve Bank of India is also needed where the scheme of amalgamation contemplates issue of share/payment of cash to non-resident Indians or foreign national under the provisions of Foreign Exchange Management (Transfer or Issue of Security by a Person Resident Outside India) Regulations, 2000. In particular, regulation 7 of the above regulations provide for compliance of certain conditions in the case of scheme of merger or amalgamation as approved by the court.

INTIMATION TO STOCK EXCHANGE ABOUT PROPOSED AMALGAMATION

Listing agreements entered into between company and stock exchange require the company to communicate price-sensitive information to the stock exchange immediately and simultaneously when released to press and other electronic media on conclusion of Board meeting just as approval to the scheme.

APPLICATION TO COURT FOR DIRECTIONS

The next step is to make an application under section 39(1) to the High Court having jurisdiction over the Registered Office of the company, and the transferee company should make separate applications to the High Court. The application shall be made by a Judge's summons in Form No. 33 supported by an affidavit in Form No. 34.

The following documents should be submitted with the Judge's summons:

- A true copy of the Company's Memorandum and Articles
- A true copy of the Company's latest audited balance sheet
- A copy of the Board resolution, which authorises the Director to make the application to the High Court.

HIGH COURT DIRECTIONS FOR MEMBERS' MEETING

Upon the hearing of the summons, the High Court shall give directions fixing the date, time and venue and quorum for the members' meeting and appoint an Advocate Chairman to preside over the meeting and submit a report to the Court. Similar directions are issued by the court for calling the meeting of creditors in case such a request has been made in the application.

APPROVAL OF REGISTRAR OF HIGH COURT TO NOTICE FOR CALLING THE MEETING OF MEMBERS/CREDITORS

Pursuant to the directions of the Court, the transferor as well as the transferee companies shall submit for approval to the Registrar of the respective High Courts the draft notices calling the meetings of the members in Form No. 36 together with a scheme of arrangements and explanations, statement under section 393 of the Companies Act and form of proxy in Form No. 37 of the Companies (Court) Rules to be sent members alongwith the said notice. Once Registrar has accorded approval to the notice, it should be got signed by the Chairman appointed for meeting by the High Court who shall preside over the proposed meeting of members.

DESPATCH OF NOTICES TO MEMBERS/SHAREHOLDERS

Once the notice has been signed by the chairman of the forthcoming meeting as aforesaid it could be despatched to the members under certificate of posting at least 21 days before the date of meeting (Rule 73 of Companies (Court) Rules, 1959).

ADVERTISEMENT OF THE NOTICE OF MEMBERS' MEETINGS

The Court may direct the issuance of notice of the meeting of these shareholders by advertisement. In such case rule 74 of the Companies (Court) Rules provides that the notice of the meeting should be advertised in; such newspaper and in such manner as the Court might direct not less than 21 clear days before the date fixed for the meeting. The advertisement shall be in Form No. 38 appended to the Companies (Court)Rules. The companies should submit the draft for the notice to be published in Form No. 38 in an English daily together with a translation thereof in the regional language to the Registrar of High Court for his approval. The advertisement should be released in the newspapers after the Registrar approves the draft.

CONFIRMATION ABOUT SERVICE OF THE NOTICE

Ensure that at least one week before the date of the meeting, the Chairman appointed for the meeting files an Affidavit to the Court about the service of notices to the shareholders that the directions regarding the issue of notices and advertisement have been duly complied with.

HOLDING THE SHAREHOLDERS' GENERAL MEETING AND PASSING THE RESOLUTIONS

The general meeting should be held on the appointed date. Rule 77 of the Companies (Court) Rules prescribes that the decisions of the meeting held pursuant to the court order should be ascertained only by taking a poll. The amalgamation scheme should be approved by the members, by a majority in number of members present in person or on proxy and voting on the resolution and this majority must represent at least 3/4 ths in value of the shares held by the members who vote in the poll.

FILING OF RESOLUTIONS OF GENERAL MEETING WITH REGISTRAR OF COMPANIES

Once the shareholders general meeting approves the amalgamation scheme by a majority in number of members holding not less than 3/4 in value of the equity shares, the scheme is binding on all the members of the company. A copy of the resolution passed by the shareholders approving the scheme of amalgamation should be filed with the Registrar of Companies in Form No. 23 appended to the Companies (Central Government's) General Rules and Forms, 1956 within 30 days from the date of passing the resolution.

SUBMISSION OF REPORT OF THE CHAIRMAN OF THE GENERAL MEETING TO COURT

The chairman of the general meeting of the shareholders is required to submit to the Court within seven days from the date of the meeting a report in Form No. 39, Companies (Court) Rules, 1959 setting out therein the number of persons who attend either personally or by proxy, and the percentage of shareholders who voted in favour of the scheme as well as the resolution passed by the meeting.

SUBMISSION OF JOINT PETITION TO COURT FOR SANCTIONING THE SCHEME

Within seven days from the date on which the Chairman has submitted his report about the result of the meeting to the Court, both the companies should make a joint petition to the High Court for approving the scheme of amalgamation. This petition is to be made in Form No. 40 of Companies (Court) Rules. The Court will fix a date of hearing of the petition. The notice of the hearing should be advertised in the same papers in which the notice of the meeting was advertised or in such other newspapers as the Court may direct, not less than 10 days before the date fixed for the hearing (Rule 80 of Companies (Court) Rules].

ISSUE OF NOTICE TO REGIONAL DIRECTOR, COMPANY LAW BOARD UNDER SECTION 394–A

On receipt of the petition for amalgamation under section 391 of Companies Act, 1956 the Court will give notice of the petition to the Regional Director, Company Law Board and will take into consideration the representations, if any, made by him.

HEARING OF PETITION AND CONFIRMATION OF SCHEME

Having taken up the petition by the Court for hearing it will hear the objections first and if there is no objection to the amalgamation scheme from Regional Director or from any other person who is entitled to oppose the scheme, the Court may pass an order approving the scheme of amalgamation in; Form No. 41 or Form No. 42 of Companies (Court) Rules. The court may also pass order directing that all the property, rights and powers of the transferor company specified in the schedules annexed to the order be transferred without further act or deed to the transferee company and that all the liabilities and duties of the transferor company be transferred without further act or deed.

FILING OF COURT ORDER WITH ROC BY BOTH THE COMPANIES

Both the transferor and transferee companies should obtain the Court's order sanctioning the scheme of amalgamation and file the same with ROC with their respective jurisdiction as required vide section 394(3) of the Companies Act, 1956 within 30 days after the date of the Court's order in Form No. 21 prescribed under the (Central Government's) General Rules and Forms, 1956. The amalgamation will be given effect to from the date on which the High Court's order is filed with the Registrar.

TRANSFER OF THE ASSETS AND LIABILITIES

Section 394(2) vests power in the High Court to order for the transfer of any property or liabilities from transferor company to transferee company. In pursuance of and by virtue of such order such properties and liabilities of the transferor shall automatically stand transferred to transferee company without any further act or deed from the date the Court's order is filed with ROC.

ALLOTMENT OF SHARES TO SHAREHOLDERS OF TRANSFEROR COMPANY

Pursuant to the sanctioned scheme of amalgamation, the shareholders of the transferor company are entitled to get shares in the transferee company in the exchange ratio provided under the said scheme.

There are three different situations in which allotment could be given effect:

1. Where transferor company is not a listed company, the formalities prescribed under listing agreement do not exist and the allotment could take place without setting the record date or giving any advance notice to shareholders except asking them to surrender their old share certificates for exchange by the new ones.
2. The second situation will emerge different where transferor company is a listed company. In this case, the stock exchange is to be intimated of the record date by giving at least 42 days notice or such notice as provided in the listing agreement.

3. The third situation is where allotment to Non-Resident Indians is involved and permission of Reserve Bank of India is necessary. The allotment will take place only on receipt of RBI permission. In this connection refer to regulations 7, 9 and 10B of Foreign Exchange Management (Transfer or Issue of Security by a Person Resident Outside India) Regulations, 2000 as and where applicable.

Having made the allotment, the tranferee company is required to file with ROC with return of allotment in Form No. 2 appended to the Companies (Central Government's) General Rules and Forms within 30 days from the date of allotment in terms of section 75 of the Act. Transferee company shall having issued the new share certificates in lieu of and in exchange of old ones, surrendered by transferor's shareholders should make necessary entries in the register of members and index of members for the shares so allotted in terms of sections 150 and 151 respectively of the Companies Act, 1956.

LISTING OF THE SHARES AT STOCK EXCHANGE

After the amalgamation is effected, the company which takes over the assets and liabilities of the transferor company should apply to the Stock Exchanges where its securities are listed, for listing the new shares allotted to the shareholders of the transferor company.

COURT ORDER TO BE ANNEXED TO MEMORANDUM OF TRANSFEREE COMPANY

It is the mandatory requirement vide section 391(4) of the Companies Act, 1956 that after the certified copy of the Court's order sanctioning the scheme of amalgamation is filed with Registrar, it should be annexed to every copy of the Memorandum issued by the transferee company. Failure to comply with requirement renders the company and its officers liable to punishment.

PRESERVATION OF BOOKS AND PAPERS OF AMALGAMATED CO.

Section 396A of the Act requires that the books and papers of the amalgamated company should be preserved and not be disposed of without prior permission of the Central Government.

THE POST MERGER SECRETARIAL OBLIGATIONS

There are various formalities to be complied with after amalgamation of the companies is given effect to and allotment of shares to the shareholders of the transferor company is over. These formalities include filing of returns with Registrar of Companies, transfer of investments of transferor company in; the name of the transferee, intimating banks and financial institutions, creditors and debtors about the transfer of the transferor company's assets and liabilities in the name of the transferee company, etc. All these aspects along with restructuring of organization and management and capital are discussed in stage relating to post-merger reorganization of transferee company.

WITHDRAWAL OF THE SCHEME NOT PERMISSIBLE

Once the scheme for merger has been approved by requisite majority of shareholders and creditors, the scheme cannot be withdrawn by subsequent meeting of shareholders by passing Resolution for withdrawal of the petition submitted to the court under section 391 for sanctioning the scheme.

CANCELLATION OF THE SCHEME AND ORDER OF WINDING-UP

It was held by the Supreme Court in J.K (Bombay) (P) Ltd. Vs. New Kaiser-I-Hind that the effect of winding up order is that except for certain preferential payments provided in the Act, the property of the company is applied in satisfaction of its liabilities pari passu. Pari passu distribution is to be made in satisfaction of its liabilities as they exist at the commencement of the winding-up. So long as the scheme is in operation and is bind on the company and its creditors, the rights and obligations of those on whom it is binding are undoubtedly governed by its provisions.

But once the scheme is cancelled under section 392(2) on the ground that it cannot be satisfactorily worked and a winding-up order passed such an order is deemed to be for all purposes to be one made under section 433. It is not because as if the scheme has been sanctioned under section 391 that a winding-up order under section 392 (2) cannot be made.

THE SPECIALISED FORMALITIES TO COVER UP AMALGAMATION

The steps for merger or amalgamation are not the only considerations effecting merger but in addition to the above and in relation thereto a number of special formalities are also complied with which have been covered in detail in specific stages like share valuation and exchange ratio, accounting aspects of funding of reorganization plans, etc. These aspects have been given treatment under different stages. Readers may refer to relevant stages in the matter of drafting the scheme of amalgamation, carrying out valuation of the assets of the companies, calculating share exchange ratio, etc. wherever felt necessary. Case studies provided in the book are based on real happenings and provide practical insight into the procedural aspects.

11

Business Acquisition

INTRODUCTION

Business acquisition is the process of acquiring a company to build on strengths or weaknesses of the acquiring company. A merger is similar to an acquisition but refers more strictly to combining all of the interests of both companies in to a stronger single company. The end result is to grow the business in a quicker and more profitable manner than normal organic growth would allow.

PROCESS

The process begins with defining the type of business that would make a good acquisition. Generally businesses within the same segment or a highly complementary market segment are targeted. Once defined the target business is approached and if interest is shown due diligence is performed to ascertain the financial condition of the business. When the financial terms are agreed upon, and the contract is signed the merger portion of the acquisition begins. Overlapping processes, personnel and products are evaluated and the better-performing pieces are retained, while the less desirable are cut. Difficulty often arises when management teams are combined and responsibilities distributed between the acquiring business and the acquired.

SINGLE BUSINESS ACQUISITIONS AND SPLIT AND SELL

A single acquisition refers to one company buying the assets and operations of another company and absorbing what is needed while simply discarding duplicated or unnecessary pieces of the acquired business. "Split and sell" acquisitions involve buying an entire business in order to gain one or two pieces of the business.

The acquiring business may wish to retain the customer list and a product line, while moving manufacturing and other production related duties to an existing line. In this case the excess is often sold off to recapture some of the acquisition cost.

AFFILIATE ACQUISITIONS

Businesses that use affiliates to sell and market their products may find themselves in the position of losing control of the marketing portion. This presents a danger as the entire business cycle is dependent on the sales cycle, which is now external to the business. In this scenario the acquiring business may be forced into paying a premium to the affiliate, to regain control of the process without upsetting current customers and cash flow. In rare instances the affiliate will gain so much influence that it can purchase the parent company.

MERGERS AND ACQUISITIONS

Mergers and acquisitions refers to the aspect of corporate strategy, corporate finance and management dealing with the buying, selling, dividing and combining of different companies and similar entities that can aid, finance, or help an enterprise grow rapidly in its sector or location of origin or a new field or new location without creating a subsidiary, other child entity or using a joint venture. The distinction between a "merger" and an "acquisition" has become increasingly blurred in various respects, although it has not completely disappeared in all situations.

ACQUISITION

An acquisition is the purchase of one business or company by another company or other business entity. *Consolidation* occurs when two companies combine together to form a new enterprise altogether, and neither of the previous companies survives independently. Acquisitions are divided into "private" and "public" acquisitions, depending on whether the acquiree or merging company is or is not listed on public stock markets. An additional dimension or categorization consists of whether an acquisition is *friendly* or *hostile*. Achieving acquisition success has proven to be very difficult, while various studies have shown that 50% of acquisitions were unsuccessful. Whether a purchase is perceived as being a "friendly" one or a "hostile" depends significantly on how the proposed acquisition is communicated to and perceived by the target company's board of directors, employees and shareholders.

It is normal for M&A deal communications to take place in a so-called 'confidentiality bubble' wherein the flow of information is restricted pursuant to confidentiality agreements. In the case of a friendly transaction, the companies cooperate in negotiations; in the case of a hostile deal, the board and/or management of the target is unwilling to be bought or the target's board has no prior knowledge of the offer. Hostile acquisitions can, and often do, ultimately become "friendly", as the acquiror secures endorsement of the transaction from the board of the acquiree company. This usually requires an improvement in the terms of the offer and/or through negotiation.

"Acquisition" usually refers to a purchase of a smaller firm by a larger one. Sometimes, however, a smaller firm will acquire management control of a larger and/or longer-established company and retain the name of the latter for the post-acquisition combined entity. This is known as a reverse takeover. Another type of acquisition is the reverse merger, a form of transaction that enables a private company to be publicly listed in a relatively short time frame. A reverse merger occurs when a privately held company buys a publicly listed shell company, usually one with no business and limited assets. There are also a variety of structures used in securing control over the assets of a company, which have different tax and regulatory implications:

- The buyer buys the shares, and therefore control, of the target company being purchased. Ownership control of the company in turn conveys effective control over the assets of the company, but since the company is acquired intact as a going concern, this form of transaction carries with it all of the liabilities accrued by that business over its past and all of the risks that company faces in its commercial environment.
- The buyer buys the assets of the target company. The cash the target receives from the sell-off is paid back to its shareholders by dividend or through liquidation. This type of transaction leaves the target company as an empty shell, if the buyer buys out the entire assets. A buyer often structures the transaction as an asset purchase to "cherry-pick" the assets that it wants and leave out the assets and liabilities that it does not. This can be particularly important where foreseeable liabilities may include future, unquantified damage awards such as those that could arise from litigation over defective products, employee benefits or terminations, or environmental damage. A disadvantage of this structure is the tax that many jurisdictions, particularly outside the United States, impose on transfers of the individual assets, whereas stock transactions can frequently be structured as like-kind exchanges or other arrangements that are tax-free or tax-neutral, both to the buyer and to the seller's shareholders.

The terms "demerger", "spin-off" and "spin-out" are sometimes used to indicate a situation where one company splits into two, generating a second company separately listed on a stock exchange. As per the knowledge based views, firms can generate greater values through the retention of knowledge-based resources which they generate and integrate. Extracting technological benefits during and after acquisition is ever challenging issue because of organizational differences. Based on the content analysis of seven interviews authors concluded five following components for their grounded model of acquisition:

1. Improper documentation and changing implicit knowledge makes it difficult to share information during acquisition.

2. For acquired firm symbolic and cultural independence which is the base of technology and capabilities are more important than administrative independence.
3. Detailed knowledge exchange and integrations are difficult when the acquired firm is large and high performing.
4. Management of executives from acquired firm is critical in terms of promotions and pay incentives to utilize their talent and value their expertise.
5. Transfer of technologies and capabilities are most difficult task to manage because of complications of acquisition implementation. The risk of losing implicit knowledge is always associated with the fast pace acquisition.

Preservation of tacit knowledge, employees and literature are always delicate during and after acquisition. Strategic management of all these resources is a very important factor for a successful acquisition. Increase in acquisitions in our global business environment has pushed us to evaluate the key stake holders of acquisition very carefully before implementation. It is imperative for the acquirer to understand this relationship and apply it to its advantage. Retention is only possible when resources are exchanged and managed without affecting their independence.

Distinction between Mergers and Acquisitions

Although often used synonymously, the terms merger and acquisition mean slightly different things. When one company takes over another and clearly establishes itself as the new owner, the purchase is called an acquisition. From a legal point of view, the target company ceases to exist, the buyer "swallows" the business and the buyer's stock continues to be traded. In the pure sense of the term, a merger happens when two firms agree to go forward as a single new company rather than remain separately owned and operated. This kind of action is more precisely referred to as a "merger of equals". The firms are often of about the same size. Both companies' stocks are surrendered and new company stock is issued in its place. For example, in the 1999 merger of Glaxo Wellcome and SmithKline Beecham, both firms ceased to exist when they merged, and a new company, GlaxoSmithKline, was created. In practice, however, actual mergers of equals don't happen very often.

Usually, one company will buy another and, as part of the deal's terms, simply allow the acquired firm to proclaim that the action is a merger of equals, even if it is technically an acquisition. Being bought out often carries negative connotations; therefore, by describing the deal euphemistically as a merger, deal makers and top managers try to make the takeover more palatable. An example of this would be the takeover of Chrysler by Daimler-Benz in 1999 which was widely referred to as a merger at the time. A purchase deal will also be called a merger when both CEOs agree that joining together is in the best interest of both of their companies. But when the deal is unfriendly it is always regarded as an acquisition.

BUSINESS VALUATION

The five most common ways to valuate a business are:

1. Asset valuation,
2. Historical earnings valuation,
3. Future maintainable earnings valuation,
4. relative valuation,
5. Discounted cash flow valuation

Professionals who valuate businesses generally do not use just one of these methods but a *combination* of some of them in order to obtain a more accurate value. The information in the balance sheet or income statement is obtained by one of three accounting measures: a Notice to Reader, a Review Engagement or an Audit. Accurate business valuation is one of the most important aspects of M&A as valuations like these will have a major impact on the price that a business will be sold for. Most often this information is expressed in a Letter of Opinion of Value when the business is being valuated for interest's sake. There are other, more detailed ways of expressing the value of a business. While these reports generally get more detailed and expensive as the size of a company increases, this is not always the case as there are many complicated industries which require more attention to detail, regardless of size.

FINANCING M&A

Mergers are generally differentiated from acquisitions partly by the way in which they are financed and partly by the relative size of the companies. Various methods of financing an M&A deal exist:

Cash

Payment by cash. Such transactions are usually termed acquisitions rather than mergers because the shareholders of the target company are removed from the picture and the target comes under the control of the bidder's shareholders.

Stock

Payment in the acquiring company's stock, issued to the shareholders of the acquired company at a given ratio proportional to the valuation of the latter.

Which Method of Financing to Choose?

There are some elements to think about when choosing the form of payment. When submitting an offer, the acquiring firm should consider other potential bidders and think strategically. The form of payment might be decisive for the seller. With pure cash deals, there is no doubt on the real value of the bid. The contingency of the share payment is indeed removed. Thus, a cash offer preempts competitors better than securities. Taxes are a second element to consider and should be evaluated with the counsel of competent tax and accounting advisers.

Third, with a share deal the buyer's capital structure might be affected and the control of the New co modified. If the issuance of shares is necessary, shareholders of the acquiring company might prevent such capital increase at the general meeting of shareholders. The risk is removed with a cash transaction. Then, the balance sheet of the buyer will be modified and the decision maker should take into account the effects on the reported financial results. For example, in a pure cash deal, liquidity ratios might decrease. On the other hand, in a pure stock for stock transaction, the company might show lower profitability ratios. However, economic dilution must prevail towards accounting dilution when making the choice. The form of payment and financing options are tightly linked.

If the buyer pays cash, there are three main financing options:

- *Cash on hand*: it consumes financial slack and may decrease debt rating. There are no major transaction costs.
- It consumes financial slack, may decrease debt rating and increase cost of debt. Transaction costs include underwriting or closing costs of 1% to 3% of the face value.
- *Issue of stock*: it increases financial slack, may improve debt rating and reduce cost of debt. Transaction costs include fees for preparation of a proxy statement, an extraordinary shareholder meeting and registration.

If the buyer pays with stock, the financing possibilities are:

- Issue of stock.
- *Shares in treasury*: it increases financial slack may improve debt rating and reduce cost of debt. Transaction costs include brokerage fees if shares are repurchased in the market otherwise there are no major costs.

In general, stock will create financial flexibility. Transaction costs must also be considered but tend to have a greater impact on the payment decision for larger transactions. Finally, paying cash or with shares is a way to signal value to the other party, *e.g.*: buyers tend to offer stock when they believe their shares are overvalued and cash when undervalued.

SPECIALIST M&A ADVISORY FIRMS

Although at present the majority of M&A advice is provided by full-service investment banks, recent years have seen a rise in the prominence of specialist M&A advisers, who only provide M&A advice. These companies are sometimes referred to as Transition companies, assisting businesses often referred to as "companies in transition." To perform these services in the US, an advisor must be a licensed broker dealer, and subject to SEC regulation. More information on M&A advisory firms is provided at corporate advisory.

MOTIVES BEHIND M&A

The dominant rationale used to explain M&A activity is that acquiring firms seek improved financial performance.

The following motives are considered to improve financial performance:

- *Economy of scale*: This refers to the fact that the combined company can often reduce its fixed costs by removing duplicate departments or operations, lowering the costs of the company relative to the same revenue stream, thus increasing profit margins.
- *Economy of scope*: This refers to the efficiencies primarily associated with demand-side changes, such as increasing or decreasing the scope of marketing and distribution, of different types of products.
- *Increased revenue or market share*: This assumes that the buyer will be absorbing a major competitor and thus increase its market power to set prices.
- *Cross-selling*: For example, a bank buying a stock broker could then sell its banking products to the stock broker's customers, while the broker can sign up the bank's customers for brokerage accounts. Or, a manufacturer can acquire and sell complementary products.
- *Synergy*: For example, managerial economies such as the increased opportunity of managerial specialization. Another example are purchasing economies due to increased order size and associated bulk-buying discounts.
- *Taxation*: A profitable company can buy a loss maker to use the target's loss as their advantage by reducing their tax liability. In the United States and many other countries, rules are in place to limit the ability of profitable companies to "shop" for loss making companies, limiting the tax motive of an acquiring company. Tax minimization strategies include purchasing assets of a non-performing company and reducing current tax liability under the Tanner-White PLLC Troubled Asset Recovery Plan.
- *Geographical or other diversification*: This is designed to smooth the earnings results of a company, which over the long term smoothens the stock price of a company, giving conservative investors more confidence in investing in the company. However, this does not always deliver value to shareholders.
- *Resource transfer*: resources are unevenly distributed across firms and the interaction of target and acquiring firm resources can create value through either overcoming information asymmetry or by combining scarce resources.

- *Vertical integration*: Vertical integration occurs when an upstream and downstream firm merge. There are several reasons for this to occur. One reason is to internalise an externality problem. A common example is of such an externality is double marginalization. Double marginalization occurs when both the upstream and downstream firms have monopoly power, each firm reduces output from the competitive level to the monopoly level, creating two deadweight losses. By merging the vertically integrated firm can collect one deadweight loss by setting the downstream firm's output to the competitive level. This increases profits and consumer surplus. A merger that creates a vertically integrated firm can be profitable.
- *"Acqui-hire"*: An "acq-hire" may occur especially when the target is a small private company or is in the startup phase. In this case, the acquiring company simply hires the staff of the target private company, thereby acquiring its talent. The target private company simply dissolves and little legal issues are involved. Acqui-hires have become a very popular type of transaction in recent years.
- Absorption of similar businesses under single management: similar portfolio invested by two different mutual funds namely united money market fund and united growth and income fund, caused the management to absorb united money market fund into united growth and income fund.

However, on average and across the most commonly studied variables, acquiring firms' financial performance does not positively change as a function of their acquisition activity. Therefore, additional motives for merger and acquisition that may not add shareholder value include:

- Diversification: While this may hedge a company against a downturn in an individual industry it fails to deliver value, since it is possible for individual shareholders to achieve the same hedge by diversifying their portfolios at a much lower cost than those associated with a merger.
- Manager's hubris: manager's overconfidence about expected synergies from M&A which results in overpayment for the target company.
- Empire-building: Managers have larger companies to manage and hence more power.
- Manager's compensation: In the past, certain executive management teams had their payout based on the total amount of profit of the company, instead of the profit per share, which would give the team a perverse incentive to buy companies to increase the total profit while decreasing the profit per share.

EFFECTS ON MANAGEMENT

A study published in the July/August 2008 issue of the Journal of Business

Strategy suggests that mergers and acquisitions destroy leadership continuity in target companies' top management teams for at least a decade following a deal. The study found that target companies lose 21 per cent of their executives each year for at least 10 years following an acquisition–more than double the turnover experienced in non-merged firms. If the businesses of the acquired and acquiring companies overlap, then such turnover is to be expected; in other words, there can only be one CEO, CFO, et cetera at a time.

BRAND CONSIDERATIONS

Mergers and acquisitions often create brand problems, beginning with what to call the company after the transaction and going down into detail about what to do about overlapping and competing product brands. Decisions about what brand equity to write off are not inconsequential. And, given the ability for the right brand choices to drive preference and earn a price premium, the future success of a merger or acquisition depends on making wise brand choices.

Brand decision-makers essentially can choose from four different approaches to dealing with naming issues, each with specific pros and cons:

- Keep one name and discontinue the other. The strongest legacy brand with the best prospects for the future lives on. In the merger of United Airlines and Continental Airlines, the United brand will continue forward, while Continental is retired.
- Keep one name and demote the other. The strongest name becomes the company name and the weaker one is demoted to a divisional brand or product brand. An example is Caterpillar Inc. keeping the Bucyrus International name.
- Keep both names and use them together. Some companies try to please everyone and keep the value of both brands by using them together. This can create a unwieldy name, as in the case of Pricewaterhouse Coopers, which has since changed its brand name to "PwC".
- Discard both legacy names and adopt a totally new one. The classic example is the merger of Bell Atlantic with GTE, which became Verizon Communications. Not every merger with a new name is successful. By consolidating into YRC Worldwide, the company lost the considerable value of both Yellow Freight and Roadway Corp.

The factors influencing brand decisions in a merger or acquisition transaction can range from political to tactical. Ego can drive choice just as well as rational factors such as brand value and costs involved with changing brands. Beyond the bigger issue of what to call the company after the transaction comes the ongoing detailed choices about what divisional, product and service brands to keep. The detailed decisions about the brand portfolio are covered under the topic brand architecture.

THE GREAT MERGER MOVEMENT

The Great Merger Movement was a predominantly U.S. business phenomenon that happened from 1895 to 1905. During this time, small firms with little market share consolidated with similar firms to form large, powerful institutions that dominated their markets. It is estimated that more than 1,800 of these firms disappeared into consolidations, many of which acquired substantial shares of the markets in which they operated. The vehicle used were so-called trusts. In 1900 the value of firms acquired in mergers was 20% of GDP. In 1990 the value was only 3% and from 1998–2000 it was around 10–11% of GDP.

Companies such as DuPont, US Steel, and General Electric that merged during the Great Merger Movement were able to keep their dominance in their respective sectors through 1929, and in some cases today, due to growing technological advances of their products, patents, and brand recognition by their customers. There were also other companies that held the greatest market share in 1905 but at the same time did not have the competitive advantages of the companies like DuPont and General Electric.

These companies such as International Paper and American Chicle saw their market share decrease significantly by 1929 as smaller competitors joined forces with each other and provided much more competition. The companies that merged were mass producers of homogeneous goods that could exploit the efficiencies of large volume production. In addition, many of these mergers were capital-intensive. Due to high fixed costs, when demand fell, these newly-merged companies had an incentive to maintain output and reduce prices. However more often than not mergers were "quick mergers". These "quick mergers" involved mergers of companies with unrelated technology and different management.

As a result, the efficiency gains associated with mergers were not present. The new and bigger company would actually face higher costs than competitors because of these technological and managerial differences. Thus, the mergers were not done to see large efficiency gains, they were in fact done because that was the trend at the time. Companies which had specific fine products, like fine writing paper, earned their profits on high margin rather than volume and took no part in Great Merger Movement.

Short-run Factors

One of the major short run factors that sparked The Great Merger Movement was the desire to keep prices high. However, high prices attracted the entry of new firms into the industry who sought to take a piece of the total product. With many firms in a market, supply of the product remains high. A major catalyst behind the Great Merger Movement was the Panic of 1893, which led to a major decline in demand for many homogeneous goods. For producers of homogeneous goods, when demand falls, these producers have more of an incentive to maintain output and cut prices, in order to spread out the high fixed costs these producers faced and the desire to exploit efficiencies of maximum volume production. However, during the Panic of 1893, the fall in demand led to a steep fall in prices. Another economic model proposed by Naomi R. Lamoreaux for explaining the steep price falls is to view the involved firms acting as monopolies in their respective markets. As quasi-monopolists, firms set quantity where marginal cost equals marginal revenue and price where this quantity intersects demand. When the Panic of 1893 hit, demand fell and along with demand, the firm's marginal revenue fell as well. Given high fixed costs, the new price was below average total cost, resulting in a loss. However, also being in a high fixed costs industry, these costs can be spread out through greater production. To return to the quasi-monopoly model, in order for a firm to earn profit, firms would steal part of another firm's market share by dropping their price slightly and producing to the point where higher quantity and lower price exceeded their average total cost.

As other firms joined this practice, prices began falling everywhere and a price war ensued. One strategy to keep prices high and to maintain profitability was for producers of the same good to collude with each other and form associations, also known as cartels. These cartels were thus able to raise prices right away, sometimes more than doubling prices. However, these prices set by cartels only provided a short-term solution because cartel members would cheat on each other by setting a lower price than the price set by the cartel. Also, the high price set by the cartel would encourage new firms to enter the industry and offer competitive pricing, causing prices to fall once again. As a result, these cartels did not succeed in maintaining high prices for a period of no more than a few years. The most viable solution to this problem was for firms to merge, through horizontal integration, with other top firms in the market in order to control a large market share and thus successfully set a higher price.

Long-run Factors

In the long run, due to the desire to keep costs low, it was advantageous for firms to merge and reduce their transportation costs thus producing and transporting from one location rather than various sites of different companies as in the past. Low transport costs, coupled with economies of scale also increased firm size by two- to fourfold during the second half of the nineteenth century. In addition, technological changes prior to the merger movement within companies increased the efficient size of plants with capital intensive assembly lines allowing for economies of scale. Thus improved technology and transportation were forerunners to the Great Merger Movement. In part due to competitors and in part due to the government, however, many of these initially successful mergers were eventually dismantled. The U.S.

government passed the Sherman Act in 1890, setting rules against price fixing and monopolies. Starting in the 1890s with such cases as Addyston Pipe and Steel Company v. United States, the courts attacked large companies for strategizing with others or within their own companies to maximize profits. Price fixing with competitors created a greater incentive for companies to unite and merge under one name so that they were not competitors anymore and technically not price fixing.

Merger Waves

The economic history has been divided into *Merger Waves* based on the merger activities in the business world as:

Period	Name	Facet
1897–1904	First Wave	Horizontal mergers
1916–1929	Second Wave	Vertical mergers
1965–1969	Third Wave	Diversified conglomerate mergers
1981–1989	Fourth Wave	Congeneric mergers; Hostile takeovers; Corporate Raiding
1992–2000	Fifth Wave	Cross-border mergers
2003–2008	Sixth Wave	Shareholder Activism, Private Equity, LBO

Deal Objectives in More Recent Merger Waves

During the third merger wave corporate marriages involved more diverse companies. Acquirers more frequently bought into different industries. Sometimes this was done to smooth out cyclical bumps, to diversify, the hope being that it would hedge an investment portfolio. Starting in the fourth merger wave and continuing today, companies are more likely to acquire in the same business, or close to it, firms that complement and strengthen an acquirer's capacity to serve customers. Buyers aren't necessarily hungry for the target companies' hard assets. Now they're going after entirely different prizes. The hot prizes aren't things—they're thoughts, methodologies, people and relationships. Soft goods, so to speak. Many companies are being bought for their patents, licenses, market share, name brand, research staffs, methods, customer base, or culture. Soft capital, like this, is very perishable, fragile, and fluid. Integrating it usually takes more finesse and expertise than integrating machinery, real estate, inventory and other tangibles.

CROSS-BORDER M&A

In a study conducted in 2000 by Lehman Brothers, it was found that, on average, large M&A deals cause the domestic currency of the target corporation to appreciate by 1% relative to the acquirers. The rise of globalization has exponentially increased the necessity for MAIC Trust accounts and securities clearing services for Like-Kind Exchanges for cross-border M&A. In 1997 alone, there were over 2333 cross-border transactions, worth a total of approximately $298 billion. Due to the complicated nature of cross-border M&A, the vast majority of cross-border actions have unsuccessful anies seek to expand their global footprint and become more agile at creating high-performing businesses and cultures across national boundaries.

Even mergers of companies with headquarters in the same country are very much of this type and require MAIC custodial services. After all, when Boeing acquires McDonnell Douglas, the two American companies must integrate operations in dozens of countries around the world. This is just as true for other supposedly "single country" mergers, such as the $29 billion dollar merger of Swiss drug makers Sandoz and Ciba-Geigy.

M&A FAILURE

Despite the goal of performance improvement, results from mergers and acquisitions are often disappointing. Numerous empirical studies show high failure rates of M&A deals. Studies are mostly focused on individual determinants. A book by Thomas Straub "Reasons for frequent failure in Mergers and Acquisitions" develops a comprehensive research framework that bridges rival perspectives and promotes a modern understanding of factors underlying M&A performance. The first important step towards this objective is the development of a common frame of reference that spans conflicting theoretical assumptions from different perspectives. On this basis, a comprehensive framework is proposed with which to understand the origins of M&A performance better and address the problem of fragmentation by integrating the most important competing perspectives in respect of studies on M&A Furthermore just as to the existing literature relevant determinants of firm performance are derived from each dimension of the model.

For the dimension strategic management, the six strategic variables: market similarity, market complementarities, production operation similarity, production operation complementarities, market power, and purchasing power were identified having an important impact on M&A performance. For the dimension organizational behaviour, the variables acquisition experience, relative size, and cultural differences were found to be important. Finally, relevant determinants of M&A performance from the financial field were acquisition premium, bidding process, and due diligence. Three different ways in order to best measure post M&A performance are recognized: Synergy realization, absolute performance and finally relative performance.

MERGER INTEGRATION

Merger integration, or post-merger integration refers to the aspect of an organizational merger that involves combining the original socio-technical systems of the merging organizations into one such newly-combined system. The process of combining two or more organizations into a single organization involves several organizational systems, such as people, resources and tasks. The process of combining these systems is known as 'integration'. Integration fits within an organizational life-cycle or specific business mergers and acquisitions cycle where businesses buy, integrate then dispose of other businesses:

- Definition of vision and strategy
- Selection of growth method: organic vs inorganic
- Target identification
- Pre-deal evaluation and due diligence
- Negotiation and deal completion
- Post-merger integration
- Acquisition Integration
- Ongoing improvement
- Disposal

INTEGRATION STRATEGY

Well-intentioned acquirers often opt for a merger integration strategy that involves a rather slow, measured pace in making changes. The logic influencing executives to proceed in this fashion appears sound, but is deceiving. The rationale, as explained by executives, is that too much change, coming too quickly, could be overwhelming for employees. They conclude that it would be better to make incremental changes in a deliberate, carefully staged fashion, allowing time for a dose of change to be assimilated before administering another. But instead of worrying about having people "OD" on change, the primary concern should be to finish the merger and put an end to the suffering.

It's the uncertainty and ambiguity that create the most stress—not knowing what will happen, when it will happen, or how one will be affected. The longer these issues go unanswered, the more merging firms are likely to lose productivity, as well as their people. Human beings can handle a high level of change. They adjust and adapt remarkably well—if there is something solid they can adjust to. But people have an uncanny, intuitive feel for when the transition and change of a merger is actually over. Certainly they are savvy and perceptive enough not to be lulled into thinking that carefully paced changes are somehow less threatening to their careers. Companies that string out the integration process invariably come under harsh criticism from people at all levels of the organization. Given their preference, employees would vote in favour of expediting the process—for example, integrate, consolidate, terminate, reorganize, or redirect as necessary. They just want to get on with it, so they can get on with their careers and make their personal adjustments to whatever happens to them as individuals. Another very strong argument for moving rapidly in making merger-related changes relates to the "time window" for change.

It works like this. Being acquired or merged has a profound impact on the target company. It destabilizes the organization. Things get knocked around in this time of upheaval. The organization is in a state of flux—up in the air—and there is a brief opportunity to reshape many aspects of the company before things settle back down and crystallize into the same old routines. But the window of opportunity is open only for a brief and unspecific period of time. People are expecting change, and the circumstances are right. Top management should seize the opportunity before the window closes. The same changes, sought at a later date, after the time window has shut and the organizational dissonance has faded, can meet with extreme resistance.

ACQUISITION INTEGRATION

Integration Management should begin immediately when the deal is announced. Otherwise, you're going to be running behind, and the bulk of your time will be spent trying to fix problems rather than prevent them. You'll get caught in a crossfire—on one hand needing to develop your integration strategy, and on the other hand having to deal with problems that have a headstart on you. A wait-and-see attitude puts you and the organization at a severe disadvantage. You'll end up being reactive, instead of proactive. Rather than being effectively positioned to shape circumstances, you'll be a victim of them.

ORGANIZING FOR INTEGRATION

Mergers and acquisitions heat up the management atmosphere. There is so much to do at once and so much at stake. It is crucial to proceed with a clear sense of priorities, and this calls for a carefully structured approach. Good integration management is characterized by discipline, focus, and dedicated resources. A project group should be formed to manage the transition, and it should operate as a parallel organization focusing purely on the integration process. This organization needs to be adequately staffed, with people's roles and responsibilities clearly defined.

Several individuals should plan to devote their time fully to the project during the transition so that the integration process has the necessary direction and continuity. Disorganization gets dangerous during transition. Merging is confusing enough even when good project management practices are in place. Without that kind of discipline, the situation can all too easily spin out of control. This is a highly charged political climate where people operate with very different, personalized agendas. There are so many pressure points, conflicting points of view, and management distractions. Unless you employ a carefully orchestrated project management approach, it is almost impossible to get through the integration without damaging the potential of the deal. Treating the transition period like a special project helps management achieve adherence to schedule, effective use of resources, a focus on true priorities, and responsible management of risk. That certainly makes it worth the effort. But beyond all that, taking a project management approach actually makes it much easier to get through the demanding integration process successfully. It helps prevent the haphazard, floundering efforts so often seen where a lack of good organization results in wasted motion, false starts, and divergent initiatives that emotionally drain the people involved, while producing very poor outcomes.

PROJECT STRUCTURE AND ROLES

An efficient and serviceable structure for the project group consists of three different layers: a steering committee, a merger team, and a variety of task-force teams. Assuming that the appropriate people are assigned to these slots, the group is in a position to do a good job of integration management. Typically, the steering committee is small, consisting of two to four individuals, all of whom are senior-level people. The focus of this group is to provide direction to the integration effort as it relates to strategy and policy. While not committed full-time to the process, this group should meet on a regularly scheduled basis to approve integration plans and review progress.

The steering committee may have a majority of its members coming from the acquirer. But representation from both organizations helps ensure that key financial, operational, or cultural aspects are not overlooked during the integration process. Executive sponsorship is critical to the success of the integration. As the integration moves forward, there will be resistance from both individuals and departments. This opposition may result from a conflict with some operating priority or protection of the status quo. Senior-level personnel who serve on the steering committee may be the only ones with the necessary clout to get past these obstacles. The steering committee will also need to act as the final decision point for resource allocation and prioritizing of the recommended initiatives.

The merger team, consisting of some three to five full-time people, is the real workhorse responsible for driving the integration forward and keeping good project-management discipline in place. One member of this team should be designated as the integration project leader and given the overall responsibility for the project's progress. As a whole, this team's purpose is to provide the guidance and day-to-day decision making that will allow the integration process to move forward on a timely basis. The third level of the project management structure consists of a number of task-force teams. These units ordinarily contain three to five people and are formed to address specific organizational issues needing attention because of the merger/acquisition event. They can be either resource driven, such as finance, human resources, information technology, and so on, or operations driven just as to business unit, product line, or perhaps geographic location. The resource-driven teams will have tasks of their own to complete but also will need to support the operating groups in the completion of their respective tasks. The task-force teams commonly have individuals working both full-time and part-time on the integration and should have one person designated as the team leader. The assortment of task-force teams take their marching orders from, and report to, the merger team.

In turn, the merger team is ultimately accountable to the steering committee. Under the day-to-day direction of the integration project leader, the merger team has responsibility for coordinating all of the analyses and recommendations for action that the task-force teams generate.

COMMON MISTAKES IN INTEGRATION PROJECT MANAGEMENT

These errors are seen all too often even in well-run companies with highly capable executives at the helm:

- *Lack of a clearly defined project leader*: Make sure one person is put in charge of the integration effort. Assigning individual accountability and responsibility is the best way to get a strong action orientation in support of the integration project. Some organizations choose one person from each organization to serve as co-leaders in the process. While this may seem equitable, it can lead to confusion as to who has formal sign-off over a given task or activity, or who is ultimately responsible for the success or failure of the transition effort. Generally it's a good idea to make sure that individuals from both organizations are present on the team, but it works best when only one person is in charge.
- *Failure to execute against plan*: Transition teams often find it is easier to develop a plan than it is to execute one. The programme for action should not be so complicated that it cannot be carried out. The role of the merger team is to ensure that the plan is manageable and that the task-force teams do not become sidetracked.
- *Declaring victory on the 20-yard line*: Avoid the temptation to proclaim that the merger is over just because some important, top-level issues have been settled. The chairman of a large managed care company came before his people, stating that the integration was complete once the senior management team had been identified. He felt that each executive would handle integration concerns within their respective operating areas. For lack of a coordinated ongoing effort, the integration proceeded at different speeds in different parts of the organization. The result was a clumsy, poorly executed integration.
- *Skimping on the investment in the integration effort*: Companies often invest heavily in due diligence, then get remarkably stingy in terms of their willingness to spend on the integration effort. This helps explain why so many good deals go bad. A strategy for growth

through mergers is carefully conceived but poorly implemented. The economics argue strongly in favour of allocating sufficient resources—money and people—to support a sophisticated integration process.

- *Presuming that all people are at the same point*: Senior management typically spends months planning a merger or acquisition. Invariably, they are way ahead of the rest of the people in terms of having adjusted to the situation. They've had access to information, time to wrestle with the issues, and—likely as not—already have closure on how they personally will be affected by the deal. Other folks will be lagging far behind. Remember this when communicating to the rest of the organization. Design an aggressive communication plan to get people the information they need. Move at top speed to give them closure on the "me issues."
- *Leaving too much on the table*: Too many integration efforts are far too superficial. Often, companies are satisfied if they can merely get the benefits outlined in the initial deal announcement. But usually more juice can be squeezed out of the merger. For example, is there a technology in one of the companies that can be used in the product line of the other company? Has each task-force team taken a good, hard look at the combined organization to find every possible benefit? Seek out every possible synergy? Continue to look for cost cutting and revenue growth beyond what the deal makers originally identified.

TURNOVER IN MERGERS

It is not surprising that people often choose to leave an organization or "de-commit" during a merger or acquisition. The widespread turmoil created by change turns people's thoughts inward, away from their job and towards personal concerns. Self-protective thoughts swirl through their minds, leaving people to wonder about the wisdom in waiting to see what will happen to their careers. The big concerns people are wrestling with reflect their uncertainty about how they will fare in the new scheme of things.

For example, they worry, "What will happen to my job, my pay, my security?" These doubts and unanswered questions create a great feeding ground for headhunters and company recruiters, who naturally step up their efforts to pick off the best talent. These recruiters who are circling the merger scene have the advantage of being able to buzz in fast and lay a hard offer in front of a person. This immediately provides the individual with an alternative to the ambiguity, uncertainty, and personal concerns he or she is experiencing. The turnover statistics associated with mergers and acquisitions are staggering.

Based on studies by Pritchett, LP, when no coordinated retention actions are taken, 47 per cent of all senior managers in an acquired firm leave within the first year of the acquisition. But the exodus doesn't stop there. Within the first three years, 72 per cent end up heading for the door. Turnover peaks at two times in the typical merger scenario. The first vulnerable point is early on—during the first several weeks—when the integration process is just getting under way. The second exodus occurs some months later, as the new organization finally takes shape and people get an accurate sense of what it's going to be like to work in the merged organization. At this point the wait-and-see period is over. Now comes the second turnover surge, as some of the people who were patient enough to "give it a shot" decide the merger hasn't worked in their best interests. This crew is harder to re-recruit. The secret lies in starting early and being willing to invest as much time and effort as you would have to spend in attracting replacement personnel.

CULTURAL INTEGRATION

When integrating cultures, people can get fussy about a lot of trivial stuff. Practically everybody has a pet issue or two—that is, their own cultural priorities or sensitivities. These may be aspects of the culture that they personally want somebody to "fix." Or traits that they feel shouldn't be tampered with at all. Obviously, senior management can't keep everyone happy when it comes to culture change. Therefore, executive teams should not get scattered trying to address all the cultural preference items people make noise about or tiptoe around the delicate culture issues if they're crucial and need to be hit head-on. Focus sharply on what's mission critical.

Ordinarily, only about 5 per cent of the cultural issues truly qualify as mission critical. This small handful of traits accounts for about 95 per cent of culture's influence on operating performance. These are the "vital few." The cultural matters that remain are more or less noise, the "trivial many." And it's a mistake for the organization to get distracted by these lightweight issues.

Why? Because this remaining 95 per cent that's basically noise will soak up people's attention, yet account for only 5 per cent of culture's overall impact on business results. Look across any organization, and you'll see all kinds of cultural hot buttons. The challenge is to keep the change effort focused on the 5 per cent of culture that's mission critical. The company can't afford to get distracted by the multitude of cultural issues that don't drive the business.

MERGER CONTROL

Merger control refers to the procedure of reviewing mergers and acquisitions under antitrust/ competition law. Over 60 nations worldwide have adopted a regime providing for merger control. Merger control regimes are adopted to prevent anti-competitive consequences of concentrations.

Accordingly most merger control regimens provide for one of the following substantive tests:

- Does the concentration substantially lessen competition?

- Does the concentration significantly impede effective competition?
- Does the concentration lead to the creation or strengthening of a dominant position?

In practice most merger control regimes are based on very similar underlying principles. Simplified, the creation of a dominant position would usually result in a substantial lessening of or significant impediment to effective competition. Modern merger control regimes are of an *ex-ante* nature, *i.e.* the antitrust authority has the burden of predicting the anti-competitive outcome of a concentration. While it is indisputable that a concentration may lead to a reduction in output and result in higher prices and thus in a welfare loss to consumers, the antitrust authority faces the challenge of applying various economic theories and rules in a legally binding procedure.

UNILATERAL EFFECT

Unilateral effect is a competition law term used in the area of merger control. It refers to the ability of post-merger firms to raise prices because of the removal of competitive constraints resulting from the merger, irrespective of the pricing decisions and actions of their competitors. Such anti-competitive effects can be pronounced when two significant competitors merge to create a large, but not dominant player on a market with only a few other competitors. In such a case, particularly when the two merging companies have highly substitute good, it will be rational for the merged company to raise prices to some degree, because it will recapture some of the customers who would have switched away from the product in favour of what was previously a competing product. Such a price increase does not depend on the merged firm being the dominant player in the market. The likelihood and magnitude of such an increase will instead depend on the substitutability of the products in question–the closer the substitute,the greater the unilateral effects.

FEATURES OF FINANCING MERGERS AND ACQUISITIONS IN RUSSIA

The peculiarity of financing mergers and acquisitions in Russia due to the transition mechanisms of corporate control. Most Russian companies were formed in the process of privatization and corporatization. Privatization of companies is going through their allocation of state structures and the transfer to private owners. This allows us to consider acquisitions in the privatization process as the first mechanism to implement the strategy of mergers and acquisitions, which continues to play an important role in modern Russian conditions. The second mechanism of transition of corporate control, which is characteristic for Russia, we can assume the accumulation of debts absorbed by the company and its conversion to its shares in the process of bankruptcy. When conducting bankruptcy procedures may be signing a settlement agreement, under which the lender receives its debt stock company. Another five or six years ago, often used third transition mechanism for corporate control, which consists of participation in corporate governance, the target company. If control over it could not be established through participation in its equity, the composition of its leadership instilled a number of persons loyal to the company or group exercising absorption. By adopting certain management decisions, legal clarity that remains in question, the basic production assets of the company for a symbolic sum transferred to a specially created entities. Then, depending on the likelihood of the trial and the decision to return assets last to resell or pledge. As a result, within the same production co-existed two legal entities: the old company, whose assets were listed in uncollectible receivables for removing the equipment and are often just as hopeless a large accounts payable, and a new company with significant assets of a particular corporate group.

The three transition mechanism of corporate control are non-market nature. The fourth mechanism - the acquisition of shares in the share capital - is quite a market. It is most prevalent in Western countries, and most recently - and in Russia.

MANDATORY AND VOLUNTARY REGIMES

A merger control regime is described as "mandatory" when the parties are indefinitely prevented from closing the deal until they have received merger clearance. A distinction can also be made between "local" and "global" bars on closing/implementation; some mandatory regimes provide that the transaction cannot be implemented within the particular jurisdiction and some provide that the transaction cannot be closed/implemented anywhere in the world prior to merger clearance. South Africa has a merger control regime which imposes a global bar on closing.

A merger control regime is described as "voluntary" when the parties are not prevented from closing the deal and implementing the transaction in advance of having applied for and received merger clearance. In these circumstances the merging parties are effectively taking the risk that the competition authority will not require them to undo the deal if in due course it is found that the transaction is likely to have an anti-competitive effect. The UK has a voluntary merger control regime.

However, the Office of Fair Trading can request the parties to a merger that has already completed to hold the two businesses separate pending an investigation. Mandatory regimes are more effective in preventing anticompetitive concentrations since it is almost impossible to unravel a merger once it has been implemented.

MATERIAL ADVERSE CHANGE

A material adverse change also formulated as a Material adverse event or Material adverse effect contingency is a legal provision often found in mergers and acquisitions contracts and venture financing agreements that enables the acquirer to refuse to complete the acquisition or merger or financing with the party being acquired if the target suffers such a change. The rationale for such a clause is a means to protect the acquirer from major changes that make the target less attractive as a purchase. Large transactions often require a long period of time between actual agreement and the completion of the transaction. This time is used to obtain governmental or regulatory approvals to obtain shareholder or labour consents, and any other required third-party consents.

During this period, the target continues to function pending the completion of the merger, and is subject to the normal risks of its business, the economy or acts beyond its control. Each merger agreement that contains such a clause has a different definition of what, in its particular context, constitutes a material adverse change. Often this is one of the few or some times, the only way that an acquiring party can refuse to complete a contemplated acquisition. When the acquiring party cites the occurrence of a material adverse change to refuse to complete a merger or acquisition, litigation may ensue. One notable occurrence is the planned acquisition of SLM Corporation by a group including Bank of America and JPMorgan Chase.

In the United States, much of this litigation occurs in the Delaware Court of Chancery as many large American companies are organized under Delaware law. An acquirer seeking to avoid completion of a transaction based upon a MAC provision bears the burden of proving that a material adverse change as defined by the parties' agreement has in fact occurred. It is also used in "Gas Sale and Purchase Agreements" and "LNG Sale and Purchase Agreements" and usually the party suffering from the effects of Material Adverse Change can apply for contract price revision.

EQUITY METHOD

Equity method in accounting is the process of treating equity investments, usually 20–50%, in associate companies. The investor keeps such equities as an asset. The investor's proportional share of the associate company's net income increases the investment and proportional payment of dividends decreases it. In the investor's income statement, the proportional share of the investee's net income or net loss is reported as a single-line item. The ownership of more than 50% of voting stock creates a subsidiary. Its financial statements consolidate into the parent's. The ownership of less than 20% creates investment position carried at historic book or fair market value in the investor's balance sheet.

FAIRNESS OPINION

A fairness opinion is a professional evaluation by an investment bank or other third party as to whether the terms of a merger, acquisition, buyback, spin-off, or going private are fair. It is rendered for a fee.

CONTROVERSY

Controversy in financial and management circles surrounds the question of the objectivity of fairness opinions, as one aspect of the duty of care in the fairness of a transaction. A potential exists for a conflict of interest when an entity rendering an opinion may benefit from the transaction either directly or indirectly· Directors and officers of the companies also may have an interest in the outcome of the proposed transaction· In response, the Financial Industry Regulatory Authority issued its Rule 2290 to require disclosure by its members to minimize abuses; this was approved in 2007 by the Securities and Exchange Commission·

EQUITY AND FAIRNESS

Stockholder lawsuits are in the courts.The Delaware Court of Chancery has required sufficient disclosures to "provide a balanced, truthful account of all matters" and said "When a document ventures into certain subjects, it must do so in a manner that is materially complete and unbiased by the omission of material facts." In a Memorandum Opinion in the CheckFree/ Fiserv merger Chancellor Chandler underlined that the earlier *In re Pure Resources* Court had established the proper frame of analysis for disclosure of financial data: "[S]tockholders are entitled to a fair summary of the substantive work performed by the investment bankers upon whose advice the recommendations of their board as to how to vote on a merger or tender rely." The certification hypothesis fairness opinions may also serve the interest of the shareholders by mitigating informational asymmetries in corporate transactions. First empirical evidence of fairness opinions in Europe indicates their relevance for shareholders.

FLIP-OVER

A flip-over is one of five types of poison pills in which current shareholders of a targeted firm will have the option to purchase discounted stock after the potential takeover. Introduced in late 1984 and adopted by many firms, the strategy gave a common stock dividend in the form of rights to acquire the firm's common stock or preferred stock under market value. Following a takeover, the rights would "flip over" and allow the current shareholder to purchase the unfriendly competitor's shares at a discount. If this tool is exercised, the number of shares held by the unfriendly competitors will realise dilution and price devaluation.

FREEZE-OUT MERGER

A freeze-out merger is a technique by which one or more shareholders who collectively hold a majority of shares in a corporation gain ownership of remaining shares in that corporation. The majority shareholders incorporate a second corporation, which initiates a merger with the original corporation. The shareholders using this technique are then in a position to dictate the plan of merger. They force the minority stockholders in the original corporation to accept a cash payment for their shares, effectively "freezing them out" of the resulting company.

CRITICISM

The legal community has criticised the present rules with regard to freeze-out mergers as being biased against the interests of the minority shareholders. For example, if a gain in stock value is anticipated by the majority, they can deprive the frozen-out minority of its share of those gains. Although a LBO is an effective tool for a group of investors to use to purchase a company, it is less well suited to the case of one company acquiring another. An alternative is the freeze-out merger: The Laws on tender offers allow the acquiring company to freeze existing shareholders out of the gains from merging by forcing non-tendering shareholders to sell their shares for the tender offer price. Here is how it is accomplished. An acquiring company makes a tender offer at an amount slightly higher than the current target stock price. If the tender offer succeeds, the acquirer gains control of the target and merge its assets into a new corporation, which is fully owned by the acquirer. In effect, the non-tendering shareholders lose their shares because the target corporation no longer exists. In compensation, non tendering shareholders get their right to receive the tender offer price for their shares. The bidder, in essence, gets complete ownership of the target for the tender offer price. Because the value the non-tendering shareholders receive for their shares is equal to the tender price, the law recognizes it as fair value and non-tendering shareholders have no legal recourse.

Under these circumstances, existing shareholders will tender their stock, reasoning that there is no benefit to holding out: if the tender offer succeeds, they get the tender price anyway; if they hold out, they risk jeopardizing the deal and forgoing the small gain. Hence the acquirer is able to capture almost all the value added from the merger and, as in the leveraged buyout, is able to effectively eliminate the free rider problem. This freeze-out tender offer has a significant advantage over a LBO because an acquiring corporation need not make an all-cash offer. Instead of paying the target's shareholders in cash, it can use shares of its own stock to pay for the acquisition. In this case, the bidder offers to exchange each shareholder's stock in the target for stock in the acquiring company. As long as the exchange rate is set so that the value in the acquirer's stock exceeds the premerger market value of the target stock, the non-tendering shareholders will receive fair value for their shares and will have no legal recourse.

GOLDEN PARACHUTE

A golden parachute is an agreement between a company and an employee specifying that the employee will receive certain significant benefits if employment is terminated. Sometimes, certain conditions, typically a change in company ownership, must be met, but often the cause of termination is unspecified. These benefits may include severance pay, cash bonuses, stock options, or other benefits. They are designed to reduce perverse incentives—paradoxically they may create them.

Proponents of golden parachutes argue that they provide three main benefits:

1. Golden parachutes make it easier to hire and retain executives, especially in industries more prone to mergers.
2. They help an executive to remain objective about the company during the takeover process.
3. They dissuade takeover attempts by increasing the cost of a takeover, often part of a Poison Pill strategy,

Critics have responded to the above by pointing out that:

1. Dismissal is a risk in any occupation, and executives are already well compensated.
2. Executives already have a fiduciary responsibility to the company, and should not need additional incentives to stay objective.
3. Golden parachute costs are a very small percentage of a takeover's costs and do not affect the outcome.

The use of golden parachutes have caused some investors concern since they don't specify that the executive has to perform successfully to any degree. The first known use of the term "golden parachute" dates back to when creditors sought to oust Howard Hughes from control of TWA airlines. The creditors provided Charles C. Tillinghast Jr. an employment contract—dubbed a golden parachute in likely reference to the protection a parachute offered—with protection against the almost definite job loss Tillinghast would have faced if famed aviator Howard Hughes had successfully maintained control of TWA.

The use of the term "golden parachute" has significantly increased in 2008 because of the global economic recession, especially being used by news media and in the 2008 Presidential Debates. The use of golden parachutes expanded greatly in the early 1980s in response to the large increase in the number of takeovers and mergers. The French executives' golden parachutes are the highest in Europe, and equivalent to the funds received by 50% of the American executives. In contrast, the French standard revenues for executives located themselves in the European average. French executives receive roughly the double of their salary and bonus in their golden parachute.

WILLIAMSON TRADE-OFF MODEL

The Williamson trade-off model is a theoretical model in the economics of industrial organization which emphasizes the trade-off associated with horizontal mergers between gains resulting from lower costs of production and the losses associated with higher prices due to greater degree of monopoly power.

The model was first presented by Oliver Williamson, co-laureate of the 2009 Nobel prize in economics, in his 1968 paper "Economics as an Anti-Trust Defence: The welfare trade-offs" in the *American Economic Review*. Williamson argued that ignoring efficiencies that may result from proposed mergers in antitrust law "fail(ed) to meet the basic test of economic rationality".

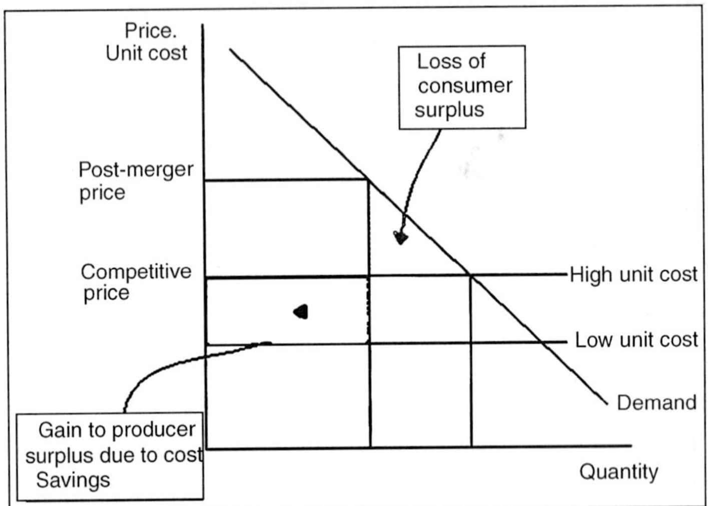

BASIC IDEA OF THE MODEL

Suppose that a given industry is initially characterized by perfect competition and has a constant unit cost of production equal to *c1*. Because of competition the market price of the good produced will be equal to this unit cost, which means that firms in the industry earn normal profits, as captured by the producer surplus. Suppose further that after a merger between firms in the industry takes place, unit costs fall to $c2<c1$ as a result of economies of scale or other forms of synergy. However, the industry is now less competitive, with a monopoly being the most extreme example.

Since the firm is no longer a price taker, the price it charges will be above the unit cost. For a monopoly, for example, the price will be set where the unit/marginal cost intersects marginal revenue. This means that the amount of consumer surplus, the area below the demand curve and above the price, will be lower. The change in overall social surplus of the market depends on whether the increase in producer surplus due to lower production costs is larger or smaller than the fall in consumer surplus due to higher prices. Note that it is theoretically possible that the fall in unit costs due to the merger could be sufficiently large that the post merger monopoly price ends up being lower than the pre merger competitive price in which case both producer and consumer surplus would increase. In that situation no trade-off exists and the merger is unambiguously beneficial to all market participants. More generally however, a horizontal merger can involve both costs and benefits.

APPLICATIONS IN ANTI-TRUST POLICY

One implication of the Williamson model is that the gains from cost reduction do not have to be "large" in order to outweigh the losses that result from higher prices. This is because the welfare losses associated with the latter tend to be "second-order" while the gains tend to be "first-order". What this means is that the gains from the merger would have to be very small, or alternatively, the demand for the good in question would have to be relatively quite inelastic for social surplus to decrease. A broader conclusion of the model is that antitrust, or competition, policy should be "discretionary". That is, government regulators who are faced with a proposed merger need to examine each proposal on a case by case basis. In some instances, the cost savings might make it worth it, while in others they will not. This is in contrast to a "non-discretionary" policy where regulators set certain standards that any industry must meet - for example, that no firm has more than 20% market share. Then, they do not actually examine the potential gains or losses to consumer or producer surplus from a proposed merger, but only its impact on meeting the set standard - for example, whether or not the merger will increase a single firm's market share above 20%. The model has been applied to the study of mergers in the US rail freight industry and the US food industry, among others. It has also been used in evaluation of actual antitrust laws by American legal scholar and judge Robert Bork. A regulatory approach based on the model was popular in the United States in the 1980s and influenced much antitrust legislation.

CRITICISMS AND LIMITATIONS

- The "trade-off" in the Williamson model involves a gain in producers' surplus and a loss in consumers' surplus. Thus, in focusing the analysis on total surplus, it neglects distributional issues and treats changes in both consumers' and producers' welfare symmetrically. However, anti-trust policy as actually practiced in many countries appears to have the goal of maximizing consumer surplus. In that sense, as long as the post-merger market price is higher than pre-merger, the fact that producer surplus and firm profits rise is immaterial from the point of view of the regulators. In that case, only those mergers in which the fall in unit cost is sufficiently large to ensure a lower price after the merger should be permitted. For this reason, the Williamson model is not applicable in European Community competition law and is controversial in Canada.

- The simplest version of the model compares a situation where initially the market is competitive to a situation where the post-merger market is not. However, if initially price exceeds marginal cost, further increases in price have a "first order" effect on consumer surplus.
- The model is limited in that it only considers the effect of the merger on price charged by the firm(s). However, in most real life situations, firms compete on many other aspects other than price, for example; product quality, capacity, research and development, and product differentiation. These variables are also likely to be affected by a merger and the basic model does not capture these effects. However, the model can and has been extended in these directions by more recent work.
- The model ignores the possibilities that similar gains in cost reductions and efficiencies may instead arise due to growth of market demand and the firms on their own without any need for a merger.

WHITE KNIGHT (BUSINESS)

In business, a white knight, or "friendly investor" may be a corporation, or a person that intends to help another firm. There are many types of white knights. Alternatively, a *grey knight* is an acquiring company that enters a bid for a hostile takeover in addition to the target firm and first bidder, perceived as more favourable than the *black knight* but less favorable than the white knight. The first type, the white knight, refers to the friendly acquirer of a target firm in a hostile takeover attempt by another firm.

The intention of the acquisition is to circumvent the takeover of the object of interest by a third, unfriendly entity, which is perceived to be less favorable. The knight might defeat the undesirable entity by offering a higher and more enticing bid, or strike a favorable deal with the management of the object of acquisition. The second type refers to the acquirer of a struggling firm that may not necessarily be under threat by a hostile firm. The financial standing of the struggling firm could prevent any other entity being interested in an acquisition. The firm may already have huge debts to pay to its creditors, or worse, may already be bankrupt. In such a case, the knight, under huge risk, acquires the firm that is in crisis. After acquisition, the knight then rebuilds the firm, or integrates it into itself.

WHITE SQUIRE

A *white squire* is similar to a white knight, except that it only exercises a significant minority stake, as opposed to a majority stake. A white squire doesn't have the intention, but rather serves as a figurehead in defence of a hostile takeover. The white squire may often also get special voting rights for their equity stake.

HOSTILE FIRM'S STRATEGIES

- The strategy that is usually employed by the Hostile Firm is making an offer more lucrative than the White Knight's, so that the shareholders consider rejecting the White Knight's bid. This, however, can lead to bidding wars and finally to overpaying, by one or the other, for the target firm.
- Another option is known as the NL strategy. Here, the hostile firm allows the white knight to move ahead and waits for the acquisition to take place. Once things are settled between the two entities, the Hostile Firm launches a takeover offer for the White Knight. This takeover offer is generally a hostile one. The target can enter into standstill agreements with the White Knight to prevent it from turning Gray Knight.

VOTING PLAN

A voting plan or voting rights plan is one of five main types of poison pills that a target firm can issue against hostile takeover attempts. These plans are implemented when a company charters preferred stock with superior voting rights to common shareholders. If an unfriendly bidder acquired a substantial quantity of the target firm's voting common stock, it would not be able to exercise control over its purchase. For example, ASARCO established a voting plan in which 99% of the company's common stock would only harness 16.5% of the total voting power.

VOTING INTEREST

Voting interest in business and accounting means the total number of votes entitled to be cast on the issue at the time the determination of voting power is made, excluding a vote which is contingent upon the happening of a condition or event which has not occurred at the time. This notion is different from economic interest that refers to a percentage of all the equity issued, including preferred stock, warrants, and so on. Ownership of more than 50% of voting shares gives the right of control and consolidation. In special cases, control is possible without having to own more than 50% of voting stock. For example, if agreed, shareholders may pass control to a chosen one owning much fewer shares.

VIRTUAL DATA ROOM

A virtual data room is an online repository of information that is used for the storing and distribution of documents. In many cases, a virtual data room is used to facilitate the due diligence process during an M&A transaction, loan syndication, or private equity and venture capital transactions. This due diligence process has traditionally used a physical data room to accomplish the disclosure of documents. For reasons of cost, efficiency and security, virtual data rooms have widely replaced the more traditional physical data room. An alternative to the physical data room involves the setting up of a virtual data room in the form of an extranet to which the bidders and their advisers are given access via the internet. An extranet is essentially an Internet site with limited controlled access, using a secure log-on supplied by the vendor, which can be disabled at any time, by the vendor if a bidder withdraws. Much of the information released is confidential and restrictions are applied to the viewer's ability to release this to third parties. This can be effectively applied to protect the data using Digital Rights Management. In the process of Mergers and Acquisitions, the data room is set up as part of the central repository of data relating to companies or divisions being acquired or sold.

The data room enables the interested parties to view information relating to the business in a controlled environment. Confidentiality is paramount and strict controls for viewing, copying and printing are imposed. Conventionally this is achieved by establishing a supervised, physical data room in secure premises with controlled access. In most cases, with physical data room, only one bidder team can access the room at a time. This becomes time consuming. A virtual data room has exactly the same strengths as a conventional data room - controlling access, viewing, copying and printing as well as setting time limits on viewing and logging. It has none of the disadvantages of being in a standard location, needing couriers to move documents or transporting of key staff and personnel back and forth. It is also accessible 24/7 over the allowed period. With a virtual data room, documents reach the regulators and investors in a more efficient and timely manner. Due to improvements in efficiency and speed, a virtual data room typically pays for itself in a single M&A transaction. A virtual data room is quick to set up. Scanned data and existing electronic files can be mixed, information can be added or eliminated at any time and any or all information can be restricted to any or all registered viewers at any time.

DISADVANTAGES OF A PHYSICAL DATA ROOM

- Time consuming
- Narrow bandwidth
- Expensive
- Cost of travel
- Paper intensive

BENEFITS OF A VIRTUAL DATA ROOM

The largest financial benefits accrue to the seller although buyers also benefit. For the former, advantages include:

- Improvement in the number of bidders.
- Increased bid throughout if the virtual data room is accessible 24/7 over the allowed period.

- Increased control and understanding of bidders.
- Resulting 20%-30% higher bid values.
- Increased speed of transactions owing to improved accessibility
- Enhanced information secures more deals at higher prices. Conventional physical data rooms restrict the bidder or buyers' ability to get the correct people to the room simply due to the physical location. However, Virtual Data Room opens up global markets for M&A, takeovers and property deals compared with purely face-to-face and hardcopy document transactions.
- Information cannot be downloaded and taken away in a true Virtual Data Room - only viewed by a user with the correct permissions

TRANSITION COMPANIES

Transition companies are professional mergers and acquisitions companies that assist middle market business owners in the transition from one person's ownership to another. Services offered are often referred to as Transition Management services.

THE TRANSITION COMPANIES

The Transition Companies - "TTC" - is the name of a Company in Addison, Texas which is a International M&A Firm serving the lower middle market privately held business owner. This is the leading Mergers and acquisitions - "M&A" - and consulting firm specializing in maximizing the value realised by the owners of privately-held companies when transitioning their business. Gene Sartin originally formed The Transition Companies in 1988 as SUCCEL, Inc which merged with Interprise M&A in 2008 to become The Transition Companies. The Transition Companies provide lower middle market business owners with a custom strategy for the sale of the company, recapitalization, management buyouts or some other fully customised Exit strategy. Business optimization techniques are a unique part of The Transition Company's consulting model. This process facilitates their middle market client in controlling the value his or her entity will bring in the open market in a highly confidential manner.

TRADE IN SERVICES STATISTICS

Trade in services statistics are economic statistics which detail international trade in services. They received a great deal of focus at the advent of services negotiations which took place under the Uruguay Round, which became part of the General Agreement on Trade in Services, one of the four principal pillars of the WTO trade treaty, also called the "WTO Agreement".

The GATS Four Modes of Supply comprises:

- Mode 1 Cross border trade, which is defined as delivery of a service from the territory of one country into the territory of other country;

- Mode 2 Consumption abroad - this mode covers supply of a service of one country to the service consumer of any other country;
- Mode 3 Commercial presence - which covers services provided by a service supplier of one country in the territory of any other country, *i.e.* foreign direct investment undertaken by a service provider;
- Mode 4 Presence of natural persons - which covers services provided by a service supplier of one country through the presence of natural persons in the territory another economy.

Statistics which correspondent to the GATS Four Modes of Supply comprise quantitative data addressing:

- Trade in services, which is defined as delivery of a service from the territory of one country into the territory of other country, specific disaggregation as per GATS Four Modes of Supply may not apply, *i.e.* this depends on decisions taken by each country;
- Foreign direct investment Cross-border foreign investment as per IMF guidelines. *Roughly correspondent to Mode 3*
- Foreign Affiliate Trade Statistics Statistics, or corporate data detailing the operations of foreign direct investment-based enterprises, including sales, expenditures, profits, value-added, inter- and intra-firm trade, exports and imports; *Roughly correspondent to Mode 3*

Statistics which detail commercial services trade taking place under the GATS are in a state of development in most countries. Most countries don't have information which details trade as per the GATS Four Modes of Supply, which makes trade negotiations in this realm difficult, especially for developing country WTO Members. The United States Bureau of Economic analysis produces rich statistics in this area, but they do not address the GATS Four Modes of Supply directly, rather, they address only cross-border services, generally defined, and statistics related to foreign direct investment, or FDI. Foreign affiliate trade statistics, known as FATS, are collected by the United States BEA, and several other OECD countries.

TERMINATION FEE

A termination fee is a charge levied when a party wants to break the term of an agreement or long-term contract. They are stipulated in the contract or agreement itself, and provide an incentive for the party subject to them to abide by the agreement. Early Termination Fee–The total fee that will be charged for early termination of a contract or agreement. If the contract has a declining rate "Early Termination Fee" refers to the initial or starting amount. Early Termination Fee Amount–The fee that would be assed at a point in time. If the contract has a flat fee, the fee remains constant for the period described in the contract. If the contract has a declining fee the fee decreases at a rate described in the contract as a period of time elapses. Early Termination Fee Rate–The Rate at which an Early Termination Fee declines.

SERVICE INDUSTRIES

Termination fees are common to service industries such as cellular telephone service, subscription television, and so on, where they are often known as early termination fees. For instance, a customer who purchases cellular phone service might sign a two-year contract, which might stipulate a $200 fee if the customer breaks the contract. Consumer interest groups have criticized such fees as being anti-competitive because they prevent users from migrating to superior services.

MERGERS AND ACQUISITIONS

In mergers and acquisitions termination fees are often levied in the event that one party fails to consummate a merger—for instance, because it was unsuccessful in getting shareholder approval or because it agreed to a competing offer. For instance, in 2005 Johnson and Johnson agreed to acquire Guidant, but Guidant later accepted a competing offer and was subject to a termination fee of $705 million. These termination fees have been criticized as well. Shareholders in companies being purchased sometimes believe that termination fees are too high, and instead of representing the costs that the purchasing party would suffer should the deal fall through, instead act as a way of forcing shareholders and directors to accede to the deal.

TAKEOVER

In business, a takeover is the purchase of one company by another. In the UK, the term refers to the acquisition of a public company whose shares are listed on a stock exchange, in contrast to the acquisition of a private company.

TYPES OF TAKEOVER

Friendly Takeovers

Before a bidder makes an offer for another company, it usually first informs the company's board of directors. If the board feels that accepting the offer serves shareholders better than rejecting it, it recommends the offer be accepted by the shareholders. In a private company, because the shareholders and the board are usually the same people or closely connected with one another, private acquisitions are usually friendly. If the shareholders agree to sell the company, then the board is usually of the same mind or sufficiently under the orders of the equity shareholders to cooperate with the bidder. This point is not relevant to the UK concept of takeovers, which always involve the acquisition of a public company.

Hostile Takeovers

A hostile takeover allows a suitor to take over a target company whose management is unwilling to agree to a merger or takeover. A takeover is considered "hostile" if the target company's board rejects the offer, but the bidder continues to pursue it, or the bidder makes the offer directly after having announced its firm intention to make an offer. A hostile takeover can be conducted in several ways. A tender offer can be made where the acquiring company makes a public offer at a fixed price above the current market price. Tender offers in the United States are regulated by the Williams Act. An acquiring company can also engage in a proxy fight, whereby it tries to persuade enough shareholders, usually a simple majority, to replace the management with a new one which will approve the takeover. Another method involves quietly purchasing enough stock on the open market, known as a creeping tender offer, to effect a change in management. In all of these ways, management resists the acquisition but it is carried out anyway.

The main consequence of a bid being considered hostile is practical rather than legal. If the board of the target cooperates, the bidder can conduct extensive due diligence into the affairs of the target company, providing the bidder with a comprehensive analysis of the target company's finances. In contrast, a hostile bidder will only have more limited, publicly-available information about the target company available, rendering the bidder vulnerable to hidden risks regarding the target company's finances.

An additional problem is that takeovers often require loans provided by banks in order to service the offer, but banks are often less willing to back a hostile bidder because of the relative lack of information about the target available to them.

Reverse Takeovers

A reverse takeover is a type of takeover where a private company acquires a public company. This is usually done at the instigation of the larger, private company, the purpose being for the private company to effectively float itself while avoiding some of the expense and time involved in a conventional IPO.

However, under AIM rules, a reverse take-over is an acquisition or acquisitions in a twelve month period which for an AIM company would:

- Exceed 100% in any of the class tests; or
- Result in a fundamental change in its business, board or voting control; or
- In the case of an investing company, depart substantially from the investing strategy stated in its admission document or, where no admission document was produced on admission, depart substantially from the investing strategy stated in its pre-admission announcement or, depart substantially from the investing strategy.

An individual or organization-sometimes known as corporate raider-can purchase a large fraction of the company's stock and in doing so get enough votes to replace the board of directors and the CEO. With a new superior management team, the stock is a much more attractive investment, which would likely result in a price rise and a profit for the corporate raider and the other shareholders.

Backflip Takeovers

A backflip takeover is any sort of takeover in which the acquiring company turns itself into a subsidiary of the purchased company. This type of takeover rarely occurs·

FINANCING A TAKEOVER

Funding

Often a company acquiring another pays a specified amount for it. This money can be raised in a number of ways. Although the company may have sufficient funds available in its account, remitting payment entirely from the acquiring company's cash on hand is unusual. More often, it will be borrowed from a bank, or raised by an issue of bonds. Acquisitions financed through debt are known as leveraged buyouts, and the debt will often be moved down onto the balance sheet of the acquired company. The acquired company then has to pay back the debt. This is a technique often used by private equity companies. The debt ratio of financing can go as high as 80% in some cases. In such a case, the acquiring company would only need to raise 20% of the purchase price.

Loan Note Alternatives

Cash offers for public companies often include a "loan note alternative" that allows shareholders to take a part or all of their consideration in loan notes rather than cash. This is done primarily to make the offer more attractive in terms of taxation. A conversion of shares into cash is counted as a disposal that triggers a payment of capital gains tax, whereas if the shares are converted into other securities, such as loan notes, the tax is rolled over.

All Share Deals

A takeover, particularly a reverse takeover, may be financed by an all share deal. The bidder does not pay money, but instead issues new shares in itself to the shareholders of the company being acquired. In a reverse takeover the shareholders of the company being acquired end up with a majority of the shares in, and so control of, the company making the bid. The company has managerial rights.

STRATEGIES

There are a variety of reasons why an acquiring company may wish to purchase another company. Some takeovers are opportunistic - the target company may simply be very reasonably priced for one reason or another and the acquiring company may decide that in the long run, it will end up making money by purchasing the target company. The large holding company Berkshire Hathaway has profited well over time by purchasing many companies opportunistically in this manner. Other takeovers are strategic in that they are thought to have secondary effects beyond the simple effect of the profitability of the target company being added to the acquiring company's profitability.

For example, an acquiring company may decide to purchase a company that is profitable and has good distribution capabilities in new areas which the acquiring company can use for its own products as well. A target company might be attractive because it allows the acquiring company to enter a new market without having to take on the risk, time and expense of starting a new division. An acquiring company could decide to take over a competitor not only because the competitor is profitable, but in order to eliminate competition in its field and make it easier, in the long term, to raise prices. Also a takeover could fulfill the belief that the combined company can be more profitable than the two companies would be separately due to a reduction of redundant functions. Takeovers may also benefit from principal-agent problems associated with top executive compensation. For example, it is fairly easy for a top executive to reduce the price of his/her company's stock - due to information asymmetry. The executive can accelerate accounting of expected expenses, delay accounting of expected revenue, engage in off balance sheet transactions to make the company's profitability appear temporarily poorer, or simply promote and report severely conservative estimates of future earnings.

Such seemingly adverse earnings news will be likely to reduce share price.. There are typically very few legal risks to being'too conservative' in one's accounting and earnings estimates. A reduced share price makes a company an easier takeover target. When the company gets bought out-at a dramatically lower price - the takeover artist gains a windfall from the former top executive's actions to surreptitiously reduce share price. This can represent tens of billions of dollars transferred from previous shareholders to the takeover artist. The former top executive is then rewarded with a golden handshake for presiding over the fire sale that can sometimes be in the hundreds of millions of dollars for one or two years of work..

This is just one example of some of the principal-agent/ perverse incentive issues involved with takeovers. Similar issues occur when a publicly held asset or non-profit organization undergoes privatization. Top executives often reap tremendous monetary benefits when a government owned or non-profit entity is sold to private hands. They can facilitate this process by making the entity appear to be in financial crisis - this reduces the sale price, and makes non-profits and governments more likely to sell. It can also contribute to a public perception that private entities are more efficiently run, reinforcing the political will to sell off public assets.

PERCEIVED PROS AND CONS OF TAKEOVER

While perceived pros and cons of a takeover differ from case to case, there are a few worth mentioning.

Pros:

- Increase in sales/revenues
- Venture into new businesses and markets
- Profitability of target company
- Increase market share
- Decrease competition
- Reduction of overcapacity in the industry
- Enlarge brand portfolio Increase in economies of scale
- Increased efficiency as a result of corporate synergies/redundancies

Cons:

- Goodwill, often paid in excess for the acquisition.
- Reduced competition and choice for consumers in oligopoly markets.
- Likelihood of job cuts.
- Cultural integration/conflict with new management
- Hidden liabilities of target entity.
- The monetary cost to the company.
- Lack of motivation for employees in the company being bought up.

Takeovers also tend to substitute debt for equity. In a sense, government tax policy of allowing for deduction of interest expenses but not of dividends, has essentially provided a substantial subsidy to takeovers. It can punish more conservative or prudent management that don't allow their companies to leverage themselves into a high risk position. High leverage will lead to high profits if circumstances go well, but can lead to catastrophic failure if circumstances do not go favorably. This can create substantial negative externalities for governments, employees, suppliers and other stakeholders.

OCCURRENCE

Corporate takeovers occur frequently in the United States, Canada, United Kingdom, France and Spain. They happen only occasionally in Italy because larger shareholders often have special board voting privileges designed to keep them in control. They do not happen often in Germany because of the dual board structure, nor in Japan because companies have interlocking sets of ownerships known as keiretsu, nor in the People's Republic of China because the state majority owns most publicly-listed companies. A number of western government officials are expressing concern over the commercial information for corporate acquisitions, hostile or otherwise, being sourced by sovereign governments and state enterprises.

Index

L

N

O

R

S

T

V